THE NEW CAMBRIDGE
T. S. EL

Drawing on the latest developments in scholarship and criticism, *The New Cambridge Companion to T. S. Eliot* opens up fresh avenues of appreciation and inquiry to a global twenty-first century readership. Emphasizing major works and critical issues, this collection of newly commissioned essays from leading international scholars provides seven full chapters reassessing Eliot's poetry and drama; explores important contemporary critical issues that were untreated in the previous *Companion*, such as the significance of gender and sexuality; and challenges received accounts of his controversial critical reception. Complete with a chronology of Eliot's life and work and an up-to-date select bibliography, this authoritative and accessible introduction to Eliot's complete oeuvre will be an essential resource for students.

Jason Harding is Reader in the Department of English Studies at Durham University. He is the author or editor of six books, including *T. S. Eliot in Context* (Cambridge University Press) and (with Ronald Schuchard)*The Complete Prose of T. S. Eliot: The Critical Edition: Volume 4, English Lion, 1930–1933*.

A complete list of books in the series is at the back of this book.

THE NEW CAMBRIDGE COMPANION TO T. S. ELIOT

THE NEW CAMBRIDGE COMPANION TO
T. S. ELIOT

JASON HARDING
Durham University

CAMBRIDGE
UNIVERSITY PRESS

One Liberty Plaza, 20th Floor, New York, NY 10006, USA

Cambridge University Press is part of the University of Cambridge.

It furthers the University's mission by disseminating knowledge in the pursuit of education, learning and research at the highest international levels of excellence.

www.cambridge.org
Information on this title: www.cambridge.org/9781107691056

First published 2017

Printed in the United States of America by Sheridan Books, Inc.

A catalog record for this publication is available from the British Library.

Library of Congress Cataloging in Publication Data
Names: Harding, Jason, editor.
Title: The new Cambridge companion to T. S. Eliot / edited by Jason Harding.
Description: New York : Cambridge University Press, 2016. | Series: Cambridge companions to literature | Includes bibliographical references and index.
Identifiers: LCCN 2015042947 | ISBN 9781107037014 (hardback)
Subjects: LCSH: Eliot, T. S. (Thomas Stearns), 1888–1965 – Criticism and interpretation. | BISAC: LITERARY CRITICISM / European / English, Irish, Scottish, Welsh.
Classification: LCC PS3509.L43 Z7958 2016 | DDC 821/.912–dc23
LC record available at http://lccn.loc.gov/2015042947

ISBN 978-1-107-03701-4 Hardback
ISBN 978-1-107-69105-6 Paperback

CONTENTS

NOTES ON CONTRIBUTORS

JEWEL SPEARS BROOKER, Professor Emerita, Eckerd College, has held numerous visiting appointments, most recently at Hebrew University of Jerusalem and Merton College, Oxford. She is the author or editor of nine books, including *Reading The Waste Land: T. S. Eliot and the Limits of Interpretation* (1990), *Mastery and Escape: T. S. Eliot and the Dialectic of Modernism* (1994) and *T. S. Eliot: The Contemporary Reviews* (2004). She is the co-editor with Ronald Schuchard of *T. S. Eliot: Apprentice Years 1905–1918* (2014), volume 1 of *Eliot's Complete Prose* (2014), and is also co-editing volume 8. She is writing a book on Eliot's mind and art.

JOHN XIROS COOPER, Professor Emeritus, University of British Columbia, has published articles and chapters on twentieth-century literature, modernism, poetry and fiction. His books include *T. S. Eliot and the Politics of Voice: the Argument of The Waste Land* (1987); *T. S. Eliot and the Ideology of Four Quartets* (1995); *The Modern British Novel* (1997); *T. S. Eliot's Orchestra: Critical Essays on Poetry and Music* (2000); *Modernism and the Culture of Market Society* (2004) and *The Cambridge Introduction to T. S. Eliot* (2006). He is translating the *Maximes* (1664) of La Rochefoucauld into English and has just finished writing a novel, *The Wasp's Sting*.

ANTHONY CUDA is Associate Professor of English at the University of North Carolina, Greensboro, where he teaches courses in modernism and twentieth-century poetry. He is the author of *The Passions of Modernism* (2010) and co-editor with Ronald Schuchard of *The Complete Prose of T. S. Eliot: The Critical Edition, Volume 2: The Perfect Critic, 1919–1926* (2014).

RICK DE VILLIERS has taught in the Humanities Faculty and in the Department of English at the University of Pretoria. He has published articles on T. S. Eliot, Samuel Beckett, and J. M. Coetzee in the *English Academy Review*, *English Studies in Africa* and the *Journal of Literary Studies*. His postgraduate thesis was titled "'The Concitation of the Backward Devils': A Revaluation of the Quatrain Poems in T. S. Eliot's *Poems* (1920)" (2011).

STEVE ELLIS is Professor of English Literature at the University of Birmingham. His writing on T. S. Eliot includes *The English Eliot: Design, Language and Landscape in "Four Quartets"* (1991) and *T. S. Eliot: A Guide for the Perplexed* (2009), as well as the opening chapter in his most recent book *British Writers and the Approach of World War II* (2014). He has also written books on a range of other authors including Dante, Chaucer and Virginia Woolf, and has published three volumes of poetry and a verse translation of Dante's *Inferno*.

JASON HARDING is Reader in English Studies at Durham University. He is the author of *The Criterion: Cultural Politics and Periodical Networks in Interwar Britain* (2002), co-editor with Giovanni Cianci of *T. S. Eliot and the Concept of Tradition* (2007) and editor of *T. S. Eliot in Context* (2011). He is also the co-editor with Ronald Schuchard of *The Complete Prose of T. S. Eliot: The Critical Edition, Volume 4: English Lion, 1930–1933* (2015).

SARAH KENNEDY is Research Fellow and Director of Studies in English at Downing College, Cambridge. Her research interests fall within twentieth-century and contemporary Anglophone poetry, and are informed by questions of metaphor, landscape, poetic influence and the literary afterlives of poets. She has published articles on T. S. Eliot and the Australian poet Judith Wright. She is currently working on a monograph on Eliot's later poetry and the creative imagination.

GAIL MCDONALD is Senior Lecturer in American Literature and Culture at Goldsmiths, University of London, and Director of the T. S. Eliot International Summer School. A founder and past president of the Modernist Studies Association, her publications include *Learning to Be Modern: Pound, Eliot, and the American University* (1993) and *American Literature and Culture, 1900–1960* (2007). With David Chinitz, she is co-editor of *A Companion to Modernist Poetry* (2014).

MICHAEL O'NEILL is Professor of English at Durham University. His more recent books include *The All-Sustaining Air: Romantic Legacies and Renewals in British, American, and Irish Poetry since 1900* (2007) and, with Michael D. Hurley, *Poetic Form: An Introduction* (2012). He is an editor of volume 3 of *The Complete Poetry of Percy Bysshe Shelley* (2012), editor of *The Cambridge History of English Poetry* (2010) and co-editor (with Mark Sandy and Sarah Wootton) of *Venice and the Cultural Imagination* (2012) and *The Persistence of Beauty: Victorians to Moderns* (2015). He has published three collections of poems: *The Stripped Bed* (1990), *Wheel* (2008) and *Gangs of Shadow* (2014).

LAWRENCE RAINEY is Professor of Modern Literature, University of York. He is the author of *Ezra Pound and the Monument of Culture* (1991), *Institutions of Modernism* (1998) and *Revisiting "The Waste Land"* (2005). He has edited *The Annotated Waste Land with Eliot's Contemporary Prose* (2005), *Modernism: An Anthology* (2005) and *Futurism: An Anthology* (2009). He is the founding editor of the journal *Modernism/modernity*.

BARRY SPURR is Professor of Poetry and Poetics at the University of Sydney. He is the author of numerous articles and chapters on poetry, and of books on liturgical language, including *Studying Poetry* (2006), *See the Virgin Blest: Representations of the Virgin Mary in English Poetry* (2007) and an account of T. S. Eliot's religious faith and practice, *"Anglo-Catholic in Religion": T. S. Eliot and Christianity* (2010). He has contributed a chapter, "Religions East and West," to the *Cambridge Companion to "The Waste Land"* (2015).

ANNE STILLMAN is Fellow and College Lecturer in English at Clare College, Cambridge. Her research interests lie predominantly in American and British Literature of the nineteenth and twentieth centuries (especially poetry). She has published numerous articles and reviews in *Essays in Criticism, Thinking Verse*, and *The Cambridge Quarterly*.

HELEN THAVENTHIRAN is a Fellow of Robinson College, where she is Director of Studies for English, and an affiliated lecturer of the Faculty of English, University of Cambridge. Her first book is *Radical Empiricists: Five Modernist Close Readers* (2015). She is currently preparing a new edition of William Empson's *The Structure of Complex Words* (forthcoming in 2016).

PREFACE

In his preface to the 1994 *Cambridge Companion to T. S. Eliot*, A. David Moody remarked: "For a time after his death in 1965 Eliot himself seemed in danger of becoming simply another monument, frozen in a fixed idea of his achievement. But there is too much life in his work for the accepted idea to contain it; and a new generation of readers, coming to it in the frame of mind of this end of century, are finding that there is much in it which answers to current preoccupations."[1] Over the succeeding twenty years, major developments have transformed the landscape of our current preoccupations in Eliot studies, leading one Eliot scholar to claim: "Critical work on T. S. Eliot has undergone a renaissance since the early 1990s, bringing new ideas and methods to bear on a much-studied writer whose depths, by then, were long supposed to have been plumbed."[2] As Gail McDonald observes in her contribution to this volume, the dynamic and controversial subject of Eliot's engagement with gender and sexuality was not treated in the 1994 volume. Furthermore, with the release of a mass of hitherto restricted archive material into the public domain, new generations of readers are asking their own questions of T. S. Eliot. Since 2009, six volumes of *The Letters of T. S. Eliot* have been published and four volumes of *The Complete Prose of T. S. Eliot*, taking us up to 1933. A two-volume Faber edition of *The Poems of T. S. Eliot*, building on the principles established in the 1996 edition of Eliot's early notebook, *Inventions of the March Hare*, will provide an authoritative text for new readers. These authorised, fully annotated new editions must undoubtedly re-inflect ongoing debates about this complex and challenging poet-critic. Moody's collection was sensitively and intelligently constructed as a gateway for Eliot's readers in 1994, but given the seismic upheaval in Eliot scholarship and criticism since then, it is time for a revised *Companion* to address the needs of a twenty-first century audience.

The contributors to *The New Cambridge Companion to T. S. Eliot* share many of the same goals and animating concerns of Moody's volume; in particular, the emphasis on detailed examination of major works and critical issues. However, this volume is conceived with significant differences. The introductory opening chapter, an overture to the key themes addressed in subsequent chapters, offers an analysis of the interrelations between Eliot's life and art across his career. It contains a cautionary invitation to new readers of Eliot to "unravel" some of the received orthodoxies about his life and the claims made about the impersonality of his poems. Seven chapters are devoted to Eliot's achievement as a poet and verse dramatist. One chapter is focused on Eliot's modernist handling of poetic form – at the level of rhyme, metre, lineation and allusion – as a creative transformation of (generic) poetic traditions. Crucial chapters, drawing on recent specialist scholarship, re-examine the masterpieces of *The Waste Land* and *Four Quartets*, and others re-contextualise their fresh readings of long cherished poems by devoting fuller coverage to the early poetic notebook, the satirical quatrain poems, and the transitional Ariel Poems than the 1994 *Companion*. Eliot's drama is revisited by an award-winning editor of his seminal prose writings on dramatic verse during the years 1919–26. The chapters on Eliot's literary and social criticism are informed by a number of important critical studies – books, articles and reviews – that have emerged over the past twenty years, and by a familiarity with the material in 200 prose items added to Donald Gallup's bibliography. As mentioned previously, a chapter places Eliot in the lively arena of contemporary debate regarding gender and sexuality, and a chapter on Eliot's formative reading in philosophy and anthropology is enriched by original research undertaken during the editing and annotating of Eliot's postgraduate essays and his Ph.D. thesis. The final chapter offers an account of how Eliot's daily practices as a Christian bear on his oeuvre and his reputation. In common with the original 1994 *Companion*, there is no separate chapter devoted to the "critical heritage": this international team of scholars has taken due account of the contested nature of Eliot's reception in presenting his work to a modern audience. We are all indebted to the indispensable studies by the scholars and critics listed in the Select Bibliography. In spite of the reordering and reemphasis, then, occasioned by the passage of twenty years, this *New Cambridge Companion to T. S. Eliot* reaffirms the aspiration of its predecessor, in seeking to open up subtle, incisive and rewarding avenues of inquiry to generations of readers who wish to experience the pleasure of a first-hand encounter with a living classic rather than pay a dutiful visit to a frozen monument.

NOTES

1 "Preface", *The Cambridge Companion to T. S. Eliot*, ed. A. D. Moody (Cambridge: Cambridge University Press, 1994), xiii.
2 David Chinitz, "Preface", *A Companion to T. S. Eliot*, ed. David Chinitz (Oxford: Wiley-Blackwell, 2009), xiv.

CHRONOLOGY OF ELIOT'S LIFE AND WORKS

1888	Thomas Stearns Eliot born on 26 September in St Louis, Missouri, the seventh and youngest child of Henry Ware Eliot and Charlotte Champe Stearns.
1898	Attends Smith Academy in St Louis until 1905.
1905	Spends one year at Milton Academy in preparation for his university education at Harvard.
1906	Enters Harvard University studying classics, German, French, English literature, and comparative literature as an undergraduate.
1908	Reads Arthur's Symons's *The Symbolist Movement in Literature*; encounters the work of Jules Laforgue for the first time.
1909	Joins the board of Harvard's literary magazine, the *Advocate*. Receives B.A. from Harvard.
1910	Receives M.A. from Harvard. Studies at the Sorbonne in Paris and attends the lectures of Henri Bergson at the Collège de France. Strikes up a friendship with Jean Verdenal, a French medical student.
1911	Composes "The Love Song of J. Alfred Prufrock." Travels to London, Munich, and Northern Italy. Returns to Harvard in the autumn, undertaking graduate studies in philosophy.
1912	Meets Emily Hale.
1913	Becomes president of the Philosophical Club at Harvard. Studies under Josiah Royce.

1914 Meets Bertrand Russell (who is visiting Harvard as a guest lecturer). Awarded the Sheldon Travelling Fellowship in Philosophy. Studies briefly at the University of Marburg, Germany, before the outbreak of the war. Continues study at Merton College, Oxford, under the tutelage of Harold Joachim. Meets Ezra Pound.

1915 Teaches at High Wycombe, then at Highgate Junior School (until 1917) while completing his thesis on F. H. Bradley. Jean Verdenal killed at the Battle of Gallipoli. Marries Vivien Haigh-Wood on 26 June, two months after their first meeting. Writes first review for the *New Statesman*, which marks the start of an intense and protracted period of reviewing.

1916 Completes doctoral dissertation but is prevented from returning to Harvard due to the war.

1917 Begins work for Lloyds Bank in the Colonial and Foreign Department. *Prufrock and Other Observations*. Becomes assistant editor of the *Egoist*. Delivers university extension lectures until 1918. With Pound, begins experimenting with the quatrain form using Théophile Gautier's *Émaux et Camées* as a model.

1919 Publication of *Poems* (1919). Goes on a walking tour of southern France with Pound. Publishes "Tradition and the Individual Talent" in the *Egoist*. Death of father.

1920 Publication of *Poems* (1920), *Ara Vos Prec*, and *The Sacred Wood*.

1921 Writes a draft of *The Waste Land*. Approaches Lady Rothermere with a proposal for a new journal, the *Criterion*. Takes a three-month break from Lloyds on medical advice; checks into a clinic in Lausanne, Switzerland.

1922 Becomes editor of the *Criterion* (until its closure in 1939). *The Waste Land* published in the *Criterion*. Receives Dial Award of $2,000 for *The Waste Land*.

1923 Begins work on his first verse play, *Sweeney Agonistes*.

1925 "The Hollow Men" and *Poems 1909–1925* published. Resigns from Lloyds Bank to join publishing firm Faber and Gwyer.

1926 Launches the *New Criterion*. Delivers the Cambridge Clark lectures on metaphysical poetry.

1927 Baptised and confirmed in the Church of England, and becomes a naturalized British citizen. Publishes "Journey of the Magi."

1928 "A Song for Simeon" and *For Lancelot Andrewes: Essays on Style and Order*. Takes a vow of celibacy.

1929 "Animula." Death of mother.

1930 "Marina" and *Ash-Wednesday*.

1931 *Coriolan* and *Thoughts after Lambeth*.

1932 Returns to America for the first time since 1915. Delivers Charles Eliot Norton Lectures at Harvard. These lectures are collected as *The Use of Poetry and the Use of Criticism* (1933).

1933 Presents the Page-Barbour Lectures at the University of Virginia, published as *After Strange Gods* (1934). Separates from Vivien.

1934 Opening of *The Rock* in London. Resides in the presbytery of St. Stephen's Church, Kensington. Visits Burnt Norton with Hale.

1935 Premiere of *Murder in the Cathedral* in Canterbury Cathedral. Subsequently opens in London.

1936 *Collected Poems, 1909–35* (includes *Burnt Norton*). Undertakes visits to Little Gidding in Huntingdonshire and East Coker, the ancestral home of the Eliots in Somerset.

1939 *The Idea of a Christian Society*. Premiere of *The Family Reunion* in London. Publishes *Old Possum's Book of Practical Cats*.

1940 *East Coker*.

1941 *The Dry Salvages*.

1942 *Little Gidding*.

1943 *Four Quartets*.

1946 Takes up residence in John Hayward's mansion flat in Chelsea.

1947 Receives honorary doctorates from Harvard, Yale, and Princeton. Death of Vivien.

1948	Awarded the Order of Merit and the Nobel Prize for Literature.
1949	*Notes towards the Definition of Culture. The Cocktail Party* premieres in Edinburgh.
1953	*The Confidential Clerk* premieres in Edinburgh.
1954	"The Cultivation of Christmas Trees."
1956	Lectures at the University of Minnesota to a crowd of 14,000.
1957	Marries Valerie Fletcher, his secretary at Faber & Faber. Publication of *On Poetry and Poets.*
1958	Awarded the Dante Gold Medal at the Italian Institute in London. *The Elder Statesman* premieres in Edinburgh.
1963	*Collected Poems 1909–1962.*
1964	Awarded U.S. Medal of Freedom.
1965	Dies on 4 January in London. His ashes are interred at St. Michael's Church in East Coker.

LIST OF ABBREVIATIONS

ASG	*After Strange Gods* (London: Faber & Faber, 1934).
Brooker	*T. S. Eliot: The Contemporary Reviews*, ed. Jewel Spears Brooker (Cambridge: Cambridge University Press, 2004).
CP1	*The Complete Prose of T. S. Eliot: The Critical Edition, Volume 1: Apprentice Years, 1905–1918*, eds. Jewel Spears Brooker and Ronald Schuchard (Baltimore: Johns Hopkins University Press & London: Faber & Faber, 2014).
CP2	*The Complete Prose of T. S. Eliot: The Critical Edition, Volume 2: The Perfect Critic, 1919–1926*, eds. Anthony Cuda and Ronald Schuchard (Baltimore: Johns Hopkins University Press & London: Faber & Faber, 2014).
CP3	*The Complete Prose of T. S. Eliot: The Critical Edition, Volume 3: Literature, Politics, Belief, 1927–1929*, eds. Frances Dickey, Jennifer Formichelli, and Ronald Schuchard (Baltimore: Johns Hopkins University Press & London: Faber & Faber, 2015).
CP4	*The Complete Prose of T. S. Eliot: The Critical Edition, Volume 4: English Lion, 1930–1933*, eds. Jason Harding and Ronald Schuchard (Baltimore: Johns Hopkins University Press & London: Faber & Faber, 2015).
CPP	*The Complete Poems and Plays of T. S. Eliot* (London Faber & Faber, 1969).
ICS	*The Idea of a Christian Society* (London: Faber & Faber, 1939)
IMH	*Inventions of the March Hare: Poems 1909–1917*, ed. Christopher Ricks (London: Faber & Faber, 1996)
L1	*The Letters of T. S. Eliot, Volume 1: 1898–1922*, revised edition, eds. Valerie Eliot and Hugh Haughton (London: Faber & Faber, 2009).

L2	*The Letters of T. S. Eliot, Volume 2: 1923–1925*, eds. Valerie Eliot and Hugh Haughton (London: Faber & Faber, 2009).
L3	*The Letters of T. S. Eliot, Volume 3: 1926–1927*, eds. Valerie Eliot and John Haffenden (London: Faber & Faber, 2012).
L4	*The Letters of T. S. Eliot, Volume 4: 1928–1929*, eds. Valerie Eliot and John Haffenden (London: Faber & Faber, 2013).
L5	*The Letters of T. S. Eliot, Volume 5: 1930–1931*, eds. Valerie Eliot and John Haffenden (London: Faber & Faber, 2014).
NTDC	*Notes towards the Definition of Culture* (London: Faber & Faber, 1948).
OED	*Oxford English Dictionary* (Oxford: Clarendon Press, 2013).
OPP	*On Poetry and Poets* (London: Faber & Faber, 1957).
SE	*Selected Essays*, 3rd edition (London: Faber & Faber, 1951).
TCC	*To Criticize the Critic* (London: Faber & Faber, 1965).
TLS	*Times Literary Supplement.*
UPUC	*The Use of Poetry and the Use of Criticism*, 2nd edition (London: Faber & Faber, 1964).
WLF	*The Waste Land: A Facsimile and Transcript of the Original Drafts*, ed. Valerie Eliot (London: Faber & Faber, 1971).

I

JASON HARDING

Unravelling Eliot

> There is a kind of fun in unravelling the twists & obliquities of this remarkable man.
>
> Virginia Woolf, diary entry on T. S. Eliot, 14 September 1925.

In 1927, T. S. Eliot told the Shakespeare Association: "About anyone so great as Shakespeare, it is probable that we can never be right; and if we can never be right, it is better that we should from time to time change our way of being wrong" (*CP3* 245). In this lecture, Eliot wittily disposes of several "up-to-date" Shakespeares proposed by contemporary critics. His gesture reveals an awareness of the difficulties of addressing a scholarly audience on the subject of the most studied author in the English language. Eliot's approach to the canon was often marked by iconoclasm: *Hamlet* was judged "most certainly an artistic failure"; Milton "writes English like a dead language"; Shelley was "humourless, pedantic, self-centred"; Tennyson's poetry is condescendingly placed as "beautiful but dull."[1] These extravagant judgements are indicative of an anxiety about the potentially numbing dead weight of canonical reputations. For today's readers of Eliot, seeking fresh interpretations of his work, the challenge that "we should from time to time change our minds" (*CP3* 245) is no less daunting than the position that confronted Eliot when he addressed the Shakespeare Association.

The relationship of an author's life to his work is crucial in reassessing Eliot's achievement as a poet, critic and dramatist but can require a certain amount of careful unravelling or untangling of the received opinions that have shaped his reputation. In "Tradition and the Individual Talent" (1919), Eliot famously claims "the more perfect the artist, the more completely separate in him will be the man who suffers and the mind which creates." He advances an "Impersonal theory of poetry" (*CP2* 109, 108). However, many critics have ignored Eliot's own separation of poet and poems. Ezra Pound contended that Eliot "arrived at the supreme Eminence among English critics largely through disguising himself as a corpse."[2] Pound felt that Possum's pontifical authority camouflaged the avant-garde affront to conventional taste represented by *The Waste Land*. By contrast, Helen Gardner's *The Art of T. S. Eliot* (1949), a book which Eliot recommended as the best study of his poetry, placed the emphasis on *Four Quartets*, characterized as the work of a devout Anglican. In a discussion of Eliot's later poetry, Gardner remarked: "Nobody can underrate the momentousness for any mature person of acceptance of all that membership of the Christian Church entails."[3] Hugh Kenner's sophisticated study *The Invisible Poet: T. S. Eliot* (1959) pondered the enigma of Eliot's private life glimpsed through an anti-romantic theory. "He is the Invisible Poet in an age of systematized literary scrutiny" observed Kenner, as he traced a delicate effacement of personality in this formidably difficult poet, "the archetype of poetic impenetrability."[4] It is noteworthy that many subtle and influential exegetes of Eliot's poetry – including Gardner and Kenner – have been Christians.

On the centenary of Eliot's birth, Lyndall Gordon confidently announced that: "The idea that Eliot's poetry was rooted in private aspects of his life has now been accepted." Gordon's approach is predicated on what she characterizes as Eliot's "insistent search for salvation ... his conversion to Anglo-Catholicism."[5] She is less concerned with a conservative public figure than with the poet's enduring fascination with mystical experience. The title of the second part of her biography, *Eliot's New Life*, alluding to Dante's *Vita Nuova* or "new life," suggests the passing of a spiritual watershed when Eliot became a practising Christian. In the words of the King James Bible: "Therefore if any man be in Christ, he is a new creature: old things are passed away; behold all things become new" (2 Corinthians 5:17). Although assiduously researched, Gordon's teleology of a spiritual pilgrimage, sketching the paradigm of Saint Augustine's exemplary self-reflexive narrative of spiritual autobiography, has not pleased all literary critics. In particular, Gordon's emphasis on Eliot's intimate friend Emily Hale, depicted as a Dantesque intercessor guiding him to a new life, provoked Frank Kermode to a rare fit of pique: "[Gordon's handling of all this], her religiose attitude to the facts, a sort of muckraking sublimity, affects her prose as well as her argument, and the whole pseudo-allegorical and hagiographical enterprise is vaguely disgusting, though I ought to add that it might seem just right to readers of different disposition."[6]

If there has always been an appetite for muckraking gossip about this most impersonal poet, who instructed his literary executrix not to facilitate the writing of any biography of him, there is scant evidence for it. Published volumes of Eliot's letters have disappointed reviewers by their quotidian character. In a 1933 lecture, Eliot said: "The desire to write a letter, to put down what you don't want anybody else to see but the person you are writing to, but which you do not want to be destroyed, but perhaps hope may be preserved for complete strangers to read, is ineradicable" (*CP4* 847). The guilty pleasure of spying a secret which was not intended for us is rarely to be found reading Eliot's letters. John Haffenden has disputed Peter Ackroyd's claim that sifting through correspondence in the archives of worldwide research libraries for his 1984 biography had enabled him to discover "a coherence of personality and a consistency of aim."[7] Haffenden countered: "letters may be used to flatter self-esteem, to propound opinion, to influence and manipulate others; the notion that they are more honest and open than other forms of writing is plainly absurd."[8] Eliot's letters must be interpreted with tact; they are no less rhetorical constructions than his other writings and cannot be straightforward evidence of the poet's personal experience. Haffenden, as general editor of the *Letters of T. S. Eliot*, has revised his opinion of the significance of these missives, now "all the very best building blocks of a biography" (*L5* xxxiii) and yet his earlier misgivings about the epistolary form should not be discarded. Eliot was a prolific but guarded letter writer. Subsequent published volumes of his letters are more likely to be supplementary than revelatory when it comes to the patient interpretation of an oeuvre that has been intensively discussed for a century. The opening up of Eliot's correspondence with Emily Hale in 2020 will offer insights into the nature of their lengthy and tangled relationship, but love letters, if they are such, will not provide a key to the linguistic or imaginative texture of the intricate, allusive poetics explored by Michael O'Neill's chapter in this *Companion*.

In his 1927 Shakespeare lecture, Eliot spoke of the "struggle – which alone constitutes life for a poet – to transmute his personal and private agonies into something rich and strange, something universal and impersonal" (*CP3* 253). In the searching analysis of *T. S. Eliot and Prejudice* (1988), Christopher Ricks probed the occasions when Eliot failed to transmute personal prejudices – including anti-Semitism – into great poetry. Anthony Julius's adversarial critique in *T. S. Eliot, anti-Semitism and Literary Form* (1995) was impatient with claims of impersonality when considering charges of anti-Semitism. The focus of Ronald Schuchard's *Eliot's Dark Angel: Intersections of Life and Art* (1999), built on a painstaking examination of the extant archival record, was designed to place tendentious critiques stressing the harmful effects of Eliot's life on his work in a sympathetic biographical context. "In view of the swelling barrier reef of reductive and formulaic criticism," Schuchard laments, "we may never hear the low and high registers of despair and love, horror and vision; we may never awaken to the intersecting planes and voices of a life lived intensely in art."[9] Robert Crawford, Eliot's most recent biographer, in attempting to take account of a mass of newly published material, offers a measured assessment of the value of biographer's role in providing "not a reductive explanation that undoes the mystery of an author's gift, but a form of artistic narrative that averts caricature and illuminates both poet and poetry."[10]

Eliot himself ridiculed critics who had "reconstructed" his personal biography "from passages which I got out of books, or which I invented out of nothing because they sounded well" and complained of then "having my biography invariably ignored in what I *did* write from personal experience" (*CP3* 246). In "The Perfect Critic" he reflected on the inextricable interrelations between literature and life: "For in an artist these suggestions made by a work of art, which are purely personal, become fused with a multitude of other suggestions from multitudinous experience, and result in the production of a new object which is no longer purely personal, because it is a work of art itself" (*CP2* 265). In "A Brief Introduction to the Method of Paul Valéry" (1924), Eliot framed these issues resonantly: "not our feelings, but the pattern which we make of our feelings, is the centre of value" (*CP2* 562). The inwardness of subjectivity, then, endures to the extent that it is rendered in an achieved work of art. Analogous to the techniques of modern art, Eliot's poetic theory proposes an objectification of emotion through a dynamic transformation of personal feelings onto the plane of impersonal structural relations. While it is clear that the personae of the poet cannot be mapped straightforwardly onto the biographical details of Thomas Stearns Eliot, critics will continue to unpick Eliot's advocacy of the detachment of his writing, "with only the technical experience preserved" (*L1* 212), as a mask for the strains of his personal life appearing in that work. This remains a contentious area. In what follows, I provide a biographical context for the succeeding chapters of this *Companion* but raise caveats that encourage an unravelling of overdetermined readings of the oeuvre.

"A writer's art" Eliot suggested, "must be based on the accumulated sensations of the first twenty-one years" (*CP1* 616). Eliot's first twenty-one years were spent in the United States. Not many letters survive from these formative years and reconstruction of young Tom's emotional life is a fertile ground for conjecture. He was born in St Louis in 1888 to parents in their mid-forties. The youngest child, he had one brother and five sisters, one of whom had died in infancy two years before he was born. His father Henry Ware Eliot was a successful businessman, who rose to be president of the Hydraulic-Press Brick Company, which flourished as industrial St Louis grew. His mother Charlotte Champe Stearns was a social welfare reformer who wrote religious verses. Strong-willed and protective of her youngest child, Charlotte had ambitions that were frustrated by her lack of a university education. She took a keener pleasure than her husband in the literary achievements of their son. In 1926, Eliot wrote an introduction to his mother's dramatic poem on the Florentine martyr Savonarola.

Born with a congenital double hernia and obliged to wear a truss, Eliot was bookish rather than sporty, a shy child who was painfully self-conscious about his large ears. According to Crawford, he was a "mischievous but sometimes rather priggish little boy."[11] Eliot had a privileged, sheltered and relatively strict upbringing, but he recalled his childhood in a predominantly female household as happy and he was devoted to his nurse, Annie Dunne, a Catholic Irish-American. The family house at 2635 Locust Street was situated close to African American communities and ragtime rhythms were an abiding memory. His paternal grandfather, the Reverend William Greenleaf Eliot (who died a year before Tom was born) had supported the abolition of slavery. Charlotte's biography of him, *William Greenleaf Eliot: Minister, Educator, Philanthropist* (1904), was dedicated to her children, "Lest They Forget." Eliot called him the family patriarch, a Moses-like figure. A Unitarian minister whose sense of religious duty drew him from Harvard Divinity School to the Midwest, Reverend Eliot established the Church of the Messiah in St Louis as well as three educational institutions in the city: Washington University; Mary Institute, a girls' school; and its male counterpart, Smith Academy, where Eliot's first steps as a literature student were promising rather than outstanding, although his graduation ode signalled an extra-academic promise. Summer months were spent on the New England coast – Henry had built a house overlooking Gloucester – where as a teenager Eliot enjoyed sailing a catboat (sea sounds and images permeate his poetry), clambering over granite rock-pools in search of crabs, and observing migratory birds. In 1902, Charlotte presented this avid amateur ornithologist with a cherished copy of Chapman's *Handbook of Birds of Eastern North America*, cited in the notes to *The Waste Land*.

In 1905, as preparation for attending Harvard University, Eliot was sent to Milton Academy, a boarding school near Boston, where he pursued a "somewhat miscellaneous course" (*L1* 4) of studies and joined a social and cultural elite. In Unitarian Boston, he was more conscious of his ancestry among the New England Eliots (family relations included two U.S. presidents, a president of Harvard, and an intellectual aristocracy of New England writers, notably Hawthorne and Melville). The Eliots provided several leaders of the American Unitarian Church and belonged to the caste Oliver Wendell Holmes had christened the Boston Brahmins. Eliot later claimed he had been raised outside the Christian faith, since Unitarianism does not believe in the doctrine of the Incarnation. In a 1933 lecture at a Boston Unitarian church, he warned the congregation against a desire to "trim your ideals down to fit the behavior of the nicest people" and of the dangers of a complacent self-conceit leading to "spiritual pride" (*CP4* 816). He distrusted the high-minded liberal humanitarianism of Unitarianism and rejected its optimism about social progress. In a review of *The Education of Henry Adams*, Eliot poured scorn on the intellectual scepticism that he labelled the "Boston doubt," the product of an over-refined education. Cultivated and snobbish, Eliot's family "looked down on all southerners and Virginians" (*L4* 138); in Boston he became conscious of his own Missouri accent. Crawford surmises that an outsider's desire to ingratiate himself in this milieu was partly responsible for Eliot's frat-boy taste for swapping ribald jokes with contemporaries, such as Howard Morris, who also graduated from Milton and roomed with Eliot at Harvard. Morris was a recipient of Eliot's obscene King Bolo verses.

At Harvard, Eliot, a well-mannered and well-dressed young man, was educated in the elective system introduced by President Charles W. Eliot, a distant relative. Eliot complained that this system led to "wide but disorderly reading, intense but confused thinking, and utter absence of background and balance and proportion" (*L1* 100). He took undergraduate courses in English and comparative literature, classics, modern languages, philosophy, history, politics, fine arts and science. In his senior year, Eliot applied himself assiduously. As Herbert Howarth has argued, Eliot's "debt to Harvard was considerable ... he often fell back on memories of his Harvard classes."[12] Dante studies flourished at Harvard under Charles Grandgent, Professor of Romance Languages, stimulating Eliot's endeavour to puzzle out Dante's Italian in his 1909 Temple Classics edition, which contained a facing English translation. He read John Donne's poetry as a freshman in Dean Briggs's class, and in his fourth year he studied Elizabethan and Jacobean drama with G. P. Baker. Eliot pursued a master's degree at Harvard specialising in literature and philosophy. Two of his teachers were inspirational and left an indelible mark on his development. Eliot took courses with George Santayana, whom he recalled as "a brilliant philosopher and man of letters" (*CP4* 58). He took a keen interest in Santayana's reflections on the system-building of philosophical poetry. Irving Babbitt's class on French literature was also germinal. It instilled in Eliot a lifelong advocacy of the order and authority of classicism over the individualism of romanticism. However, Eliot later rejected the ethical foundation of Babbitt's "New Humanism" since it was insufficiently grounded in religious dogma.

In December 1908, Eliot borrowed from the Harvard Union Library Arthur Symons's *The Symbolist Movement in Literature* which, as Anne Stillman's chapter suggests, had a profound effect on his experimentation with serio-comic masks. In Jules Laforgue, whom Symons described as a poet of the "nerves," Eliot discovered a temperamental affinity.[13] He sent off to Paris for the three volumes of Laforgue's *Oeuvres Complètes*, which arrived in spring 1909. By 1910, Eliot had begun drafting poems in a notebook titled "Inventions of the March Hare," representing a clean break from the apprentice work he had published in the *Harvard Advocate*. He started to sketch fragments of the poems "Portrait of a Lady," "Preludes" and "The Love Song of J. Alfred Prufrock." Eliot learned from Laforgue's wistful and ironic treatment of romantic ardour. He imitated the style and technique of the French poet's innovations in line length, rhythm and diction, but redirected his work towards American subjects, from urban squalor ("First Caprice in North Cambridge" and "Prelude in Roxbury") to genteel high culture (the atmosphere of Adeline Moffat's downtown Boston salon is conjured in "Portrait of a Lady"). "Inventions of the March Hare" reveals the first gestures of an astonishing breakthrough in twentieth-century poetry. The nervous hypersensitivity of these poems, with an undercurrent of sexual neurosis beneath the dandyish pose of detached urbane observation, is indebted to Laforgue's example but, in those poems collected in 1917 in *Prufrock and Other Observations*, Eliot has recognisably found his own poetic voice. "Of Jules Laforgue," he observed in an address acknowledging his debt to Dante, "I can say that he was the first to teach me how to speak, to teach me the poetic possibilities of my own idiom of speech" (*TCC* 125).

When Charlotte Eliot heard of her son's plans to study French literature in Paris in the academic year 1910–11, the prospect filled her with trepidation. "I cannot bear to think of your being alone in Paris, the very words give me a chill," she wrote to her son, adding: "I do not admire the French nation, and have less confidence in individuals of that race than in [the] English" (*L1* 12). Eliot overcame his parents' objections and spent a year in the cosmopolitan Latin Quarter. This does not mean that he visited every exhibition, concert, theatre and café in the city. Although Paris was the world's leading city of avant-garde activity in the years before World War I – the city of Picasso, Apollinaire and Stravinsky – aside from applying himself diligently to his academic studies in philosophy, sociology and psychology at the Sorbonne, he appears to have been (as his mother worried) quite lonely, spending evenings reading in French the novels of Dostoevsky and Charles-Louis Philippe. Eliot recorded a "temporary conversion" to Henri Bergson's philosophy of vitalism following attendance at celebrated public lectures at the College de France, society events, but his later rejection of Bergson's anti-intellectualism was pronounced.[14] The isolation of a visiting overseas student was mitigated by Eliot's friendship with his French tutor, Alain-Fournier, a novelist who was associated with the Parisian monthly magazine *La Nouvelle Revue Française*, and with a fellow lodger at his *pension*, Jean Verdenal, a medical student who was killed in battle in the Dardanelles in 1915. Eliot dedicated *Prufrock and Other Observations* to Verdenal: a mark of respect and of grief at his battlefield death, not as some critics have strangely contended evidence of a homosexual relationship.[15] Eliot and Verdenal shared a passion for the operas of Richard Wagner and an interest in the extreme right-wing French nationalist Charles Maurras whose royalist (some historians have argued proto-fascist) Action Française movement clashed with police in streets close to Eliot's lodgings. Maurras's writings provided a blueprint for a reactionary political philosophy.

Eliot recalled that in his early twenties he was "very immature for my age, very timid, very inexperienced" (*L1* xix). In a letter to a fellow editor of the *Harvard Advocate*, Conrad Aiken, who was already married and a published poet, he confided that he had been unable to visit the brothels he read about in Philippe's novels: "One walks about the street with one's desires, and one's refinement rises up like a wall whenever opportunity approaches. I should be better off, I sometimes think, if I had disposed of my virginity and shyness several years ago: and indeed I still think sometimes that it would be well to do so before marriage" (*L1* 82). Gail McDonald's chapter sympathetically yet critically addresses Eliot's sexuality and his expressions of misogyny. Sexual anxiety was exacerbated by his father's fierce belief that syphilis was God's punishment. An American Puritan background exerted its transatlantic pull. Eliot later recalled that he had considered settling in Paris and writing poetry in French, revealing doubts about his academic future at Harvard. Contemporary French poets, however, were no longer in tune with the aesthetics of Symons's Symbolists and nothing came of this pipe dream.

On his return to America, Eliot delivered a paper as president of the Harvard Philosophical Club criticising Bergson's philosophical inconsistencies. Bergson's emphasis on intuition had found support from liberal modernists within the Catholic Church but had excited vehement attacks from more conservative quarters. A central preoccupation of Eliot's graduate studies in philosophy at Harvard was the concern to reconcile religious beliefs with advances in science, addressing what Josiah Royce called in a 1913 book *The Problem of Christianity*. Eliot enrolled in Royce's seminar on scientific method in 1913–14. His student essay for Royce's seminar entitled "The Interpretation of Primitive Ritual" is a fascinating document. Eliot doubts there can be a science of religion and advances a sophisticated theory of interpretation that is more relativist than Royce's own idealist position in which self and community are forged by social acts of interpretation. The essay revealed Eliot's wide reading in cultural anthropology and the psychology of religion (notably, the rival theories of Sir James Frazer and Lucien

Lévy-Bruhl). Together with seminars on metaphysics, ethics and logic, Eliot took courses in Eastern philosophy with Charles Lanman and James Woods, which required him to study texts in Pali and Sanskrit, but which ultimately left him, looking back, "in a state of enlightened mystification" (*ASG* 40). Eliot also attended a class on "Schools of the Religious and Philosophical Thought of Japan, as compared with those of China and India," taught by a Japanese scholar, Masaharu Anesaki. The diversity and difficulty of these courses led Crawford to conclude: "No other major twentieth-century poet was so thoroughly and strenuously educated."[16]

In 1914 Eliot took up a Sheldon Travelling Fellowship to Merton College, Oxford, to study the work of the eminent British philosopher, F. H. Bradley, and also Aristotelean thought with Harold Joachim. The previous year Eliot had purchased Bradley's *Appearance and Reality* (1893). Eliot rejected Bradley's Absolute as a postulate of his metaphysical system: in effect, an act of faith. Once his academic year at Oxford concluded in the summer of 1915, Eliot worked hard writing up his doctoral dissertation which was completed in April 1916. It was received in the Harvard Philosophy Department as the work of an expert, but due to the wartime dangers of crossing the Atlantic it was not defended at a viva voce. Eliot was never enthusiastic about his dissertation. He praised the grace of Bradley's expository prose style and repeated his maxim that philosophy was the finding of reasons to justify what one believes on instinct. However, in a 1915 letter to a Harvard acquaintance, Norbert Wiener, Eliot expressed grave reservations about his philosophical studies: "I took a piece of fairly technical philosophy for my thesis, and my relativism made me see so many sides to questions that I became hopelessly involved, and wrote a thesis perfectly unintelligible to anyone but myself." He also explained to Wiener that: "For *me*, as for Santayana, philosophy is chiefly literary criticism and conversation about life" (*L1* 89, 88). Disenchantment with the sterility of academic Oxford encouraged Eliot to rebel against his parents and mix among avant-garde poets and artists in London. He later suggested that a desire to escape from returning to the philosophy department at Harvard contributed to his precipitous decision to marry Vivien Haigh-Wood in June 1915 and to settle in London – against strong family disapproval – first as a teacher at private schools and then from March 1917 as an employee of Lloyds Bank.[17]

The technical aspects of Eliot's philosophical writings are examined in detail in Jewel Spears Brooker's chapter, but it is important to note here that it is unwise to ascribe a too systematic theoretical programme to his creative writing. Eliot was not, in Santayana's terms, a philosophical poet. He made a firm distinction between the two activities: "Without doubt, the effort of the philosopher proper, the man who is trying to deal with ideas in themselves, and the effort of the poet, who may be trying to *realize* ideas, cannot be carried on at the same time" (*CP2* 228). Eliot's training in philosophy, however, is evident in his early articles, essays and book reviews for the *International Journal of Ethics*, the *Monist*, the *New Statesman* and for the *Egoist*, an avant-garde magazine of literature and philosophy which Eliot joined as assistant editor in 1917. In the *Egoist*, Eliot reconceived the concept of a modernising tradition in contradistinction to the radical individualism promoted elsewhere in its pages by Dora Marsden, and in dialogue with Pound's modernist aesthetics. The framework of Bradley's predilection for system and a coherence theory of truth have been discerned behind Eliot's doctrine of tradition in "Tradition and the Individual Talent," published in the final two issues of the *Egoist* in 1919. The magisterial tone of this essay cloaks its subversive intent – an act of creative criticism that sought to demolish moribund pre-war literary standards.

In 1920, Eliot assembled a coherent selection of his literary journalism in *The Sacred Wood*, drawing on "longer and better" (*L1* 354) essays for the *Athenaeum*, an advanced weekly arts journal. He reprinted his criticism of the structural and the psychological weaknesses of *Hamlet* in which Shakespeare had apparently failed to find an "objective correlative" (*CP2* 125) to express Hamlet's emotions towards his mother. William Empson linked this striking assertion to Eliot's need to reconcile his own family drama after the death of his father in January 1919, observing: "One ought to have realised at the time that only some great personal distraction could account for so bizarre a judgement."[18] Eliot's formulation of the objective correlative is allied to the attack on romantic theories of self-expression contained in his impersonal theory of poetry. Helen Thaventhiran's chapter examines the rhetorical tactics of Eliot's critical prose: his revaluations of particular works and elucidatory epitomes of well-chosen passages of poetry. *The Sacred Wood*, soon to be reinforced by a series of leading reviews for the *TLS*, collected as *Homage for John Dryden* in 1924, represented a thoroughgoing challenge to the London literary establishment, including thinly veiled attacks on figures such as Sir Edmund Gosse. Eliot conceived of the thirteen essays in *The Sacred Wood* as "a single distinct blow" (*L1* 431) and the collection's title, as commentators have noted, invokes the violent succession enacted by the priest of Nemi as retold in Frazer's *The Golden Bough*. It is remarkable how Eliot followed Wordsworth's injunction (to the original writer) to "create the taste by which he is to be realised" (Brooker xxii).

Eliot's collection *Poems* was published by the Woolfs' Hogarth Press in 1919. It was through Bertrand Russell, who, as a visiting professor, had taught Eliot at Harvard, that he gained an entrée into Ottoline Morrell's

Garsington set and to the Bloomsbury Group, with whom the Eliots' relations were sometimes fractious. Due to the Eliots' financial difficulties, Vivien stayed in Russell's London flat. By 1917 they had begun an affair which Eliot is likely to have known about. Eliot later told Morrell, Russell's ex-mistress, that he believed Russell "has done Evil."[19] There is a darkening of tone in the poems Eliot composed in the years 1917 to 1919. His satire is sharper and the invitations to prejudice are more sinister. "Burbank with a Baedeker: Bleistein with a Cigar" is a poem redolent of sexual intrigue and an atmosphere of evil. Eliot described the poem as "intensely serious" (*L1* 441). Rick de Villiers's chapter finds sexual betrayal at the heart of the savage comedy of Eliot's quatrain poems (whose form was modelled on Gautier's *Émaux et Camées*). Anthony Julius is more troubled by the menace of anti-Semitism he detects in these poems. Eliot's state of mind was not sweetened by the effects of the war which he told E. M. Forster "crippled me as it did everyone else; but me chiefly because it was something I was neither honestly in nor honestly out of" (*L4* 573). Vivien's brother, Maurice, passed on harrowing details of trench warfare. Unlike Russell and some of his Bloomsbury acquaintances, Eliot was not a pacifist but his protracted attempts to join the U.S. military were fruitless. Complications over the situation of U.S. nationals living in wartime Britain led this "resident alien" to take the first official steps (frequently interrupted) towards becoming a British citizen.

After the war, Eliot shared John Maynard Keynes's dismay at the peace treaty concluded at Versailles. He dealt with punitive German war reparations in his duties concerning foreign loans at Lloyds Bank. For Eliot, this was a dispiriting period of illness, overwork and a misery that bordered on despair. "Gerontion," the opening poem of *Ara Vos Prec* (1920), is a dramatic monologue spoken by an embittered little old man. It is no straightforward mask for self-expression; rather, as Peter Ackroyd has suggested: "there is an immediate sense of release into an expansive, elaborate and allusive mode of address."[20] "Gerontion" is saturated in Elizabethan and Jacobean rhetoric (Chapman, Shakespeare, Jonson, Middleton, Bishop Andrewes) which Eliot had studied intensively for his 1918 adult education class on Elizabethan literature, the foundation of his scholarship in this field. The nervous and turbulent energy of the lines, "I that was near your heart was removed therefrom / To lose beauty in terror, terror in inquisition" (*CPP* 38) adapts Beatrice's terrifying confession in Middleton's *The Changeling*, a tragic story of murder and sexual betrayal that Eliot described as an impassioned exposure of fundamental passions: "it is the tragedy of the not naturally bad but irresponsible and undeveloped nature, suddenly caught in the consequences of its own action" (*CP3* 123) and he expressed a haunted fascination with Jacobean drama's "tentacular roots reaching down to the deepest terrors and desires" (*CP2* 156–7).

In 1921, Eliot embarked in earnest on writing the long poem that became *The Waste Land*. He had drafted the first two sections by May, before work was interrupted by the summer visit of members of his family. After the prolonged tension of managing the testy relations between his elderly mother and chronically ill wife, Eliot suffered a nervous breakdown, taking three months of leave from the bank in the autumn. He spent a month at the seaside town of Margate ("On Margate Sands. / I can connect / Nothing with nothing" [*CPP* 70]), where he drafted parts of section three before travelling to Lausanne on the shore of Lake Geneva or Leman ("By the waters of Leman I sat down and wept" [*CPP* 67]) in Switzerland, where he underwent a rest cure at the sanatorium of the psychiatrist Dr Roger Vittoz. Responding well, Eliot emerged from his debilitating self-diagnosed *aboulie* (or loss of will) to complete the apocalyptic closing section of *The Waste Land* in a burst of creativity. Eliot thought this was the finest part of the poem, later observing that "some forms of illness are extremely favourable ... to artistic and literary composition" (*CP4* 340). In Paris in January 1922, Pound took his blue pencil to nineteen pages of drafts, removing three long narrative sections, pruning and polishing, and effectively giving the poem its final structure. It is the most remarkable collaboration between two major poets since Wordsworth and Coleridge laboured on *Lyrical Ballads*.

A forbiddingly erudite and angular poem, a fragmentary text full of allusion, parody and pastiche, *The Waste Land*, as Lawrence Rainey's chapter shows, is built on the dislocations and recoveries of lexis and syntax. It was awarded the New York *Dial*'s lucrative $2,000 annual prize for modern literature, but it was received frostily by distinguished London critics. In the *London Mercury*, Sir John Squire complained "what is language but communication, or art but selection and arrangement" and he dismissed the poem as incoherent: "A grunt would serve equally well" (Brooker 115). On the other hand, Edmund Wilson, who wrote an insightful review for the *Dial*, was moved to remark: "we feel that he is speaking not only for a personal distress, but for the starvation of a whole civilization" (Brooker 86). That the poem was a cri de coeur is supported by Eliot's (otherwise misleading) reported comment that far from being an attempt to capture a widespread spirit of post-war disillusionment, the poem "was only the relief of a personal and wholly insignificant grouse against life" (*WLF* 1). *The Waste Land*'s ghostly "Unreal City" (*CPP* 62), inhabited by Dante's souls in Limbo, transforms the real City of London, where Eliot took lunchtime walks from his basement office at Lloyds to the refuge of nearby churches. Eliot's most chilling retrospective statement on the poem was that his marriage brought no happiness but "the state of mind out of which came *The Waste Land*" (*L1* xix). The comment is suggestive in the light of those sections dramatizing failed sexual relationships. The jagged dialogue of the neurotic couple in "A Game of Chess" was admired by Vivien as "wonderful" and described by Pound as "photography" (*WLF* 10). Seamus Perry is correct to say that the transmutation of this multivocal multilingual poem (a modernist experiment to rival Joyce, Picasso and Stravinsky), transcends mere autobiography: "to interpret the poem merely as an expression of Eliot's local melancholy would be seriously to undersell the amplitude of the poem's ambition."[21] Moreover, as Jim McCue says of the notes added to the first American book edition of *The Waste Land*: "Purporting to explain it, they complete it, complicate it and undermine it."[22]

One biographer contends that Eliot's "relationship with Vivien lay behind the composition of what is arguably his major work, written between 1917 and 1930."[23] Vivien was certainly a valued commentator on the drafts of *The Waste Land*, even if she recoiled from the misogyny of her husband's Fresca couplets. Childless Vivien suggested the line "What you get married for if you don't want children?" (*CPP* 66), which was incorporated into the published version of "A Game of Chess." The sexual politics of this section have been given a twist by the revelation offered by Eliot's second wife that it was Vivien who asked for a cryptic line, "The ivory men make company between us" (*WLF* 12), to be left out (it was restored in 1960). Eliot thought that Vivien was a talented writer, and throughout 1924 and 1925 he supported his wife's pseudonymous career as an author of prose sketches – until a crushing rejection letter from Marianne Moore at the *Dial*, which sparked an apoplectic response from Eliot, contributed to the collapse of Vivien's confidence and an alarming downturn in her well-being. Her letters from this time indicate that her state of mind was tortured, unstable and morbid.

"The Hollow Men" sequence of 1925 represents the lowest ebb of Eliot's poetry, with its flat pulse of utterance and arid desert imagery. In this year, Eliot told John Middleton Murry that he had "made myself into a *machine* … in order to endure, in order not to feel" (*L2* 627), claiming he had done so to avoid destroying his partner. "The Hollow Men" appeared in *Poems 1909–1925*, which Eliot inscribed to Vivien as a collection "no one else will quite understand."[24] Although countless commentators have been willing to explain Tom and Vivien's unhappy marriage by fabricating links between a tissue of letters, rumours and fictional literature, the complexities of their domestic intimacies are beyond posthumous reconstruction from second-hand scraps or from correspondence (to repeat Haffenden's words) "used to flatter self-esteem, to propound opinion, to influence and manipulate others." Pondering Eliot's marriage, Crawford warns us against the dangers of "advancing theories for which evidence is so slender."[25] When Vivien's biographer, Carole Seymour-Jones, writes, "It was the horror of Eliot's life with Vivien which motivated him to write *Sweeney Agonistes*," this highly experimental jazz-age drama is reduced in her reading to an "exposé of marital disconnectedness" in which Vivien appears as the prostitute Doris and Eliot performs the role of brutal and inarticulate Sweeney, who wants "to do a girl in."[26] Anthony Cuda's chapter in this *Companion* proposes a more nuanced reading of the labyrinthine entanglements of Eliot's life in his verse drama.

Vivien's prose fiction was published alongside work by Joyce, Woolf, Pound, Yeats, Wyndham Lewis, Huxley and Lawrence in the *Criterion*, the small-circulation highbrow quarterly review launched by Eliot in 1922 with the financial backing of Lady Rothermere. Eliot later dated the beginning of his "adult life" to the foundation of the *Criterion* "and the development of relations with men of letters in the several countries of Europe."[27] Eliot's desire to strengthen a European ideal of "classicism" – "the European idea – the idea of a common culture of western Europe" (*CP*2 778) – led him to solicit contributions from major European authors: Hesse, Valéry, Proust, Pirandello. Eliot's poetry took a back seat during the nerve-wracking period in which he established the *Criterion*'s phalanx of like-minded critics in literary London. Some of Eliot's best critical articles, for example on the music-hall artiste Marie Lloyd and on the conventions of Elizabethan drama, date from the early years of the *Criterion*. An Arnoldian restatement of his critical position in the 1923 *Criterion* essay "The Function of Criticism" provoked a lengthy debate with John Middleton Murry, editor of the rival *Adelphi* magazine, on the respective claims of the traditions of classicism and romanticism. In spite of the sarcasm Eliot directed at the "Whiggery" of Murry's reliance on the "Inner Voice" (*CP*2 463), compounded by ad hominem barbs, in 1925 Murry generously recommended Eliot to succeed him as Cambridge Clark lecturer.

Eliot followed Murry's Clark lectures on Keats and Shakespeare with a series of eight lectures on the nature of metaphysical poetry. He redefined his contentious theory of a "dissociation of sensibility" (*CP*2 380) rupturing thought from feeling in the poetry written after the English Civil War, by tracing the "disintegration of the intellect" (*CP*2 609) back to the thirteenth century. Dante and the *trecento* poets were Eliot's chief exemplars of an undissociated sensibility. He scolded the exhibitionism that he found in the elaborate extended conceits in the poetry of Donne and Cowley. Private criticism of these lectures by Mario Praz discouraged Eliot from publishing them immediately as a book and the rejection of an over-ambitious research proposal on seventeenth-century culture, crafted for a research fellowship at

All Souls College, Oxford, was a measure of how this bold poet-critic was still viewed with suspicion by some established scholars, thereby frustrating hopes of an academic career in English literature. Fortunately, a conversation between Charles Whibley and Geoffrey Faber at All Souls led to Eliot being recruited as a director of the new publishing venture of Faber and Gwyer. He resigned from Lloyds Bank in the autumn of 1925.

In 1926, in the midst of one of Vivien's bouts of suicidal despair, Eliot fell to his knees before Michelangelo's Pietà in St Peter's Basilica in Rome. This was an indication of a deepening attraction towards religion that eventually led to his baptism in June 1927 by his friend William Force Stead and his confirmation as an Anglican by the Bishop of Oxford. As Barry Spurr's chapter points out, Eliot rejected the evangelical idea that he had been converted, preferring to see his religious belief not as a leap of faith but rather as the gradual accumulation (echoing Newman's words) of "powerful and concurrent" (*CP4* 342) reasons, in which doubt and scepticism played their part. Eliot informed Stead that "nothing could be too ascetic" (*L4* 128) for him. Spurr explains that Eliot worshipped as an Anglo-Catholic deeply committed to the sacraments of penance and confession. In 1928, withdrawing further from Vivien, who often stayed for several weeks in a Paris sanatorium, Eliot took a vow of celibacy. He later confided to John Hayward that he had never slept with a woman to whom he felt any strong physical attraction. Challenged by Irving Babbitt to make a formal public statement of his religious and political position, Eliot announced an all-too-quotable credo in the preface to *For Lancelot Andrewes* (1928): "classicist in literature, royalist in politics, and anglo-catholic in religion" (*CP3* 513).

For Lancelot Andrewes signalled a realignment of Eliot's critical values, what he called in the 1928 preface to the second edition of *The Sacred Wood*, "not so much a change or reversal of opinions, as an expansion or development of interests" (*CP3* 413). This expansion was received with consternation by former admirers. In a review of *For Lancelot Andrewes*, Jacob Bronowski bemoaned "the moments when [Eliot] is near becoming the intolerant cleric" (Brooker 149). Eliot used his editorials in the *Criterion* (acquired by Faber in 1927) to shield the magazine from accusations it was too "Frenchified" or that it actively promoted "a reactionary Latin philosophy" as "a repressive instrument of literary criticism."[28] The *Criterion*'s antagonists had essays from Eliot's Parisian acquaintances Maurras, Henri Massis and Jacques Maritain on their minds. Increasingly preoccupied by the problem of poetry and belief, Eliot admired Maritain's neo-Thomist aesthetics, advocating the primacy of the spiritual and a strict separation between poetry and religion, and detached himself from I. A. Richards's influential interpretation of *The Waste Land* as a poem bereft of belief. Eliot defended

Maurras against condemnation from the Vatican. He claimed that this atheist (who paid a politically motivated lip-service to French Catholicism) had drawn him closer to faith. Eliot dedicated his 1929 study of Dante (the heart of his prose criticism) to Maurras and, in a *Criterion* symposium on fascism and communism, he said that he found Maurras's monarchism more palatable than Mussolini's fascism. Eliot's own brand of Tory royalism attracted misunderstanding and hostility among fellow British political commentators (he had been naturalised as a citizen at the end of 1927).

If Eliot's post-Christian prose criticism witnessed a readjustment of values, it is an over-simplification, as Sarah Kennedy's chapter reveals, to gloss the poems Eliot composed in the years 1927 to 1931 as "conversion" poems. Those critics who read the Ariel poems as the solution to a dilemma should be mindful of Eliot's exasperated letter to Paul Elmer More, complaining that it is "rather trying to be supposed to have settled oneself into an easy chair, when one has just begun a long journey afoot" (*L4* 567). Eliot's Ariel poems dramatize the difficulties of faith. Christopher Ricks writes powerfully about these transitional poems. He is attentive to a redemptive suffering unlocked by profound Shakespearean allusions in "Marina" (1930), described as "the greatest of the between-poems, being the one where the energies of animosity are at once acknowledged to be substantial and believed to be so transcendable that they can 'become unsubstantial'."[29] Lyndall Gordon's biographical approach risks becoming an escape from poetry when she identifies a real person, Emily Hale, as the elusive "Lady of silences" (*CPP* 91) in *Ash-Wednesday*, "a dream of sexual purity" leading the poet towards faith; a figure that is "set against Vivien" (Eliot had dedicated the poem "To My Wife").[30] Yet when Eliot introduced Hale to his London acquaintances, she elicited acerbic comments in respect of a bossy "sergeant major" manner towards Eliot.[31] It is doubtful whether Hale's voluminous correspondence with Eliot could certify Gordon's vision of her as an angelic lady of "silences" and it does appear hyperbolic to liken Eliot's modest reunion with the middle-aged Hale as "a replay of Dante's reunion with Beatrice on the verge of Paradise."[32]

After the death of his mother in 1929, Eliot's marriage deteriorated. Vivien's behaviour, affected by a cocktail of prescription drugs, became worryingly erratic, as testified by numerous contemporary reports. Richard Aldington's caustically satirical presentation of the Eliots' marriage in *Stepping Heavenward* (1931) caused the couple a great deal of distress. Eliot's best critical essays from this period reveal a lacerating self-scrutiny. For example, an introduction to Christopher Isherwood's translation of Baudelaire's *Intimate Journals* (1930) broods on the vertiginous divide separating salvation from damnation and asserts that "recognition of the reality of Sin is a New Life" (*CP4* 161). His remarkable preface to a 1931 edition of Pascal's *Pensées* places the emphasis on Original Sin and strenuous, ascetic self-discipline as a stay against illness and suffering. He remained a prominent critic of seventeenth-century literature, teasing out in a series of leading *TLS* reviews the "personality" of major and minor dramatists of the age from the "pattern" of their oeuvres. However, Paul Elmer More, a Princeton theologian and close confidant, pondered in a review of Eliot's *Selected Essays* (1932) whether a clear division had opened up between "the older poet and the newer critic" (Brooker 216): that is, between the radical poet of *The Waste Land* and the Anglican moralist apparent in "Thoughts after Lambeth" (1931), in which Eliot denied that *The Waste Land* represented the disillusionment of a generation – "I may have expressed for them their own illusion of being disillusioned" (*CP4* 226) – and offered conservative Christian opinions on birth control, youth movements, modern science and the calls for a reunion of Christian churches (Eliot satirised Evangelicals and Anglican Modernists).

In September 1932, Eliot travelled to the United States for the first time in seventeen years to take up the Norton professorship of poetry at Harvard. During nine months he delivered over forty public talks across America, the most significant of which were the eight Norton lectures on *The Use of Poetry and the Use of Criticism: Studies in the Relation of Criticism to Poetry in England*, which, in spite of hurried preparation, furnishes fascinating reflections on the conscious sources of his poetry (and on unconscious "depths of feeling into which we cannot peer" or "feelings too obscure for the authors even to know quite what they were" [*CP4* 688]) as well as compelling, if combative, confrontations with the history of English literary criticism from the age of Shakespeare, through the Augustans and Romantics, to the modern avant-garde. In February 1933, in the middle of the Norton series, Eliot instructed his solicitors in London to draw up a Deed of Separation from Vivien. The stress of this irrevocable decision appears in his lecture on Shelley and Keats, where Eliot betrays an antipathy to Shelley's advocacy of free love and calls him a "blackguard" (*CP4* 642). In a short preface to a posthumous collection of Harold Monro's poetry, written at this time, Eliot declared: "the compensations for being a poet are grossly exaggerated; and they dwindle as one becomes older, and the shadows lengthen, and the solitude becomes harder to endure" (*CP4* 524). A few months later, Eliot told the graduating class at Milton Academy that if he could address his teenage self he would tell him: "See what a mess you have made of things" (*CP4* 818).

In his Harvard undergraduate course on contemporary English literature, Eliot displayed distaste for the representation of human sexuality in the novels of Hardy and Lawrence. He elaborated more fully on this topic in his May 1933 Page-Barbour lectures at Virginia University, published in 1934 as *After Strange Gods: A Primer of Modern Heresy*. Herbert Read's neo-romantic theory of the spontaneity of the poet's "personality" was included in a heresy appendix. Although, in Eliot's view, heretics have a "profound insight, of some part of the truth" (*ASG* 24), reviewers were either shocked or amused by his strictures on the role of the devil in modern literature. Ezra Pound crossed swords with him on the subjects of religion, economics and ethics in the pages of the *New English Weekly*. The centrality of Christian orthodoxy to *After Strange Gods* occasioned a notorious, subsequently regretted, statement that, "reasons of race and religion combine to make any number of free-thinking Jews undesirable" (*ASG* 20). *After Strange Gods* anticipates the dogmatism of "Religion and Literature" (1935): "literary criticism should be completed by criticism from a definite ethical and theological standpoint" (*SE* 388).

On his return to London in 1933, Virginia Woolf noted in her diary that Eliot spoke with asperity about the failure of his marriage but in his forties "wants to live, to love."[33] After residence in a series of temporary lodgings, Eliot settled in the presbytery of St Stephen's Church, Kensington. The flamboyant vicar, the Reverend Eric Cheetham, appointed him as the churchwarden. Although a Faber secretary in the mid-1930s recalled Eliot as "an unhappy man ... crouched over his desk in an attic in Russell Square,"[34] his daily contact with authors and the jovial company of his fellow Faber directors, who held regular soirées at John Hayward's Kensington flat in Bina Gardens, provided welcome respite. (Witty verses composed at these gatherings were privately published as *Noctes Binanianae* in 1937.) As a director of Faber, Eliot has been recognised for his "kindness, his active helpfulness to young writers."[35] Another social circle was opened up by his commitment to the Church of England. Bishop George Bell encouraged Eliot to take an interest in the revival of religious drama, leading to commissions to write prose dialogue and verse choruses for a pageant play, *The Rock*, and, following that, *Murder in the Cathedral* for the Canterbury Festival.

Performances of these plays were attended by Vivien (who paid unannounced visits to Russell Square, where she was prevented from confronting her husband). Her diaries record that she was a supporter of Oswald Mosley's British Union of Fascists and that she was "very nearly insane already with the cruel pain of losing Tom."[36] In 1938, after she was discovered by the police wandering in a distraught and confused state, her brother Maurice sought medical approval to commit her to a London nursing home (where she died in 1947). It has been supposed that the "restless shivering painted shadow" (*CPP* 290) in *The Family Reunion* (1939) is Eliot's portrait of his wife. Seymour-Jones asserts that the guilt-ridden protagonist of this play, Harry, Lord Monchensey, is "patently Eliot."[37] But Ackroyd resists such a "banal identification of author and character" on the grounds that it is "at best hypothetical, since it implies that Eliot was unconsciously propelled towards some instinctual revelation of his own guilt and horror."[38] Eliot himself acknowledged a closer self-resemblance to Harry's uncle, Charles. Whatever the truth, Seymour-Jones's hypothesis requires more tact to convince doubters like Ackroyd that it could be seamlessly and illuminatingly woven into a literary-critical appreciation of this play.

In a series of BBC radio broadcasts during the 1930s, Eliot established himself as a public intellectual, or as he told Paul Elmer More, "a new type of intellectual, combining the intellectual and the devotional" (*L4* 567). In "The Modern Dilemma" BBC series, Eliot spoke as an Anglican moralist attacking what he took to be the corrosive claims advanced by communism, psychology and modern science. In 1931 his signed *Criterion* editorial "Commentaries" doubled in length to deal with political and economic crises. Eliot was dismissive of the National Coalition government and the materialist basis of party politics. He called for a reinvention of a modern Toryism based on Christian principles. Although his *Criterion* editorials on major social and political issues of the day (including the Abyssinian Crisis and the Spanish Civil War) exasperated contemporaries by their lack of political realism and a refusal to adopt a strident anti-fascist line, Eliot did not favour a totalitarian dismantling of democracy. He was an opponent of the British government's appeasement of Hitler. The Munich Agreement occasioned "a depression of spirits so different from any other experience of fifty years as to be a new emotion" and convinced him to close down the *Criterion* in a state of gloom at the destruction of European intellectual life. In his valedictory "Last Words," Eliot said that the *Criterion* "had brought me associations, friendships and acquaintances of inestimable value."[39] In a lecture series delivered at Cambridge in March 1939, collected as *The Idea of a Christian Society*, he espoused a critique of laissez-faire capitalism and unregulated industrialism, promoting an idea of a utopian Christian society that he had formulated in conversations with the Christendom Group of Christian Sociologists: an embodiment of the "clerisy" that he hoped would provide cultural and spiritual leadership at this bleak historical moment.

At the outbreak of World War II, Eliot was also an integral member of the ecumenical discussion group The Moot led by J. H. Oldham. In meetings of The Moot, Eliot stressed the importance for Britain of a hierarchical class-based religio-cultural stability, a rival theory to the German sociologist Karl Mannheim's intellectual elites. These wartime recommendations for post-war reconstruction were articulated in the *New English Weekly*, although by the time they were gathered in book form as *Notes towards the Definition of Culture* (1948), Eliot was completely out of step with the egalitarian spirit of the Labour Party's Welfare State. Aside from a patriotic selection of Rudyard Kipling's poetry, Eliot's war work involved BBC radio talks, lectures and addresses to learned societies. John Xiros Cooper's chapter rightly recalls that these talks were used to champion a common Latin-Christian culture, a European "unity" he underscored in a series of radio broadcasts to occupied Germany in 1946. Eliot's connections with the British Council, whose mission to promote British culture and civilization abroad was conceived by its founders as a form of cultural propaganda, started during the war. In the spring of 1942, Eliot braved German U-boats as part of a British Council delegation to neutral Sweden. In 1947, he spoke in Italy on behalf of the British Council in the midst of a highly volatile communist-backed general strike. Eliot's extensive work for the British Council was crucial in promoting his reputation globally. (Kamau Brathwaite testifies to first encountering Eliot through BBC radio broadcasts and not the literary texts.) Nor is this cultural diplomacy inconsequential when considering the Cold War context in which the Nobel Prize for literature was awarded in 1948 to this public anti-communist.

It was Eliot's achievement as a poet, however, that justified the decision of the Swedish Academy. Eliot was convinced that *Four Quartets* (1943) set a crown on a lifetime's achievement. The idea of a linked series of quartets emerged only after the wartime disruption of the London theatres. The principal themes of *Four Quartets* – meditations on time and memory, on visionary scenery, on beginnings and ends – are rehearsed in *Burnt Norton*. Steve Ellis notes that Eliot had visited Burnt Norton manor house with Hale, but his chapter is concerned with the purgatorial *via negativa* Eliot pursues in order to liberate himself from biographical and historical exigencies. The poet divests himself of worldly things in a humble embrace of the divine darkness of the "dark night of the soul"; it is an ascetic, inward struggle to apprehend a mystical "still point of the turning world" (*CPP* 175). Succeeding quartets mirror the anxious solitude of Eliot's wartime displacement, although the communal language of war does permeate passages of *East Coker* (1940) and *The Dry Salvages* (1941). His auditory imagination was quickened by memories of St Louis and the New England coast, illustrating his remark that "in its sources, in its emotional springs, [my poetry] comes from America."[40] The culminating poem of the quartets, *Little Gidding* (1942), was polished by the exacting search for *le mot juste* conducted in correspondence with John Hayward (who was credited with "improvements of phrase and construction"[41]). Hayward made several improvements to the scene set during the London Blitz. Ricks reflects thrillingly on the encounter with the elusive and allusive "familiar compound ghost" (*CPP* 193), where Eliot's experiences as an air-raid warden are transfigured in this inspired imitation of a canto from Dante.[42] Yet critics who read the confession of guilt ("awareness / Of things ill done and done to others' harm" [*CPP* 194]) as Eliot's remorse for his treatment of Vivien, or for his anti-Semitism, must reckon with the allusion to the poem "Vacillation" by W. B. Yeats, the "dead master" (*CPP* 193), whom Eliot summoned in this haunting phantasmagoria.[43] It is understandable that critics detect an intense personal anguish beneath the meditative tone of *Four Quartets*, but the thematic patterns traced by the symbolist music of this spiralling poem, yearning after the mystic's intersection with the timeless, transfigure private doubts into something rich and strange.

Stephen Spender summarises Eliot's career after *Four Quartets* as follows: "The rest of his work was an epilogue, which was not without some interesting developments for the history of poetic drama, some authoritative lessons drawn from a lifetime of combining poetry with criticism, some revealing wisdom in remarks about society and culture, and something of the grace and urbanity of a 'distinguished guest' who rises at the end of a banquet."[44] Certainly, unlike Yeats, Eliot did not write a resplendent poetry of old age, and his late criticism – polite to the point of blandness – lacks the keen edge and vigour of his early polemics. In a packed American arena in 1956, Eliot reflected on the limitations of professional academic criticism: "Perhaps the form of criticism in which the danger of excessive reliance upon causal explanation is greatest is the critical biography, especially when the biographer supplements his knowledge of external facts with psychological conjectures about inner experience." Eliot says that this is because "a critical biography of a writer is a delicate task in itself; and the critic or the biographer who, without being a trained and practising psychologist, brings to bear on his subject such analytical skill as he has acquired by reading books written by psychologists, may confuse the issues still further." Instead, a proper understanding and enjoyment of literature arises from "the whole man, a man with convictions and principles, and of knowledge and experience of life" (*OPP* 111, 116). In guarding himself against the "causal explanation" of the psychobiographer's lexicon of sublimation and transference and unconscious wishes, he is still reluctant to acknowledge the entanglements of the man who suffers and the mind that creates.

Eliot's lecture on "The Three Voices of Poetry" (1953) dredges up fascinating psychological metaphors about the "obscure impulse" or "inert embryo" in the poet's creative desire to relieve himself of a discomfort: "He is oppressed by a burden which he must bring to birth in order to obtain relief, or, to change the figure of speech, he is haunted by a demon." Eliot goes on to say that "when the words are finally arranged in the right way – or in what he comes to accept as the best arrangement he can find – he may experience a moment of exhaustion, of appeasement, of absolution, and of something very near annihilation, which is in itself indescribable" (*OPP* 98). This formulation recalls a 1931 letter in which Eliot writes movingly about "the fruit of reconciliation and relief after immense suffering" that he heard in Beethoven's late quartets, adding "I should like to get something of that into verse once before I die" (*L5* 203).

As a playwright, the Broadway success of Eliot's *The Cocktail Party* (1949) was stunning, but Kenneth Tynan's review of *The Elder Statesman* (1958) was indicative of the winds of change emanating from a generation of Angry Young Men. Now a grand old man, an elder statesman, honoured by the Order of Merit, Eliot lived in dignified frugality after the war at Hayward's Chelsea mansion flat. In spite of some tetchy disagreements with his sharp-tongued flatmate, Hayward (who was confined to a wheelchair by muscular dystrophy) helped Eliot to weather the shocks of the deaths of Vivien and his brother Henry. Hayward also provided a buffer from the personal intrusions that accompany celebrity. In 1949, Eliot declined a proposal of marriage from a fellow parishioner at St Stephen's, Mary Trevelyan, explaining that he could not give his heart to another woman. It was, therefore, an unexpected blow to Hayward, Trevelyan and Hale when in January 1957 Eliot decided to marry Valerie Fletcher, thirty-eight years his junior, and who since 1949 had been his secretary at Faber. For the remainder of his life, which was increasingly troubled by ill-health, including emphysema and irregular heartbeats, she was his loyal nurse and companion and then, following Eliot's death in 1965, the keeper of the flame. Valerie Eliot has probably done more than anyone else, as executrix and editor, to present the details of Eliot's life in dramatic chiaroscuro: from the darkness of his first marriage – "He felt he had paid too high a price to be a poet, that he had suffered too much" she remarked in an interview[45] – to the radiant glow of his second marriage to her: "To whom I owe the leaping delight / That quickens my senses" (*CPP* 522).

"In my beginning is my end," reads Eliot's memorial plaque in St Michael's Church in East Coker, the Somerset village his ancestors had departed in the 1660s for the New World. The neatness of this self-crafted epitaph has emboldened biographers to impose the narrative of a spiritual pilgrimage across his life and work – an exemplary journey through evil and existential crisis, to humility and final Christian redemption. Gordon's biographical uncovering of epiphanic "unattended" moments" (*CPP* 190) follows a schema of Augustinian conversion, even if her starring lady, Emily Hale, could recognise "mighty little of me in any poetry!"[46] Hagiography, as Aldington's *Stepping Heavenward* noted with cruel relish, is conducted on an otherworldly plane. Other contemporaries had claimed to see through a mere pose of Christian humility. New Yorker Edmund Wilson disparaged Anglican Eliot as a "completely artificial, or, rather a self-invented character" and, in the *New Yorker*, Cynthia Ozick disinterred "Eliot at 101" as a politically incorrect bogey-man: an "autocratic, inhibited, depressed, rather narrow-minded, and considerably bigoted fake Englishman."[47] Her words will bemuse lovers of the boyish feline humour of *Old Possum's Book of Practical Cats* (1939), which furnished the delightful lyrics for Andrew Lloyd Webber's smash-hit musical *Cats*. As further tranches of archival material are released into the embattled arena of Eliot studies, admirers and detractors alike will interpret them in the light of pre-existing arguments about his life and work. Reassessment of this subtle, oblique, at times perplexing poet, an acutely shy and fastidious man, will never cease to attract ardent explorers. In the original *Cambridge Companion to T. S. Eliot* (1994), Bernard Sharratt shrewdly observed: "the fact of the matter is that 'T. S. Eliot' is constructed and reconstructed according to the ways in which his work is received."[48] Or, to put it another way: we should from time to time change our way of being wrong.

NOTES

1 *CP2* 124; *OPP* 141; *CP4* 642; *SE* 332.
2 Quoted in Stefan Collini, "Eliot Among the Intellectuals," *Essays in Criticism* (April 2002), p. 101.
3 Helen Gardner, *The Art of T. S. Eliot* (London: Cresset Press, 1949), p. 103.
4 Hugh Kenner, *The Invisible Poet* (London: Methuen, 1960), p. ix.
5 Lyndall Gordon, *Eliot's New Life* (Oxford: Oxford University Press, 1988), p. v.
6 Frank Kermode, *Bury Place Papers* (London: London Review of Books, 2009), p. 105.
7 Peter Ackroyd, "A Life Measured Out," *The Times* (15 September 1984), p. 8.
8 See John Haffenden, "Life over Literature; or, Whatever Happened to Critical Biography?" in *Writing the Lives of Writers*, eds. Warwick Gould and Thomas F. Staley (London: Macmillan, 1998), p. 22.
9 Ronald Schuchard, *Eliot's Dark Angel* (New York: Oxford University Press, 1999), p. 20.
10 Robert Crawford, *Young Eliot* (London: Jonathan Cape, 2015), p. 3.
11 Crawford, *Young Eliot*, p. 5.
12 Herbert Howarth, *Notes on Some Figures behind T. S. Eliot* (London: Chatto & Windus, 1965), p. 65.
13 "It is an art of the nerves, this art of Laforgue." Arthur Symons, *The Symbolist Movement in Literature* (New York: Haskell House, 1971), p. 304.
14 See *A Sermon Preached in Magdalene College Chapel* (Cambridge: Cambridge University Press, 1948), p. 5.

15 George Watson, who researched Jean Verdenal's life, dismisses the supposition that Eliot and Verdenal had a homosexual affair. Eliot vehemently denied the insinuation of homosexual feelings contained in John Peter's article, "A New Interpretation of *The Waste Land*," *Essays in Criticism* (July 1952), pp. 242–66.
16 Crawford, *Young Eliot*, p. 172.
17 Eliot's letter to Polly Tandy of 9 September 1946 makes the connection between his marriage and abandoning a career in philosophy.
18 William Empson, *Using Biography* (Cambridge, MA: Harvard University Press, 1984), p. 198.
19 Letter to Ottoline Morrell, 14 March 1933. Quoted in Schuchard, *Eliot's Dark Angel*, p. 179.
20 Peter Ackroyd, *T. S. Eliot* (London: Hamish Hamilton, 1984), p. 93.
21 Seamus Perry, *The Connell Guide to T. S. Eliot's "The Waste Land"* (London: Connell, 2014), p. 18.
22 Jim McCue, "Editing Eliot," *Essays in Criticism* (January 2006), p. 14.
23 John Worthen, *T. S. Eliot: A Short Biography* (London: Haus, 2009), p. 2.
24 Quoted in Robert Sencourt, *T. S. Eliot: A Memoir* (London: Garnstone Press, 1971), p. 12.
25 Crawford, *Young Eliot*, p. 357.
26 Carole Seymour-Jones, *Painted Shadow: A Life of Vivienne Eliot* (London: Constable & Robinson, 2001), p. 445.
27 "Brief über Ernst Robert Curtius," in *Freudesgabe für Ernst Robert Curtius*, eds. Max Rychner and Walter Boehlich (Bern: Francke Verlag, 1956), p. 26.
28 For details of these controversies, see Jason Harding, *The Criterion: Cultural Politics and Periodical Networks in Interwar Britain* (Oxford: Oxford University Press, 2002), pp. 19, 59–61.
29 Christopher Ricks, *T. S. Eliot and Prejudice* (London: Faber & Faber, 1988), p. 234.
30 See Gordon, *Eliot's New Life*, pp. 146–90.
31 In 1935, Ottoline Morrell referred to "that *awful* American woman Miss Hale. She is like a sergeant major, quite intolerable." Quoted in Lyndall Gordon, *T. S. Eliot: An Imperfect Life* (London: Vintage, 1998) p. 218.
32 Gordon, *Eliot's New Life*, p. 12.
33 *The Diary of Virginia Woolf: 1931–1935*, ed. Anne Olivier Bell (London: Hogarth Press, 1982), p. 178.
34 Erica Schumacher (née Wright), letter to Jason Harding, 1 February 1999.
35 Hugh Sykes Davies, "Mistah Kurtz: He Dead," in *T. S. Eliot: The Man and His Work*, ed. Allen Tate (London: Chatto & Windus, 1967), p. 355.
36 Papers of Vivien Eliot's archive, Bodleian Library, Oxford. Quoted in Gordon, *An Imperfect Life*, p. 296.
37 See Seymour-Jones, *Painted Shadow*, pp. 466–7.
38 Ackroyd, *T. S. Eliot*, p. 246.
39 "Last Words," *Criterion* (January 1939), 274–5.
40 "The Art of Poetry I: T. S. Eliot" *Paris Review* (Spring–Summer 1959), p. 70.
41 *Four Quartets* (London: Faber & Faber, 1944), p. 5.
42 See Christopher Ricks, *True Friendship: Geoffrey Hill, Anthony Hecht, and Robert Lowell under the Sign of Eliot and Pound* (New Haven: Yale University Press, 2010), pp. 188–218.

43 Eliot quotes the relevant lines from Yeats's "Vacillation" – "'Things said or done / long years ago, / Or things I did not do or say / But thought that I might say or do, / Weigh me down, and not a day / But something is recalled, / My conscience or my vanity appalled" – in his Virginia lectures (*ASG* 46).
44 Stephen Spender, *Eliot* (London: Fontana, 1975), p. 242.
45 Valerie Eliot, interview in the *Observer* (20 February 1972). Quoted in Ackroyd, *T. S. Eliot*, p. 334.
46 Quoted in Gordon, *An Imperfect Life*, p. 425.
47 Wilson's remarks are quoted in Jeffrey Meyers, *Edmund Wilson: A Biography* (New York: Houghton Mifflin, 1995), p. 156. See Cynthia Ozick, "T. S. Eliot at 101," *New Yorker* (20 November 1989), pp. 119–54.
48 Bernard Sharratt, "Eliot: Modernism, Postmodernism, and after," *The Cambridge Companion to T. S. Eliot*, ed. A. D. Moody (Cambridge: Cambridge University Press, 1994), p. 224.

2

MICHAEL O'NEILL

Eliot: Form and Allusion

James Longenbach has argued that "Eliot forces his readers to feel the weight of his allusions very strongly."[1] The point is thought-provoking; forcing us to "feel the weight of ... allusions" is part of that process of "assuming a double part" which Gareth Reeves notes is acknowledged as "an articulated and articulate strategy" in the terza rima passage in *Little Gidding*.[2] In Eliot, allusion brings to mind a particular literary moment and a larger generic model. At the same time allusion finds a home in an imaginative world that is innovative.

This newness may often involve shaking us out of conventional responses, as when, in John Crowe Ransom's words, Eliot "inserts beautiful quotations into ugly contexts."[3] Ransom is discussing the use of Olivia's song from Goldsmith's *The Vicar of Wakefield* (1766) in *The Waste Land*. Here, Eliot turns lyric melancholy into a simulacrum of automatic response. He does so by making us hear the original differently. That original ("When lovely woman stoops to folly") has a tetrametric lilt and movement that are called up yet almost cancelled through the addition of "and" in line 253, "an unaccented syllable," as Jason Harding points out.[4] The reworking satirises lyric sentimentality. But it stops short of mere debunking; Eliot/Tiresias may have "foresuffered all" (*CPP* 69), yet there is something to be "suffered" in the scene, and the allusion suggests that there is, as well, residual value in the original lyric mode.

That value allows Eliot to express tacit sadness at the fate of the woman who "smoothes her hair with automatic hand, / And puts a record on the gramophone" (*CPP* 69). The quatrains of the passage's central section imitate the "automatic" nature of the sexual encounter they depict. The formal means are metronomic iambs and alternating, often sardonic rhymes: "guesses" and "caresses," "tired" and "undesired" (*CPP* 68). However, as a whole, the passage accommodates disciplined feelings of yearning. Secret sympathy for the woman insinuates itself beneath the air of detachment. Her washing "perilously spread," she is a descendant of the Keats who imagines voyages across "perilous seas, in fairy lands forlorn" ("Ode to a Nightingale," line 70).[5] The allusion may be wholly ironic, but its effect is not without poignancy. Such a mingling of attitudes derives from shifts in the passage's formal modes of being. With its vibrant "throbbing between two lives" (*CPP* 68), the opening hints at foiled expectation amidst its echo of Sappho, fragment 149 (to which Eliot's notes indirectly refer us) or Dante's *Purgatorio*, 8.1–6.

To speak of "the evening hour that strives / Homeward" (*CPP* 68) is to arouse memory of the desires evoked in those originals. And like a Dantean canto, the passage shapes surprises and change: first by introducing the spectatorial figure of Tiresias; second by the descent into near-contempt in its description of the "small house agent's clerk" whose "vanity requires no response" (*CPP* 68), a line that redeems the passage from snobbery by using the clerk to epitomise what the language suggests is a more general human failing – the line "requires [a] response" from the reader who is asked to think about the nature of "vanity"; third by turning, with a gesture very like severe solicitude, towards the woman in a set-off passage of two run-together quatrains; and fourth by announcing its end and moving into a changed key with a quotation from *The Tempest* ("'This music crept by me upon the waters'" [*CPP* 69]). Throughout, the handling of form and the workings of allusion conspire to create an original, disturbing, hauntingly multi-toned vision.

In a comparable manner, when the woman in "Portrait of a Lady" invokes "these April sunsets, that somehow recall / My buried life, and Paris in the Spring" (*CPP* 19), she induces in reader and speaker an alienated empathy. The words are affecting. Yet they are also affected. Shaping our response is the fact that the passage alludes to Arnold's extended lyric "The Buried Life" (1852). The echo of that poem's central trope in the woman's words is touching. But Eliot is dry-eyed amidst her near-sentimentality and Arnold's emotional longing. His poem is at a remove from the genre it calls to mind. Arnold's mode is lyric exploration; Eliot's is a self-aware, near-voyeuristic monodrama, the self-awareness belonging to the poem's "I" and to the supervising poet one senses beyond or behind that self.

The simultaneous calling up and questioning of feeling may sound like a self-protective strategy, a matter of eating one's cake and having it, too. There are times, as at the close of "Preludes," when Eliot seems to be spinning latter-day skeins of Romantic irony. "Wipe your hand across your mouth, and laugh" annuls the reverence for the "Infinitely suffering thing" (*CPP* 23) which had found its way into the poem; a door is slammed in the face of any miniature lyric like Tennyson's *Maud* (1855). Laforgue is a key presider over such manoeuvres, which hint, too, at a post-Byronic mobility. At their most enriching, such inflations and deflations convey an attentiveness to poetic history as well as effects. This attentiveness links with Eliot's ability to restore the full formal integrity of the line to English verse. A line in his poetry supports or contests other lines around it by being memorably itself; it also frequently suggests its place in a literary lineage. Eliot induces readers to quote quintessential examples. "For us," Stephen Spender reminisced, "his private life was summed up in the line, 'the awful daring of a moment's surrender'" (*CPP* 74).[6] Open vowels release unusual semantic suggestiveness. Hanging at the line ending, the "surrender" is vulnerable, the matter of an instant and absolute, while "awful" intimates a daring that is breath-stopping but also appalling, a faux pas.[7] Moreover, the return at this stage in the poem to a virtually regular pentameter rehearses the conflict between the "proper" and the "improper" in *The Waste Land*.[8]

Form, here as elsewhere, is the arena where Eliot stages tensions in his dealings with tradition. The hesitation between the meanings of "awful" offers a sign of Eliot's ability to crisscross between resonance and critique, to pay homage to a predecessor or previous culture, yet to distance himself, too. So, here, the start of Shelley's "Hymn to Intellectual Beauty" (1817) – "The awful shadow of some unseen Power" – traces itself behind Eliot's line, which installs its semi-ironized version ("a moment's surrender") of a Platonic "Power."[9] The idiomatic sense of "awful" contributes to that vestigial irony, and displays Eliot's gift, central to his poetic renewings, for mimicking the rhythms of speech. To apply Hugh Kenner's phrase for a Poundian quest, Eliot's gift manifests itself as "the rare cooperation of genius with common speech."[10]

Eliot's forms quicken into life, as they seek to utter what Wallace Stevens calls in "Of Modern Poetry" (1942) "the speech of the place," while remaining aware of the history of words.[11] Spender noticed that "His talk had a subdued metric quality which held my attention, as in the line once made at tea I have quoted elsewhere 'I daren't take cake, and jam's too much trouble.'"[12] There is a link with the figure who revitalises poetic drama in the knockabout dark comedy of *Sweeney Agonistes*, in which Eliot experiments with a line that is marked by its primitivist use of repeated accent. In this work Eliot ventriloquises different voices turning into the same voice, one that is banal, menaced and menacing, in keeping with the view that "Birth, and copulation, and death. / That's all the facts when you come to brass tacks" (*CPP* 122). The first line has been used earlier in the scene, thus taking on a matter-of-fact quality, holding at arm's length any doom-and-gloom portentousness. The second has a jaunty, jazz-like lilt, supplied by the internal rhyme and the kicking life of the accentual metre.

Whatever their ostensible genre, Eliot's poems are always a form of modernist lyric drama; he is a poet of voices, often of voices that fall subtly awry, as in Marie's line in "The Burial of the Dead": "I read, much of the night, and go south in the winter" (*CPP* 61). These mimicries tend to inhabit a half-numbed space between speech and thought. They show how "Eliot uses styles, quotes styles, 'as a way of putting it'," as J. C. C. Mays has argued, alluding to *East Coker*.[13] That idea, that poetry is "a way of putting it," leads to Eliot's use of a powerful sub-genre: one that might be called the confessionally metapoetic. So, in *East Coker*, the passage continues with the comment: "not very satisfactory: / A periphrastic study in a worn-out poetical fashion, / Leaving one still with the intolerable wrestle / With words and meanings. The poetry does not matter" (*CPP* 179).

The lines make evident later Eliot's experiment with a line unmoored from the pentameter, the pentameter or "heroic line" being a variously strong if modified presence, as Helen Gardner has contended, in the poetry up to and including *The Waste Land*.[14] In its place, Eliot uses a pattern of stresses, usually four, which provides the basis for his attempts to wrest design from his materials. That design makes use of false starts and failures of communication, turning them into points of departure towards enhanced understanding. In calling the preceding lyric, "What is the late November doing" (*CPP* 178), "A periphrastic study," Eliot poses his reader with a puzzle that allows him or her to re-experience the poet's own self-criticism: the poet may purposefully misrepresent his previous lines, or imply a withdrawal from a perspective which holds him and us while the lyric lasts, or suggest the temporary nature of all perspectives based on (mere) "poetry."

This use of poetic form requires that the reader works towards revelation by dwelling among misapprehension. One might argue, for instance, that, set in conjunction with and opposition to the symbolist lyric in *Burnt Norton*, section II, "Garlic and sapphires in the mud" (*CPP* 172), "What is late November doing" is less "periphrastic" than apocalyptic. Its vision of disaster opposes the previous lyric's intimations of harmony.[15] Its eighteen lines have a rhyme scheme that cunningly mimics disorder and accelerating anxiety; they constitute a form that is already self-troubled. Eliot's impressively risky challenge to the reader is to read the poetry's forms as an index of his conviction that "the pattern is new in every moment" (*CPP* 179). In his gloss on the lyric, Eliot is original in the act of conceding lack of originality. His accentual line gives his voice space in which to make its fatigued yet incisive emphases. This sense that "poetical fashion" is likely to be "worn-out" characterises Eliot's dealings with forms, but so too does his abiding commitment to "the intolerable wrestle / With words and meanings" (*CPP* 179). "Words" first, one notes, then "meanings." Meaning in Eliot seems like the aura that surrounds his involvement in the life of "words."

Such attention to speech rhythms and their re-imagined existence in poetic lines often affects those borrowings which Eliot makes his own, as when, in "La Figlia Che Piange," he concludes with the lines, "Sometimes these cogitations still amaze / The troubled midnight and the noon's repose" (*CPP* 34). Hardyesque "throbbings of noontide" subside into becalmed, subliminally troubled amazement via echoes (in the use of "amaze") of Marvell's "The Garden" (1681) and Daniel 7:28, "As for me Daniel," the prophet confesses, "my cogitations troubled me."[16] Surprising both in the King James Version and in Eliot, the Latinate "cogitations" assumes, in the poem, an air of self-mockery. It means less "Reflection previous to action," Samuel Johnson's meaning quoted in the OED (2b), than, in context, "indeterminate and possibly futile reflections on an entire poetic process," with its imperatives, hypothetical conditionals, and assertions. The same poem recycles Laforgue's "Simple et sans foi comme un bonjour," which it converts into "Simple and faithless as a smile and shake of the hand" (*CPP* 34).[17] The remodelling gives the poem's feelings "a gesture and a pose," and the line is arresting, in part, as Edmund Wilson observes, because its approach to the alexandrine has an "unstressed" quality which makes it very different from alexandrines found in Pope and Shelley.[18] Eliot brings to mind other lyric modes, including Hardy's emotional authenticity, Marvell's poise and Laforgue's *dédoublement* and handling of languorous ironies, while he offers his reader a poem whose idiom and manner compel the imagination.

To be original, for Eliot, is to be aware of tradition and to incorporate that awareness in the demeanour of a poem. From the beginning, he is freed, not weighed down, by such awareness. His ability to make his metres and rhythms work significantly is evident in earlier work in *Inventions of the March Hare*. "Paysage Triste" uses regular iambs to suggest the cool indifference to the speaker of the girl who climbed onto the bus and "answered my appreciative stare" with an "averted look without surprise" (*IMH* 52). Eliot deliberately makes his lines move "without surprise." Yet he concludes the second stanza, imagining the woman moving "about her chamber / With naked feet passing across the skies," the slight stumble in the last line's third foot among the constituents of an allusion to one of the most lyrically suggestive and unscannable lines in the canon, Wyatt's "With naked foot stalking in my chamber."[19] Wyatt's example arouses an erotic possibility unavailable in the speaker's social world, a world in which we have just been told the woman "would not have known how to sit, or what to wear" (*IMH* 52). That line, itself at odds with anything iambically regulated, is wistfully or resignedly repeated in the final stanza.

Eliot, as this early poem shows, is pervasively conscious of the authority possessed by the iambic, and especially the iambic pentameter, in the tradition of English poetry. As here, he is able to arrange his departures from the iambic tradition with stealth and cunning. He praises a passage from Ezra

Pound's "Near Perigord" (1916) because of the way it provides both "the constant suggestion and the skilful evasion of iambic pentameter" (*CP1* 513) and the praise might be returned to the giver. If the last four lines of the passage from Pound – "She who could never live save through one person, / She who could never speak save to one person, / And all the rest of her a shifting change, / A broken bundle of mirrors...!"[20] – look ahead to the use of identical rhyme and "broken images" (*CPP* 61) in *The Waste Land*, they also, with their slight but expressive shifts of accent, mirror Eliot's preference for a poetry of high rhythmic intensity that cannot and has no wish to be sustained at the length of a Swinburnian rhapsody or Tennysonian incantation. In Pound's lines, the repeated, irregular stresses on "She" and "save," for example, and the possibly fractured grammar (although "she" is initially an object, we might expect her to take on the position of a subject) bear witness to his wish to engage solely with "the poetic part of a drama the rest of which (to me the prose part) is left to the reader's imagination or implied or set in a short note."[21] The notion casts light on Eliot's imaginative and rhythmic practice in many if not all of his poems: even when relatively long, their impulse is to move in a transitional way between passages, focusing maximum although unforced readerly concentration on their line-by-line workings. It is a poetry in which each line makes something happen.

Eliot captures an essential truth about his own practice when he writes in "Reflections on *Vers Libre*" that "the ghost of some simple metre should lurk behind the arras in even the 'freest' verse; to advance menacingly as we doze, and withdraw as we rouse" (*CP1* 514). If one returns to "La Figlia Che Piange," one can see how the poem opens with iambic control, issuing directorial commands – "Stand on the highest pavement of the stair — / Lean on a garden urn." The poem finds its way with a change of key into a movement that is more conditional, hesitant, self-reflective, a movement marked by a sudden clustering of trisyllabic feet, "So he would have left" (*CPP* 34), scannable as a dactyl followed by an iamb. In the third and last section, iambic resolution is to the fore, as endings and self-aware regret assume a central position in the poem's emotions.

Highlighted as the bearer of allusive significance, the line, in Eliot, keeps readers and the poems themselves on their toes. "A Cooking Egg" provides an example. Before the last of its whimsically clever quatrains, a line, set apart ("Where are the eagles and the trumpets?"), sways affectingly between elegiac pastiche of the "ubi sunt?" motif and something close to the real thing, an effect only reinforced by the subsequent bathos of the rhyme with "buttered scones and crumpets" (*CPP* 45). Each of the five sections of *The Waste Land* concludes with a strong line that sums up and leaves behind what has gone before: the table-turning quotation from Baudelaire at the end of "The Burial of the Dead"; the allusion to *Hamlet* at the close of "A Game of Chess," where pub-talk modulates into something more elegiac; the use of a single Buddhic word "burning" after the Augustinian "O Lord thou pluckest" (*CPP* 70) at the conclusion of "The Fire Sermon" with its "collocation of ... two representatives of eastern and western asceticism" (*CPP* 79), as Eliot's note has it; the admonition to "Consider Phlebas" (*CPP* 71) at the end of "Death by Water"; and the abrupt enigma of the Sanskrit chant at the conclusion of "What the Thunder said." With its ear for liturgical patterns, *Ash-Wednesday* concludes three of its six poems with single lines: "And after this our exile" (*CPP* 95), "O my people" (*CPP* 97), "And let my cry come unto Thee" (*CPP* 99). The poet turns to a language saturated with the religious longings of others to convey his own yearning, even as the close of Part IV concedes a common "exile," the end of Part V assumes a prophet's lamenting tone, and the termination of Part VI, although personal, also voices a transpersonal desire to be heard.

The conclusion of "The Love Song of J. Alfred Prufrock" wreathes variations on couplet and tercet, wheeling adroitly between the faux-pathos of the music hall comedian, visionary fantasy and a sense of spent loss:

> I grow old ... I grow old...
> I shall wear the bottoms of my trousers rolled.
>
> Shall I part my hair behind? Do I dare to eat a peach?
> I shall wear white flannel trousers, and walk upon the beach.
> I have heard the mermaids singing, each to each.
>
> I do not think that they will sing to me. (*CPP* 16)

These six lines are each independent units; there is no enjambment, no carrying over of the sense across the line-ending. Eliot plays the lines off against one another: the lamenting repetition of "I grow old" is punctured by the pseudo-decisiveness of the trouser-rolling assertion, while the questions of the tercet's first line come into being as a contrast to this definiteness. We sense that the speaker's will has faltered, passing into the perfectly balanced pair of questions, each kicked off by an anapaest, followed by two iambs. "*Teach* me to hear mermaids singing" (emphasis added), the Donnean prompt, implicates itself in the choice of rhyme-word in the tercet here.[22] The rhyming may seem forced in the phrase "each to each," the triple chime clenched rather than clinched. But it works by spinning a web of relationship and difference. Like Prufrock, "each" mermaid is an individual; unlike him, each is "singing" to the others, as though the others were all individuals, capable of mutual song. Prufrock's sense of exclusion from the harmony he fantasises into existence provides the formal principle for the stand-alone line that follows. "I do not think that they will sing to me" marks a return to the hesitant, doubting self who has imagined self-escape in the lines which have preceded.

Eliot's criticism rewards triumphs attained by single lines, often when a concentrated "singleness" of poetic power coexists with a suggestive doubleness: Donne's "A bracelet of bright hair about the bone," for example, "where the most powerful effect is produced by the sudden contrast of associations of 'bright hair' and of 'bone' " (*CP2* 376), or Dante's description of Farinata, "*come avesso lo inferno in gran dispitto* [as though he entertained great scorn of Hell]," where the glimpse of an individual is made "memorable by a perfect phrase" (*CP3* 708). But he is alert to these moments as parts of larger wholes, relating single lines by Francesca to the entire scheme of the *Commedia*. His own work thrives on single lines having a living relationship with the overall work, but doing so through relationships of tension, juxtaposition, an off-key yet musical dissonance. *The Waste Land* closes with a congeries of such lines, sometimes broken into half lines: "These fragments I have shored against my ruins" (*CPP* 75) offers itself as a metapoetic epigraph for the work, its strong iambic pulse "shoring" the poetry "against" the "ruins" which beset it. Longenbach is among the most persuasive of those commentators who sees the reference to allusive "fragments" as presupposing some totality: "the wide field of references are folded into the present to remind us of historical continuity and show us the way out of our predicament."[23] On this line of argument, the "broken" forms of which the poem is composed have an encyclopaedic intent, aspiring after the condition of mock-epic or, indeed, epic itself. The range of allusions brings into play our awareness of a jostling crowd of literary forms, including medieval epic, Elizabethan revenge tragedy, nursery rhyme and nineteenth-century lyric. Yet the fact that fragmentation has undone so many forms may suggest, in the end, the absence of any one form as a guide to "show us the way out of our predicament."

Here, after the line about the shoring of "fragments," the next line uses the first-person singular to remind us that the poem moans round with many voices, as it stitches together two moments from *The Spanish Tragedy* (1592). The effect is of ironic juxtaposition: Hieronymo as producer of a carnage-ridden play set against the previous speaker's perilous quest for residual order. And yet it is also the case that allusion forgets its origin in the Elizabethan revenge-tragedy and takes on new life, its edge of danger glittering keenly, as though we sensed something in the author not entirely well disposed towards our mental comfort, prepared to "fit" (*CPP* 75) us to his own designs.[24]

Allusions are duplicitous in this ghosted masterpiece, just as the single line often works in juxtaposed tension with other lines. The result is a productive mirroring of uncertainty, an effect anticipated by the opening of "Prufrock." There, we reach the relative closure of a semi-colon after three lines, yet each line dwells in its own space, taking more than its allotted time, each flirting with an iambic pattern into which it never wholly settles: "Let us go then, you and I" is jaunty, intense, lilting, implying some causal antecedent in "then"; "When the evening is spread out against the sky" is almost conventionally lyrical but disturbingly not so in the prepositional violence of "out," which suggests that the evening has been spread-eagled; "Like a patient etherised upon a table" (*CPP* 13) confirms oddness, discomfort, yet also a longing for numbness. If the simile arrests us through its apparent projection of feeling onto the scene, Eliot's strategy might seem, on reflection, close kin to Browning's in "Porphyria's Lover" (1836), where the disturbed speaker hears the wind do "its worst to vex the lake."[25] Yet monologue undergoes change from Browning to Eliot. Browning's speaker has or is a definite essence; Eliot's moves between something close to a self-mocking persona and a voice that seems to flow in and out of our own thought processes. The "you and I" of whom Prufrock speaks are Eliot and persona, Prufrock and addressee, self and other, poet and reader. The subject positions steal away from certainty, much as the rhythms refuse, for all their musicality, to settle into a pattern.

Eliot's patterns, indeed, frequently refuse the reassurance of pattern. "Cousin Nancy" closes with a straight lift from a sonnet ("Lucifer in Starlight") by Meredith, "The army of unalterable law" (*CPP* 30), but it stops one line short of the unconventional, unrhymed sonnet (with sestet and octave reversed) into which it appeared to be settling; the final effect is elusively serio-comic as Cousin Nancy's errancies take on (mock) Luciferian grandeur and are juxtaposed with "unalterable law."[26] In "Prufrock" the couplet recalls its Augustan and even Byronic role of imparting order to the disparate, only to depart from that function. Not that Eliot is any less of a controlled artist than Pope or Byron, even as his use of a form associated with authorial command imbues it with trailing qualms. "I should have been a pair of ragged claws / Scuttling across the floors of silent seas" (*CPP* 15) feels as though it will rely on end-rhyme. But the premature securing of the rhyme through the internal chime of "floors" with "claws" thwarts too rounded an assertion, throwing the emphasis back on the conditionality of "should have been."

When there is a full rhyme in a couplet, as occurs at the end of the first verse paragraph ("Oh, do not ask, 'What is it?' / Let us go and make our visit"), an echo of Byronic nonchalance is audible. But the poem troubles the assurance of the ancestral voice as the rhyme sends us back to ask the question we are told not to ask. After a line space, Eliot offers another couplet, "In the room the women come and go / Talking of Michelangelo" (*CPP* 13), a couplet that is repeated some lines later. Christopher Ricks refutes the notion that the couplet indicts the women as gossips. Instead, he argues, the couplet might be thought to have a generosity following the alleged "prissy pursedness" of its predecessor.[27]

That reading may, in turn, show Ricks falling into the trap he claims the Michelangelo lines have successfully set for others: namely, of being, in effect, a screen on which readers project their prejudices. And whether the couplet is quite so tonally poker-faced as Ricks intimates is doubtful, given the poem's allusive dynamics. Prufrock is "not Prince Hamlet, nor was meant to be" (*CPP* 16), a way of putting it that fleetingly gestures towards the tragic stature that is self-denyingly refused. He fantasises being Lazarus, or even Marvell's speaker in "To His Coy Mistress" (1681), drawing an energy of utterance from the fantasy. Yet such energy is almost playfully able to see its kinship with rhetoric, even bombast. Emotions perform themselves in the speaker's head, "visions" accompanied by their attendant "revisions." So, when the Michelangelo lines are repeated, they seem themselves the screen on which Prufrock projects a recurrent scenario in which a former greatness jostles to assert itself in the presence, "the room," of a world unable to measure up to such greatness. Even the argument that the couplet resists interpretation reads the reader as much as it tells us about Eliot.

That said, Ricks's suggestion that Eliot's couplet offers us an "impalpable smell" rather than a "palpable dossier" helps us to understand the function of many formal devices in his work.[28] For all the relative failure of the Popean pastiche excised at Pound's advice from *The Waste Land*, the couplet, often without end-rhyme, is among Eliot's most formidable weapons in that poem. Couplets can embed themselves in larger syntactical units, as when the speaker, head full of Dante (*Inferno*, 3.55–57), says, "A crowd flowed over London Bridge, so many, / I had not thought death had undone so many" (*CPP* 62). There, the repeated phrase "so many" earns its authority, in part, by ironising the pointed elegance of the Augustan couplet. There is no escape from the prospect of "so many" undone by death. Rhyme is less a question of chime than of a design that works thematically, allusively, as Eliot brings into connection contemporary London and Dante's *Inferno*. Again, in "What the Thunder said," the two-line structure is vital:

> We think of the key, each in his prison
> Thinking of the key, confirms a prison

> Only at nightfall, aethereal rumours
> Revive for a moment a broken Coriolanus (*CPP* 74)

Again, repetition of the same word (here "prison") does the work of rhyme, suggesting the obsession with imprisonment. The lines return to the idea of thinking, and the unrhymed couplets "Revive for a moment," yet in modernist vein, the ways in which the form can present contrast and balance. In the first two lines, the syntax moves fluidly between "We" and "each," a movement that asserts a common fate yet suggests an individual one, too. The phrasing allows us to be "Thinking of the key" and, in so doing, confirming "a prison" – yet in its access to a larger perspective (that accorded to the speaker who can see what holds true for "us"), it permits momentary escape from complete isolation. As if building on that glimpse of escape, yet romantically overstating and thus threatening to undercut the possibility, the following two lines offer possibly the most charged vision of "revival" in the poem. The adverb "Only" signals a one-off opportunity, while "a broken Coriolanus" illustrates one of Eliot's favourite post-symbolist devices, the re-orchestration of a word within the poem's echo-chamber. He recalls, in this instance, the "heap of broken images" (*CPP* 61) with which a voice confronted us in "The Burial of the Dead." "Broken," there, suggested disintegration; here, it intimates something closer to "broken in spirit," a residual tragic dignity clinging to the word, as though we glimpsed "a broken Coriolanus" in the "moment" after he gave in to his mother's entreaties and foresaw the consequences of doing so.

Elsewhere, an unrhymed couplet possesses a sealed-off loneliness, as when a voice, as if in response to the instruction to "Think," breaks through the edgy preciosities and nerviness of "A Game of Chess" to assert: "I think we are in rats' alley / Where the dead men lost their bones" (*CPP* 65). The phrase "rats' alley" seems incongruously close to a place name, and the poem glimpses an utter lostness, even as such loss begins to breed dreams of recovery, hinted at in the subsequent return to an allusion to *The Tempest*: "I remember / Those are pearls that were his eyes" (*CPP* 65). The allusion is complicated because in Shakespeare Ariel sings Ferdinand a song about his father's supposed death; he is, in fact, alive, his supposed death part of Prospero's elaborate dramatisations. When Eliot repeats the phrase, he brings into play, yet holds at arm's length, the possibility that *The Waste Land* will stage a miracle of recovery and near-resurrection.

Eliot's use of the tercet up to the "familiar compound ghost" (*CPP* 193) passage in *Little Gidding* is rarely sustained, more a marker of suspended energies, a form that settles for the unsettled. "Marina" finishes with a three-line paragraph that seems to aim for the "peculiar lucidity" (*CP3* 702) of Dante's tercets:

> What seas what shores what granite islands towards my timbers
> And woodthrush calling through the fog
> My daughter. (*CPP* 110)

One could say of these lines, as Eliot says of Dante, that "The thought may be obscure, but the word is lucid, or rather translucent" (*CP3* 702). Obscurity is at one, in this unpunctuated, passage, with the "translucent" quality of the words: "calling through the fog" is an almost self-reflexive example. The "fog" is a "translucent" image for the speaker's acceptance of what he cannot wholly comprehend, "this grace dissolved in place" (*CPP* 109), as the poem has asserted earlier, where rhyme gives substance to the dissolution into one another of matter and spirit, longing and reality; anticipates the sought-for "face" of the next line; and betrays affectingly the speaker's desire to "dissolve" or resolve the problem named as "Death." The closing lines recall and play against the five-line section with which the poem began, dropping the "O" which had preceded "My daughter" in the fifth line, substituting "granite" for "grey" before "islands," cancelling the definite article before "woodthrush," adding the phrase "towards my timbers" and above all leaving out the earlier line: "What images return." The earlier lines still retained the interrogative note of the Senecan epigraph, but that note has now been subsumed within a mood of open-ended yet accepting wonder. As Denis Donoghue remarks, "The last three lines of the poem resume the first five, and conclude it as an exclamation rather than a question."[29] Again, because of its intra-textual patterning, the poem must be read in its own terms, even if it invites us to recall the plot of Shakespeare's *Pericles* (1609). The suggestion may be that not only do "images return" but also that in some sense the realities to which they correspond have been restored. Or it may be that the return of the images is the form that restoration can take. The speaker, at any rate, is caught up in vision, while at the same time he sees – it may be intimated – the challenges he has faced: challenges suggested by the "granite islands" that are approached by and threaten the intactness of his "timbers."

In the "familiar compound ghost" passage from *Little Gidding*, Eliot replaces the rhyme scheme of terza rima with a pattern of alternating masculine and feminine endings. In conjunction with a fluid syntax, this pattern turns from device into perfect medium. Setting the poem "In the uncertain hour before the morning / Near the ending of interminable night / At the recurrent end of the unending" (*CPP* 193), Eliot is able to convey the co-existence of the "interminable," "the unending," and a sense of "the recurrent end." Each line advances towards such a paradoxically circular "end." The poetry's rhythms, at once fatigued by watching and expectant, shape a pre-dawn space in which the German bomber turns into a shadowy paraclete, "the dark dove with the flickering tongue," that speaks a language of conflict. This language prepares for the colloquy between poet and alter ego, the measure, wording and tone attuned to an encounter in which self and other share an identity that is "Both intimate and unidentifiable," a making new of Dante that is the most emphatically accented passage of iambic pentameter in *Four Quartets*. The passage broods on questions of linguistic propriety, but, like the ghost, Eliot, with whatever self-lacerating irony, is able to "find words I never thought to speak." Those words turn into savage self-indictment in which the severe tones of eighteenth-century satire rise to the surface: "Then fools' approval stings, and honour stains" has the air of a compound allusion to Pope, Swift and Johnson, but one that works to "urge the mind to aftersight and foresight." That urging of "the mind" suggests Eliot's allusive elusiveness: "foresight" means looking ahead to what will come "after"; "aftersight" means reflecting on what has gone "before." The phrase suggests both the poetic act of looking before and after and the dream of a new meaning that occupies the space between past and future which opens up in an Eliotic allusion; it comes after an allusion to Mallarmé's "Le tombeau d'Edgar Poe" in which he writes of the hyena-dislike of the angel who was able "Donner un sens plus purs aux mots de la tribu," or as Eliot has it, adding his own ethical shading, "To purify the dialect of the tribe" (*CPP* 194).[30]

Eliot builds the sonnet's compulsion to turn and surprise into his extended meditation, as he goes on to flesh out the cruelly humiliating recognitions forced by "aftersight and foresight." And yet Dante, Yeats and *Hamlet* come to his aid in the sombre yet residually hopeful conclusion, the purgatorial joy of Arnaut Daniel, the Yeatsian vision of the "dancer" at the close of "Among School Children" (1927), and the ghost's vanishing and farewell in *Hamlet* all folding into Eliot's implicit "valediction" to his own career.[31] Touchstones of excellence in epic, lyric and drama are deftly evoked; if "next year's words await another voice" (*CPP* 194), the voice we have heard uncannily anticipates the future it prognosticates in a form that has commerce with past and imagined realisations of poetic speech. In Eliot, as his reshaping of the sestina in *The Dry Salvages* reveals, past forms move through his words as he evades them; as he permits them to return, they are invited to find new ways of inhabiting the poetic structures they help to question and rebuild.

NOTES

1 James Longenbach, "'Mature Poets Steal': Eliot's Allusive Practice," in *The Cambridge Companion to T. S. Eliot*, ed. A. David Moody (Cambridge: Cambridge

University Press, 1994), p. 176. For some theoretical speculations, see Stacy Magedanz, "Allusion as Form: *The Waste Land* and *Moulin Rouge!*" *Orbis Litterarum* 61:2 (2006): 160–79.

2 Gareth Reeves, "T. S. Eliot," in *The Cambridge History of English Poetry*, ed. Michael O'Neill (Cambridge: Cambridge University Press, 2010), p. 822.

3 John Crowe Ransom, "Waste Lands," *The Waste Land*, ed. Michael North (New York: Norton, 2001), pp. 168–9.

4 Jason Harding, "Modernist and Modern Poetry: An Overview," in *The Cambridge History of English Poetry*, p. 733.

5 Miriam Allott (ed.), *The Poems of John Keats* (London: Longman, 1970).

6 Stephen Spender, "Remembering Eliot," in *T. S. Eliot: The Man and His Work*, ed. Allen Tate (Harmondsworth: Penguin, 1971), p. 51.

7 As Seamus Perry points out, "'awful' is what he says here – full of awe, yes, but also just something you would normally avoid like you would anything awful." *The Connell Guide to T. S. Eliot's "The Waste Land"* (London: Connell, 2014), p. 107.

8 See Harriet Davidson, "Improper Desire: Reading *The Waste Land*," in *The Cambridge Companion to T. S. Eliot*, pp. 121–31.

9 Zachary Leader and Michael O'Neill (eds.), *Percy Bysshe Shelley: The Major Works* (Oxford: Oxford University Press, 2003).

10 Hugh Kenner, *The Pound Era* (London: Faber and Faber, 1975), p. 107.

11 Wallace Stevens, *Collected Poems* (London: Faber and Faber, 1954), p. 240.

12 Spender, "Remembering Eliot," p. 54.

13 J. C. C. Mays, "Early Poems: From 'Prufrock' to 'Gerontion,'" in *The Cambridge Companion to T. S. Eliot*, p. 108.

14 See Helen Gardner, *The Art of T. S. Eliot* (London: Faber and Faber, 1949), pp. 16–17n for her use of "heroic line" rather than "iambic pentameter." For the view that by the close of *Four Quartets*, Eliot had made his peace both with the pentameter and a dactylic measure, see Annie Finch, *The Ghost of Meter: Culture and Prosody in American Free Verse* (Ann Arbor: University of Michigan Press, 1993), p. 127. See also Julia M. Reibetanz, "Accentual Forms in Eliot's Poetry from 'The Hollow Men' to *Four Quartets*," *English Studies* 65 (1984): 334–9.

15 See Martin Scofield, *T. S. Eliot: The Poems* (Cambridge: Cambridge University Press, 1988), p. 218.

16 "I look into my glass," line 12, *Thomas Hardy: Selected Poems*, Tim Armstrong (ed.) (London: Longman, 1993); "The Garden," line 1, *The Poems of Andrew Marvell*, Nigel Smith (ed.) (2003; London: Longman, 2007 rev).

17 The allusion to Jules Laforgue's "Petition," where the line describes how "all women" (*toutes*) behave, is noted, among other places, in Lawrence Rainey (ed.), *Modernism: An Anthology* (Oxford: Blackwell, 2005), p. 117n.

18 Edmund Wilson, *Axel's Castle: A Study in the Imaginative Literature of 1870–1930* (London: Fontana, 1961), p. 84.

19 For the echo of Wyatt, see *IMH* 201–2.

20 "Near Perigord," in Ezra Pound, *Personae* (London: Faber and Faber, 2001), p. 154.

21 Letter of Pound to William Carlos Williams in 1908, in *Selected Letters of Ezra Pound: 1907–1941*, intro. and notes. D. D. Paige (New York: New Directions, 1971), pp. 3–4.

22 For the echo of Donne's "Song," see B. C. Southam, *A Student's Guide to the Selected Poems of T. S. Eliot* (London: Faber and Faber, 1968), p. 35.

23 Longenbach, "'Mature Poets Steal,'" p. 183.

24 For further discussion of the allusions to *The Spanish Tragedy*, see my essay "'Why then Ile Fit You': Poetry and Madness from Wordsworth to Berryman," in Corinne Saunders and Jane Macnaughton (eds.), *Madness and Creativity in Literature and Cultures* (Basingstoke: Palgrave Macmillan, 2005), p. 153.

25 Adam Roberts (ed.), *The Oxford Authors: Robert Browning*, intro Daniel Karlin (Oxford: Oxford University Press, 1997).

26 For commentary, see Longenbach, "'Mature Poets Steal,'" pp. 181–2.

27 Christopher Ricks, *T. S. Eliot and Prejudice* (London: Faber and Faber, 1988), p. 17.

28 Ricks, *T. S. Eliot and Prejudice*, p. 18.

29 Denis Donoghue, *Words Alone: The Poet T. S. Eliot* (New Haven: Yale University Press, 2000), p. 177.

30 Anthony Hartley (ed.), *Mallarmé*, with plain prose translations (Harmondsworth: Penguin, 1963). Eliot's emphasis on "aftersight" picks up a concern in Mallarmé's sonnet: that of wishing to forestall later erroneous responses to Poe through the creation of his poem's memorial.

31 For discussion of the allusions in this section of the poem, see Harry Blamires, *Word Unheard: A Guide through Eliot's "Four Quartets"* (London: Methuen, 1969), pp. 152–8, and Longenbach, "'Mature Poets Steal,'" p. 186.

3

ANNE STILLMAN

Prufrock and Other Observations

In 1917, T. S. Eliot published "Eeldrop and Appleplex," a prose dialogue between two figures modelled on caricatures of himself and Ezra Pound. Eeldrop is Eliot:

> "I test people," said Eeldrop, "by the way in which I imagine them as waking up in the morning. I am not drawing on memory when I imagine Edith waking to a room strewn with clothes, papers, cosmetics, letters and a few books, the smell of Violettes de Parme and stale tobacco. The sunlight beating in through broken blinds, and broken blinds keeping out the sun until Edith can compel herself to attend to another day. Yet the vision does not give me much pain."
>
> (*CP1* 530)

Eeldrop's test follows from a remark Appleplex makes about Edith: "'Everyone says of her, "How perfectly impenetrable!" I suspect that within there is only the confusion of a dusty garret'" (*CP1* 530). Eeldrop picks up on Appleplex's "dusty garret," but he is less explicit about the distinction between what may be within Edith's person and what may be around her; where Appleplex speculates about the kind of room within Edith's person, Eeldrop imagines her placed within a room. The expression "waking *to* a room" (emphasis added) slightly alters the expected prepositional locution of "waking in a room." As Eeldrop phrases it, Edith wakes to her setting, as if, say, waking to remorse. The specific moment of regaining consciousness is temporally afloat, as if part of Eeldrop's test is to imagine the act of waking in order to speculate when, and how, a person and the world may come together, but also to show the difficulty of locating any such finite place or time when a sharp distinction might be drawn between a person and the world. Edith wakes to a setting which is itself a threshold in the double aspect of the sunlight beating in and being kept out: the broken blinds recall the shaded peripheries between figures, rooms and worlds in Eliot's "Preludes," where the "showers beat / On broken blinds," and where "the world came back / And the light crept up between the shutters" (*CPP* 22, 23).

"Rooms," "scenes," "atmospheres," "situations" – these words repeatedly play a part in Eliot's early poems and critical prose: "the contact and cross-contact of souls, the breath and scent of the room" (*CP1* 488). Eeldrop's test is scenic, as it delineates a particular temporal and material setting: a room with some clues. "In poetry," Eliot writes, "some very small event, a dropping of a book, a turning toward the door, a silence, may give the emotion for the literary purpose" (*CP2* 220). Here, dropping the name Violettes de Parme in among a list of other clues is a small event with the power to conjure narrative curiosity. The French name for an Italian city could be perfume (or cheap eau de toilette?); it might be Edith's own scent, or the lingering trace of a guest. The name may be a joke, now out of earshot, perhaps, a chic nudge in the ribs for Appleplex, as in 1917 Violettes de Parme may have been recognisably passé. Eeldrop's test is designed not just to test a subject, but to test himself, Appleplex and us, for that "knowledge of the environment" which Eliot thought went toward an appreciation of Marie Lloyd's performances, where "one ought to know what objects a middle-aged woman of the charwoman class would carry in her bag; exactly how she would go through her bag in search of something; and exactly the tone of voice in which she would enumerate the objects she found in it" (*CP2* 419). Edith may seem to be tested by Eeldrop's scene, but the description is really asking how it is that we come to apprehend another's existence. It shows how such apprehensions are bound up with the incitement to prejudice, prompting us to think we can piece Edith together from these objects: "Now, we know what she's like."[1] Through Eeldrop, Eliot invites self-conscious considerations of how our judgements of others are staged by surroundings, and imagines, as "Preludes" puts it, a setting for another person who "comes to consciousness" (wakes up), but also how another person "comes to [one's] consciousness" (comes to be perceived) through their setting. This is put sharply when Eliot writes of Flaubert's Frédéric Moreau in *L'Éducation Sentimentale*:

> He is constructed partly by negative definition, built up by a great number of observations. We cannot isolate him from the environment in which we find him; it may be an environment which is or can be universalised; nevertheless it, and the figure in it, consist of very many observed particular facts, the actual world. Without this world the figure dissolves. (*CP2* 154)

Edith too, as Eeldrop shows us, appears to be a figure built up from observations. Such a figure seems robust under one aspect, constituted by a "great number of observations," "particular facts, the actual world" and, at the same time, a tantalising figment, dissolving at a touch, caught in a vanishing-act, and glimpsed only fleetingly under the prospect of a world that could slip away. Eeldrop calls his vision a "test," yet part of Eliot's joke on Eeldrop is that he is shown to be testing something that can't be measured in any strong sense: "without this world the figure dissolves." Where the world begins and the figure ends, neither Eeldrop nor Eliot could say. Eliot's first poetic name for a figure and a world is *Prufrock and Other Observations*.

Open *The Complete Poems and Plays* by T. S. Eliot, turn to what passes as "PRUFROCK, 1917" in the contents, and you find a collection beginning like this:

PRUFROCK
and Other Observations
1917

For Jean Verdenal, 1889–1915
mort aux Dardanelles

Or puoi la quantitate
comprender dell'amor ch'a te mi scalda,
quando dismento nostra vanitate,
trattando l'ombre come cosa salda. (*CPP* 11)

Eliot presents his first book of poems as beginning with an end, "for Jean Verdenal, 1889–1915." The curtain-raiser for a poetic life is rendered epitaphic. "Observations" and the dates of 1917, 1889–1915 melt into the shadowy world of Dante's *Purgatorio*, as if we've sunk under the mud where Jean Verdenal died, "mort aux Dardanelles," to a place of unearthly recognition. Eliot quotes the words of the poet Statius from the *Purgatorio* xxi, as he recognises Dante's guide Virgil. Statius reaches to clasp his fellow Roman poet in homage, but Virgil stops the gesture, reminding him that they are both insubstantial shadows. The moment is at once comic and wrenchingly sad. Statius replies, "Now you can understand the quantity of love that warms me towards you, so that I forget our vanity, and treat the shadows like the solid thing" (Eliot's translation, *CP3* 715). As Eliot's epigraph, the Dantean surrounding for Statius's words is palpably absent, and yet the words of mutual estrangement and love still sound purgatorial in this opening, only here in different company. Hearing the cadences of the rhymes in the Italian prompts a ghostly rhyme into being between the name "Verdenal" and his place of death, "Dardanelles"; like Statius's gesture, the faint echo clasps at shadows. Intimacy and distance are interlaced by Dante in this encounter, as the insubstantial body is both coldly isolated and burning with love. The tangible absence of intimacy sketched by the epigraph has long shadows flickering in and out of *Prufrock and Other Observations*, a collection of poems where bodies vaporise into fog, vanish across the city skies, or where beings can seem to melt into one another, only to find that isolation is all they have in common.

As Eeldrop imagines Edith waking to a scene, *Prufrock* opens up to a constellation of objects setting a scene. Title, dedication and epigraph triangulate between languages, creating a peculiar atmosphere, mixing "observations" and phantoms. The date of a first collection rubs shoulders with the end of a life, while the name "PRUFROCK" may or may not be a proper name quite in the same way that "Jean Verdenal" names a person. The title of the collection is intrinsically linked with the "J. Alfred" of "The Love Song of J. Alfred Prufrock," but we may still wonder if "PRUFROCK," on the title page, names a person or a collection, and whether the name is one observation among many "other observations," or whether "PRUFROCK" is made up, as Eliot said of Frédéric Moreau, of a "great number of observations," and so something more, although never less, than those other observations. The name "Prufrock" radiates all the distinctive indistinctiveness of Violettes de Parme. Names seem to possess the elusive scent of a person, a conjuration fascinating to Eliot's imagination. Such figments weave through this collection in shifting shapes. Miss Helen Slingsby, Mr Apollinax, Miss Nancy Ellicott, Professor Channing-Cheetah, Mrs Phlaccus, Prester John, together with Prince Hamlet, Michelangelo, Lazarus, Matthew and Waldo, Fragilion, Chopin, La Rochefoucauld (and others) – all constellate a menagerie of indistinct figures. Together they may be "other observations" making up "PRUFROCK," or they may be observations made up by "PRUFROCK." At times such figments appear to have detached themselves from their respective pieces and wandered into another part of the collection, as if the poems were different rooms, in which the figures come and go, passing through "the other masquerades / That time resumes" (*CPP* 22). The fascination in *Prufrock* with the details of interiors, with scenes in rooms, speaks to Eliot's 1918 tribute to Henry James, in which he emphasises that in James's work "the focus is a situation, a relation, an atmosphere"; Eliot writes of "memorable scenes" crafted by a writer who is "dramatic": "it is in the chemistry of these subtle substances, these curious precipitates and explosive gases which are suddenly formed by the contact of mind with mind, that James is unequalled" (*CP1* 649). In *Prufrock* curious precipitates and explosive gases are created by the contact of poem with poem.

"The Love Song of J. Alfred Prufrock" dwells on parts of bodies (eyes, arms, head), parts that seem to become further disembodied as the collection unfolds. The "head (grown slightly bald) brought in upon a platter" (*CPP* 15) rolls into "Mr. Apollinax": "I looked for the head of Mr. Apollinax rolling under a chair" (*CPP* 31); "a pair of ragged claws" (*CPP* 15) scuttles across poems, to end up in "Rhapsody on a Windy Night," as

"An old crab with barnacles on its back" (*CPP* 25). As the speaker in "The Love Song of J. Alfred" is made up of parts, the collection he finds himself in may be made up of parts of him. Or parts of his poem. Without this world the figure dissolves, and without this composite figure, "PRUFROCK," this collection dissolves. (It seems arranged with this notion of fade-out in mind, placing its biggest scene first.) The collection shows a double preoccupation with names and namelessness, as the worlds where these figures revolve are places made up of the unnameable, the undeterminable, parts of unknown wholes, "eyes that fix you in a formulated phrase" (*CPP* 14):

> One thinks of all the hands
> That are raising dingy shades
> In a thousand furnished rooms. (*CPP* 22)

Early drafts of "Preludes" from 1909 show the different sections once had names, neighbourhoods of the city of Boston. Over time, the place-names fade, but the places return, or remain, becoming a sharply unreal city by being unnamed, the placing of "one" near "thousand" tacitly conveying the oceanic quality of a real metropolis, eluding, possibly, the power of "one" to think of it as real at all or to really think at all, while the name for the rooms, "furnished," deftly sketches a short story. The rooms are rented, like Edith's room, perhaps, or like the "one-night cheap hotels" (*CPP* 13) at the opening of "The Love Song of J. Alfred Prufrock." Naming in *Prufrock*, then, is an activity framing the collection's equal fascination with indistinct identity and shared anonymity, where you find, as Dante's Statius does, your eyes meeting a seemingly solid person, only to apprehend that being slipping away, fading "behind a city block" (*CPP* 23) or dissolving into a dingy shade.

The cross-contact between poems in *Prufrock* can be heard at the end of "Portrait of a Lady" – "This music is successful with a 'dying fall' / Now that we talk of dying – / And should I have the right to smile?" – as it alludes to the beginning of *Twelfth Night*:

> If Musicke be the food of Love, play on,
> Give me excesse of it: that surfetting,
> The appetite may sicken, and so dye.
> That straine agen, it had a dying fall:
> O, it came ore my eare, like the sweet sound
> That breathes upon a bank of Violets;
> Stealing, and giving Odour.[2]

The poem folds the beginning of a play into its end, as if to double back on the earlier exclamation in "Portrait of a Lady," parenthetically emphasised and subdued, "(But our beginnings never know our ends!)"

(*CPP* 21). *Prufrock* begins with the end of a life in its dedication; here, we end up inside another beginning. Orsino's speech is itself preoccupied with hearing endings begin again. The "dying falls" of music, love, appetite, repetition, the yearning for return and the return of detumescence, combine in the atmosphere of "Portrait of a Lady" on several levels: pairs of rhymes reconfiguring across sections of the poem; "the voice" returning "like the insistent out-of-tune / Of a broken violin"; the self "returning as before" in the final section; and a "street piano, mechanical and tired" that "Reiterates some worn-out common song" (*CPP* 19, 20). The tune of Orsino's longing is perhaps just such a worn-out song. This song is playing again in "Portrait of a Lady" as the "'dying fall'" at its end follows "The Love Song of J. Alfred Prufrock": "I know the voices dying with a dying fall / Beneath the music from a farther room" (*CPP* 14).

Of wit, Eliot writes: "It involves, probably, a recognition, implicit in the expression of every experience, of other kinds of experience which are possible" (*CP2* 319). By alluding twice to the present reiteration of something played again, heard "Beneath the music from a further room," the "dying falls" in the two poems are themselves referencing the nature of allusiveness as a variety of wit. Hearing a snatch of a tune, played again, can conjure a set of remembrances which may both steal from and give to the present consciousness. Allusions are a variety of such tunes, evoking other possibilities by calling an original surrounding into being, and, at the same time, showing how another whole context can only fail to appear. By alluding both to Shakespeare, and to one another, the first two poems in Eliot's first published book of verse elicit the shadowy cross-talk between the pieces in the collection, as if the poems can hear each other "beneath the music from a farther room," rather as the two epigraphs from Dante seem to overhear one another. The individual poems might be instances of one another, "other observations," parts weaving a new whole or just reiterations of the same, worn-out common songs, "the other masquerades / That time resumes."

Dying with a dying fall is one song common to the poems published as *Prufrock and Other Observations* in 1917, if such a song may be imagined as having many strains. From the wrenching shut of "Rhapsody on a Windy Night":

> ["]The bed is open; the tooth-brush hangs on the wall,
> Put your shoes at the door, sleep, prepare for life."
>
> The last twist of the knife. (*CPP* 26)

to the fascination in "The Love Song of J. Alfred Prufrock" with words lingeringly trailing off, "'That is not it at all, / That is not what I meant, at all'" (*CPP* 16). The shape of the collection itself seems like a prolonged dying fall after its first poems. Some endings of poems in *Prufrock* seem determined to die away by falling flat, such as "The 'Boston Evening Transcript'": "If the street were time and he at the end of the street, / And I say, 'Cousin Harriet, here is the *Boston Evening Transcript*'" (*CPP* 28). A few of the shorter poems in *Prufrock* are self-consciously slight; beginning only to quickly die off and so working to dramatize the revolving concerns with tedium, routine, reiteration. *Prufrock and Other Observations* is made up of a kind of shape-shifting between the mild and the wild, at once archly dexterous and artfully clumsy, like the "dull tom-tom" beating "Absurdly" (*CPP* 19) on the fringes of "Portrait of a Lady." Or, in "The Love Song of J. Alfred Prufrock":

> And the afternoon, the evening, sleeps so peacefully!
> Smoothed by long fingers,
> Asleep ... tired ... or it malingers,
> Stretched on the floor, here beside you and me. (*CPP* 15)

The disquiet in these lines is peculiar to *Prufrock*, as it hovers between the whimsical and the menacing. The evening that was "etherised" at the beginning of the poem, here "sleeps so peacefully!" A pang of unrest is cast by the exclamation. Lingered, a motion flickering earlier in the poem, has transmuted into "malinger": to feign the symptoms of disease. (The *OED* cites Robert Browning's *Fifine at the Fair* [1872], "Be sick by stealth, Nor traffic with disease – malingering in health!") The dissemblance conjured by the word, which the dictionary also demurely tells us "is perhaps under the influence of linger" is part of the atmosphere of indecision in the lines. Whether it is "the afternoon" or "the evening" or the afternoon that has become the evening, whether this elusive "it" is indeed "asleep" or "tired" or if "it malingers," are all indecisions hovering about in the atmosphere of the lines, offset and set off-kilter by the certain certainty of "here beside you and me." In *Prufrock*, domestic interiors are lined with menace; "the bed is open" (*CPP* 26) in "Rhapsody on a Windy Night," like a wound.

The preoccupation with dwelling on interiors in these poems exists to capture the observation that we cannot stay inside. As "The afternoon, the evening" glissades into "it malingers," twilight comes inside, and the interior seeps into the world. As in "Morning at the Window":

> The brown waves of fog toss up to me
> Twisted faces from the bottom of the street,
> And tear from a passer-by with muddy skirts
> An aimless smile that hovers in the air
> And vanishes along the level of the roofs. (*CPP* 27)

The poem makes vastness appear by seeming fragmentary, as an observation is tossed up to an observer in an oceanic city, and then slips away.

"Morning at the Window" is soaked in Baudelaire's *À une passante*, but cut with an *Alice in Wonderland*'s levitating absurdity, where a smile can detach from an expression, to vanish into space and time. The threshold conjures absent faces: next to "smile" the "tear" seems both rending and lachrymal as well as an expression wrenched from a glimpse; the poem is an artful tangle, rendered and rended by tattered ways of seeing. In *Prufrock* the cusp between the street and the room is sometimes diaphanous and other times penumbral; appearances are ever "malingering" as we can't say where one inside ends and the outside begins. The poems hover or linger in the foggy regions between such places or states, the indistinct distinctions that apply to buildings and to persons, met also within Eeldrop's vision of Edith "waking to a room." The dissemblance implicit in the word "malingers" crystallises several of the states of minds at play, where a face might be prepared to meet another face, where the semblance of a countenance might act as masquerade or where an expression might slip away from a person, and where preparing a face to meet other faces is a social ritual akin to being "sick by stealth": "I feel like one who smiles, and turning shall remark / Suddenly, his expression in a glass" (*CPP* 21).

In 1928, Eliot said that "the form in which I began to write, in 1908 or 1909, was directly drawn from the study of Laforgue together with the later Elizabethan drama; and I do not know anyone who started from exactly that point" (*CP3* 518). The trans-temporal and trans-national connections between the works of a single writer and a large body of drama might not be thought of as a point from which a single form might be directly drawn, but this remark is characteristic of Eliot in its creation of what he describes elsewhere as a "cross": "Verse stands in constant need of what Samuel Butler calls a cross. The serious writer of verse must be prepared to cross himself with the best verse of other languages and the best prose of all languages" (*CP1* 679). Eliot's account of his beginnings describes how a writer might make a start from a composite masquerade, a kind of travesty. Eliot encountered Laforgue through Symons's *The Symbolist Movement in Literature*, where Symons says Laforgue "invented fantastic puppets … which dance in his prose and verse, derisively, at the end of a string." Symons describes Laforgue's work as "travesty … with which one can play, very seriously."[3] Travesty carries the general sense of a derisive imitation or grotesque misrepresentation, and like "burlesque," from the Italian *burla* ("ridicule" or "joke"), the word is associated with stage entertainment, specifically with costume and disguise; appearing *en travesti* means performing in the attire of the opposite sex. The distinction between "in the attire of" rather than "disguised as" points to the particular sense of costuming suggested by travesty, which operates like an allusion, and so implies the partial visibility of the original identity. The costume is intentionally not a completed disguise, as a travesty of a literary work requires the original to be recognisable. If a male performer appears *en travesti* as a woman, the audience is aware of the performer's true sex, the sex that they pretend, and a third state, which resembles both, but belongs to neither. Travesty thus implies the recognisable co-presence of two identities, and the simultaneous awareness of a vestigial third, not particular to either original, but the result of their interaction. In this sense, it informs Eliot's account of his beginnings, where he describes bringing two identities together to form his own, "the form *in which* I began to write" (emphasis added); his remark is revealing through the identities it adopts, as the syntax suggests that the form does not belong to him, but that temporary habitation is found within the form, as a costume or a role. Under this aspect, a form might originate at a point between possible styles. This imagines how a form might arise, not only by the espousal or rejection of a given convention or manner, but between the recognition of other possibilities; for Eliot, this is not just "a point," but a disposition. Such a cross is signalled explicitly on the title page of *Prufrock*, where levity and gravity breathe the same air.

"Prufrock," a name with comical possibilities, shares a page with a dead soldier and a purgatorial cry, a contrast we are invited to live again, or is played again, when we turn the page: hard on the heels of the title "The Love Song of J. Alfred Prufrock" are six lines from the depths of Dante's Hell. The collection acquaints you with its sudden shifts, its unprepared transitions from levity to gravity as you pass through its rooms and social gatherings and routines, as you learn to dance the steps of the masquerade, and begin to apprehend how to time the segue from the terrestrial to the subterranean:

> Shall I say, I have gone at dusk through narrow streets
> And watched the smoke that rises from the pipes
> Of lonely men in shirt-sleeves, leaning out of windows?...
>
> I should have been a pair of ragged claws
> Scuttling across the floors of silent seas. (*CPP* 15)

Here disembodied parts stand in for wholes, human and animal forms combine fantastically and are interwoven – this is a grotesque style. Eliot's verse is grotesque in the sense that Victor Hugo described, as giving voice to a double nature:

> Elle lui montre qu'il est double comme sa destinée, qu'il y a en lui un animal et une intelligence, une âme et un corps; en un mot, qu'il est le point d'intersection, l'anneau commun des deux chaînes d'êtres qui embrassent la création, matériels et de la série des êtres incorporels, la première partant de

> la pierre pour arriver à l'homme, la seconde partant de l'homme pour finir à Dieu... [Il semble, au contraire, que] le grotesque soit un temps d'arrêt, un terme de comparaison, un point de départ d'où l'on s'élève vers le beau avec une perception plus fraîche et plus excitée.[4]
>
> [It shows him that he, like his destiny, is twofold: that there is in him an animal and an intellect, a body and a soul; in a word, that he is the point of intersection, the common link of the two chains of beings which embrace all creation – of the chain of material beings and the chain of incorporeal beings; the first starting from the rock to arrive at man, the second starting from man to end at God ... On the other hand, the grotesque seems to be a halting-place, a term of comparison, a starting-point whence one rises toward the beautiful with a fresher and keener perception.]

The claim is assured as it lights on a resting place where contradictions are held together by their differences, and so may invite scepticism; but, in another way, Hugo provides a place for the practice of scepticism, as he richly imagines a style as wit, where differences are mutually conversant, understood not in each other's terms, but as terms of comparison, and imagines how a form might arise between such terms. This matters for how we understand gravity and levity in Eliot's work, as one aspect does not outweigh or diminish the other; they act as terms of comparison.

Prufrock is preoccupied with the travesty of banality, audible in the wild laughter rippling through the collection, all-consuming in "Hysteria," peculiar in "Mr. Apollinax" ("He laughed like an irresponsible foetus" [*CPP* 31]) and philosophical in "Preludes" ("wipe your hand across your mouth, and laugh" [*CPP* 23]). That banality itself is "almost ridiculous" is an aspect heightened by being flattened, sometimes through the adoption of a seemingly ingénue air, "Her hair over her arms and her arms full of flowers. / And I wonder how they should have been together!" (*CPP* 34) – or by endings that profoundly flatten ennui into a few left-overs, dying falls performing the art of sinking:

> "There was something he said that I might have challenged."
> Of dowager Mrs. Phlaccus, and Professor and Mrs. Cheetah
> I remember a slice of lemon, and a bitten macaroon. (*CPP* 31)

The poems are linked in their attention to routine and in their devotion to the surprising rupture of those routines, a texture that makes itself felt in the versification:

> The winter evening settles down
> With smell of steaks in passageways.
> Six o'clock.
> The burnt-out ends of smoky days. (*CPP* 22)

Rhythm here might be described as grotesque, as it ruptures from expectation, and so creates a "point of intersection" between terms for comparison. Those terms form a double acoustic describing twilight, but it's as if "six o'clock" speaks in a different tongue, signalling another way of marking what the rhythm of the other three surrounding lines adumbrate. Many of the poems in *Prufrock* show two, or more, voices shown in the act of telling. But Eliot's rhythms themselves conjure this ever-present possibility, even if the small speech marks palpably indicating a shift of person are not there. Magnificently, at the end of "The Love Song of J. Alfred Prufrock," a *coup de théâtre* of an end, and so ending the first poem of a first collection with a dying flourish, leaving other endings to perform emphatic fade-outs:

> I shall wear white flannel trousers, and walk upon the beach.
> I have heard the mermaids singing, each to each.
>
> I do not think that they will sing to me.
>
> I have seen them riding seaward on the waves
> Combing the white hair of the waves blown back
> When the wind blows the water white and black.
>
> We have lingered in the chambers of the sea
> By sea-girls wreathed with seaweed red and brown
> Till human voices wake us, and we drown. (*CPP* 16–17)

"The Love Song of J. Alfred Prufrock" begins in the street and ends up in the sea. The yellow city fog in the earlier part of the poem, that "Lingered upon the pools that stand in drains," the interiors behind the "window-panes," the places where you might spend "restless nights in one-night cheap hotels" (*CPP* 13) are city rooms that turn, by the end of the poem, into the chambers of the sea, another place to linger, perhaps, but not to live.

The line, "I do not think that they will sing to me," is the only line that stands alone in this way in the poem. It is hard to know where to place the stress, if vocal stress can distress this line's peculiar loneliness. Is it: "I do not think that they will sing to *me*" (because no one ever does), petulant, or maybe despondent, artfully displaying the art of loneliness, hidden in full view. Or, could it combine a wistful hope with the tentatively sceptical: "I do not *think* that they will sing to me" – but, you never know, they just might. After all, the voice that claims to "have seen them riding seaward on the waves" opens up to a rhythm that seems to retain the memory of a strange invisible song, holding the melodious sweetness and sorrows of near-repetitions, cresting in waves of minor variants: "seaward," "sea-girls," "seaweed," "blown," "blows," "back," "black," all curling in musical rip-tides, as if maybe the voice may no longer be speaking, or singing, alone, or as if the poem ends with a cadence from another world and time. The final lines of "The Love Song of J. Alfred Prufrock," like other love songs, are peculiarly nostalgic. Standing to one side is the "I" that does not think that the mermaids will sing, looking in on the "near distance" of the "I" that has seen: the poem ends in masquerade.

When, in 1917, a friend congratulated Eliot on *Prufrock and Other Observations*, he replied, "It is good of you to speak well of *Prufrock* – I fear it will simply appear a *réchauffée* to most of my friends – they are growing tired of waiting for something better from me" (*L1* 290). Here, an inquisitive "They" hovers as an audience to the collection. Eliot's remarks on *Prufrock* mirror the book; they are Prufrock-like: But they will say: "How his poems are growing thin!" The poems, mostly written before 1915, were indeed re-heated into a collection, which is not quite to say they are derivative. Eliot came to make a life's work of self-borrowing and pondering poets' re-hashings and self-borrowings, a quality he came to imagine as a force capable of imaginatively deriving original understanding from the derivative. But he had lived with these poems for some time, however elusively, before sending them out into the world. Perhaps the feeling of the *réchauffée* is part of their atmosphere, but not only as a thrifty re-heating of left-overs; rather, the sense of weariness, of second-hand objects, of malingering originality, is turned to a creative strength. Eliot's next volume, *Poems* (1920), or *Ara Vos Prec*, may have been what "they" were waiting for. There's a rare, quite sumptuous edition of *Ara Vus Prec* [sic] which comes at a hefty price, and includes the *Prufrock* volume. The strangest thing about looking at this edition in rare books rooms is that *Prufrock* is printed before *Poems* (1920). It would be odd to first encounter Eliot's poems this way around. Part of the effect of reading *Prufrock* and then *Poems* (1920) is a sudden change, habitual now perhaps, but one that the quick transitions in *Prufrock* only in part prepare for – a sharp plunge: "it looks as if a harsh, oblique light had been turned on his world."[5] The Dante epigraph which heads the volume as we read it now comes from this obliquely lit world: it was added in 1920, and then fixed itself to this collection. This chapter has treated that epigraph as part of the collection, as this is how Eliot eventually wanted it to appear. But remembering the epigraph as a later addition, as a revision of a vision, illuminates faintly how, by 1920, these poems may have come to seem like shadowy creations of a former self for Eliot. The poems recognise a belatedness of themselves, a dimly lit foreknowledge of a future perfect tense when hesitant beginnings have stalled: "After the cups, the marmalade, the tea, / Among the porcelain, among some talk of you and me"; "And would it have been worth it, after all" (*CPP* 15). This belatedness is acutely lit by the addition of the epigraph from the *Purgatorio*, where, in Beckett's words from *Krapp's Last Tape*, we enter the world of *Prufrock* from somewhere, "after all": "A late evening the future," where solid things have turned into phantoms, bodies have become shades.[6] Strange, then, to read *Poems* (1920) first, when in those later poems the tea parties are over. Gone are the niceties of drawing rooms, the Boston mantelpieces, the finer Jamesian scenes. Enter Sweeney; enter the word "fear." Cousin Nancy and Cousin Harriet, the New England nymphs, are long departed, and have left no addresses. In their place, a shady cosmopolitan crowd: Fräulein von Kulp, Madame de Tornquist, Mr Silvero. If there are parties in *Poems* (1920) then they don't take place on lawns or in drawing rooms with "cakes and ices" but in estaminets and dive bars. The pains and the pleasures of *Prufrock*, as Eliot came to fashion the collection, are that these poems, foregrounded by Statius's plaintive cry, hold a peculiar foreknowledge of their own obsolescence. They "grow old," like J. Alfred Prufrock, as they speak. Perhaps just because Eliot had lived with these poems for a while these works have stitched within their fabric as a collection a strain of nostalgia, the note of a dying fall.

It was love that spurned or burned Statius into forgetting he was a phantom body. Dante shows him lurching forward with the comic and piteously tenacious gesture of human longing – such longing as we may feel for the self we once were. By adding this epigraph, Eliot casts all the dying falls that make up *Prufrock* in a different light. Our beginnings really never do know our ends. The collected bodies, of poems, of persons, named and disembodied, come and go differently in this light. A light so dim you might be forgiven for forgetting that you were once a body; after all, "One sees little in this light."[7] Eliot's action of recasting his collection in this purgatorial shade is an act which looks back on a past self as if that person were dead. This aspect of ourselves is a past which only ever lies before us. In this way, in *Prufrock*'s trembling last shape, Eliot is addressing his past self in words remembered from Dante, words also borrowed by the poet Eugenio Montale, when he spoke to his dead wife, "It's possible, you know, to love a shadow, shadows that we are."[8]

NOTES

1 See Christopher Ricks, *T. S. Eliot and Prejudice* (London: Faber & Faber, 1988), pp. 115–18.

2 *Twelfth Night* I.1.1e First Folio (1623), repr. *A Facsimile of the First Folio* (London: Routledge, 1998).

3 Arthur Symons, *The Symbolist Movement in Literature* (London: W. Heinemann, 1899), pp. 56, 59.

4 Victor Hugo, *La Préface de Cromwell* (1827), *Oeuvres complètes*, ed. Jean Massin, 16 vols. (Paris: club français du livre, 1967–72), III, pp. 45–7.

5 Eric Griffiths, "Meeting Mr. Eliot," *TLS* (14 May 2010), p. 3.

6 *The Complete Dramatic Works of Samuel Beckett* (London: Faber & Faber, 1986), p. 215.
7 Ibid. p. 355.
8 Cited in the introduction to *Dante in English*, eds. Eric Griffiths and Matthew Reynolds (London: Penguin, 2005), p. xlix.

4

RICK DE VILLIERS

Banishing the Backward Devils: Eliot's Quatrain Poems and "Gerontion"

In the latter half of a war-torn decade, Eliot produced scores of reviews and essays but published only a handful of poems. While the most influential of his polemical pieces went on to shape literary discourse, the quatrains of *Poems* (1920) made but a negligible impression. In the wake of the positive reception of *Prufrock and Other Observations*, Eliot's formal experiments struggled to find an audience. Early critics of the quatrain poems thought them novel but "fatally impoverished of subject matter," or fit only for "readers in the waiting-room of a private sanatorium" (Brooker 21, 47). Eliot was stung by the reception of his new poetry, which he hoped could take him beyond the burdensome success of "The Love Song of J. Alfred Prufrock."[1] In a letter to his brother he reveals his estimation of the new work: "some of the new poems, the Sweeney ones, especially 'Among the Nightingales' and 'Burbank' are intensely serious, and I think these two are among the best that I have ever done. But even here I am considered by the ordinary Newspaper critic as a Wit or satirist, and in America I suppose I shall be thought merely disgusting" (*L1* 441).

Subsequent criticism has done little to rescue the quatrain poems from the early charges that were laid against them. They have been denigrated as plagiaristic, pseudo-scholarly and preparatory; they are seen to have little in common with the lyrical and psychologically poignant poems that stand on either side of these experiments. Yet Eliot's choice to trade free verse for the tautness of cross-rhymed tetrameters was deliberate. According to Ezra Pound, with whom Eliot scrutinised Théophile Gautier's quatrain poems in *Émaux et Camées* between 1917 and 1919, the two poets sought a way of addressing the lax formalism of their contemporaries. Eliot, perhaps less concerned with the general state of poetry than with framing his own thoughts, conceded in an interview that the "form gave the impetus to the content."[2] The statement is as cryptic as the content of the poetry is varied: subject matter ranges from sexual debasement to the tepidity of institutionalized religion, and the only common denominator would seem to be rhyme and rhythm. But the textual history of the quatrain poems suggests that they are also unified by an undercurrent of personal pain.

Over the course of 1919 and 1920 three books were published containing roughly the same material. First was *Poems* (1919), followed by *Ara Vos Prec* (1920) and its American counterpart, *Poems*.[3] The evolution of the titles is curious. "*Ara Vos Prec*" ("I pray you") stands in contrast to an unyielding title like *Poems*. The Provençal words are taken from Canto XXVI of the *Purgatorio* and are spoken by the troubadour, Arnaut Daniel, who is numbered among the lustful souls of the seventh terrace. In full, his supplication to Dante the pilgrim reads: "Now, by the Power that conducts you to / the summit of the stairway, I pray you: remember, at time opportune, my pain."[4]

It is tempting to think that this whispered exhortation has some bearing on Eliot's personal life at the time. That his marriage to Vivien Haigh-Wood was an unhappy one is well known. Over the union hung a cloud of financial worries, health concerns and – not least of all – the humiliation of betrayal. After their wedding, Vivien started an affair with Bertrand Russell. Though there is no corroboration of the fact in Eliot's letters, the poetry composed during this period shows a certain preoccupation with failed relationships and duplicity. For one, there is "Ode," a tortuous epithalamium published in *Ara Vos Prec* but excluded from subsequent editions. Then there is the excised second epigraph to "Sweeney Among the Nightingales," which is taken from an anonymous Elizabethan play (*The Reigne of K. Edward the Third*) that centres on infidelity. Finally, the title *Ara Vos Prec* asks the reader to take pity on one who, though not bathed in the fires of lust himself, suffered at the hands of others' illicit sexual adventures.

But in spite of the personal turmoil Eliot might have been suffering, the quatrain poems exhibit a determination to minimize subjective experience. In the first instance, their formalism bespeaks precision and restraint. Regular rhyme glazes over the content, giving bathetic touches to weighty subjects and effecting the "alliance of levity and seriousness" (*CP2* 312) that Eliot appreciated in Gautier and others. The lines, measured and regimented, serve as an aesthetic counterbalance to the loose behaviour so frequently on display. Second, detachment is the dominant mode of presentation. The Eliot family motto was "*Tace et Fac*" ("Be silent and act"), which also appears to be the governing imperative for the poetry in question. The poet shows but does not tell. There are no moments of Prufrockian introspection; instead, a speaker, aloof and out of sight, presides over the machinations of dubious characters while paring his nails. This development of technique and point of view ties in with the third instance of Eliot's impersonality: the incisive revision and editing of the poems even after publication – conscious acts to purge the work of personal taint and steer it in a new direction. Though the muted plea behind the words "*Ara vos prec*" would be lost to most, Eliot still opted in his *Collected Poems* to substitute the arcane Provençal title for the poker-faced *Poems*. It marked a clear gulf between his "observations" and his "poems."

While "The Love Song of J. Alfred Prufrock" and "Portrait of a Lady" were seen, strangely enough, as providing the "customary foundations" of poetry, the stylised quatrains had an alienating effect.[5] Form was not the issue. What made the earlier poetry palatable was its emotional direction: even first-time readers can apprehend Prufrock's self-consciousness or sense the speaker's longing in "La Figlia Che Piange." But a salacious Sweeney or a greedy Bleistein lacks the usual emotive handles. The quatrains possess, to use Eliot's phrase about Jonson, a "polished veneer" by which "no swarms of inarticulate feelings are aroused" (*CP2* 151). Their effect is intensive rather than expansive.

Taking a poem like "Burbank with a Baedeker: Bleistein with a Cigar," this appears a hard case to make. With a slippery fusion of seven sources in the epigraph, let alone an intricate plot and a larceny of other allusions, Eliot seems to implant a dispersive mechanism into the fabric of the poem. Before working out the intrigue between the poem's sordid characters, the reader must chase breathlessly after works by Gautier, Andrea Mantegna, Henry James, Ford Madox Ford, Robert Browning and John Marston. But the intertextuality calls for forensic precision and patience; only after proportionate sense has been made of each quotation does a telescoped image of Venice manifest itself.

The ostensible reference to James's *The Aspern Papers* ("*the gondola stopped, the old palace was there, how charming its grey and pink*" [*CPP* 40]) provides a useful example, situating the reader in a Venice run down by tourists – a neat parallel to the sojourn of Burbank and Bleistein. The quotation also situates Eliot's poem, self-deprecatingly, in a milieu of intellectual tourism, since James is only indirectly invoked through Ford's *Henry James: A Critical Study*. Aside from differences in punctuation, the exact phrase Eliot uses in the epigraph occurs in Ford's book in a section called "Temperaments" and is located on a page dealing flippantly with James's general "mission … to civilize his people."[6] Following this textual union, Eliot splices Shakespeare with Browning. The snippet "*goats and monkeys, with such hair too!*" directs the reader towards both *Othello* and "A Toccata of Gallupi's," but there is also a curious loop back to Ford. The chorus of the Browning poem ("Dust and ashes, dead and done with, Venice spent what Venice earned. / The soul, doubtless, is immortal – where a soul can be discerned") is eerily echoed in the fuller Ford passage: "the soul's immortal, but ... most people have not got souls." Since this sentence is meant to reflect, albeit glibly, Henry James's outlook, he too is present in the Browning allusion. Ford's usefulness as medium does not end there. One page before quoting from *The Aspern Papers*, he reproduces a phrase from James's *The Madonna of the Future*: "Cats and monkeys, monkeys and cats – all human life is there." All of a sudden there is confluence between Shakespeare, Browning, James and Ford. It arises because Eliot coerces the juxtaposition, but he is only able to do so because there is already common ground between the texts. Despite differences in time, subject and even media, the phrases of the epigraph become the collected fragments of a decayed city. Instead of representing a pristinely prelapsarian Venice, they magnify the poem's singular vision: Burbank, Bleistein and company are not new corruptors of the old world; they are inheritors of a city always-already fallen.

While Eliot compels each allusion, each action and each image along a predetermined path, he also crafts a poetic embodiment of some of his most significant theoretical formulations. The epigraph alone puts into practice the synchronic view of art that he promulgated in "Tradition and the Individual Talent" and also provides an "objective correlative" (*CP*2 125) for the poem's caustic tableau of Venice. The eight stanzas, with their submarine cross-currents of mocking and melancholy, evolve a satire akin to the kinds extolled in "Ben Jonson" and "John Dryden." In Eliot's estimation, Jonson was an artist whose work suffered because of its precocious reputation: too clever for his own good, he could not infuse his art with the same evocativeness as some of his contemporaries. The real issue, Eliot believed, was crudeness of classification: tragedy and comedy were ill-fitting masks. In a similar way, readers of Dryden, according to Eliot, did not have the necessary emotional vocabulary to appreciate the spectrum of his satire: "To those who are genuinely insensible of [Dryden's] genius ... we can only oppose illustrations of the following proposition: that their insensibility does not merely signify indifference to satire and wit, but lack of perception of qualities not confined to satire and wit and present in the work of other poets whom these persons feel that they understand" (*CP*2 350). The remark serves as an index of Eliot's belief in the subtlety and variety that satire and wit could offer. In those unable to appreciate such potential, he diagnoses a "confusion between the emotions considered to be poetic ... and the *result* of personal emotion in poetry" (*CP*2 353): if Dryden does not meet our demands for poetry, the cause is the parochial and prejudiced criteria we have for the "poetic."

The apologetics, strident and resolute, are far from dispassionate. Those quatrains which have received detailed attention have also been subject to prosaic matters of fact. Who is Sweeney really? Which Umbrian painter does the poet have in mind in "Mr. Eliot's Sunday Morning Service"? What is the nature of Pipit's relationship with the speaker of "A Cooking Egg"? The last question, for instance, sparked a famous scholarly debate in a 1953 issue of *Essays in Criticism*. It was variously and bitingly argued that she is a childhood nurse, a little girl, an estranged friend, or a sophisticated tease. The inquiry is not negligible, yet it demands considering the facts of the poem along with its feeling.

The poem explores one of Eliot's most frequent themes – regret. But the *lacrimae rerum* note is struck with such force, such exaggeration, that it becomes difficult to gauge the sincerity of feeling. The speaker's facetious bluster would suggest that Pipit in all her sad domesticity could never live up to his need for honour, capital, society and spiritual enlightenment. But while his daydream permits him handshakes with courtiers, consuls, initiates and financiers, he is inevitably led to ask where the snows of yesteryear have gone. Unlike "Burbank," which achieves its concentration through confluence, "A Cooking Egg" does so by means of divergence, distraction and a double layer of irony. On the surface is a nameless persona – clever, learned and cynical – who strews breadcrumbs leading away from the heart of the matter; deeper down, the poet implodes his speaker's every gesture of denial, empties his self-sufficiency of solace. The epigraph, taken from a work that catalogues Villon's sins and scandals, obscures only for a moment the glaring fact that the speaker's disgrace stems from inertia rather than misconduct. Similarly, the guest list he maps out in his mind suggests his own vitiated earthly existence. He would have us believe that Pipit is past her expiry date, but it is really his youth that has been squandered and his future that tenders compromise.

Eliot undermines the speaker's bravado through palimpsest. The "I shall not want" (*CPP* 44) formula has a dual basis. There is the obvious appropriation of Psalm 23, which lends the speaker's words a casual irreverence. But there is also a recasting of the unfulfilled love affair between John Ruskin and Rose La Touche. After La Touche's death, Ruskin remarked in a letter that he wanted her on earth and not in heaven, since in heaven he would keep company with Pythagoras and other thinkers. Like Ruskin, whose "Dark Tower of religious doubt" was an obstacle in the way of his relationship with La Touche, the speaker of the poem cannot bring himself to credit the "heaven" he holds up as a substitute for Pipit. He is sceptical and world-weary. He does not drink deep of his shames like Villon. He cannot believe in Sir Philip Sidney, for Sidney embodies a spirit too romantic and too remote from his own. He knows full well that he will not talk to Coriolanus, because Coriolanus hates talking. The millionaire industrialist

Alfred Mond is unlikely to be signing blank cheques, Lucretia Borgia would prove a fickle bride, and Madame Blavatsky and Piccarda de Donati are an improbable pair of spiritual guides. Ultimately, the surplus of sources serves only to underscore the void, the zero, the stale cooking egg that is the speaker's existence.

The typographical break is also the breaking of the speaker's resolve. Unable to keep up the pretence, he looks wistfully over his shoulder. Gone are the jokes, and gone is the glory. Even the quatrain sequence crumbles, and the poem terminates not on a facile rhyme, but on three plodding stresses. As in *Coriolan*, which appears about a decade later, the symbols of victory and dominion are replaced by a base need to sate hunger; the masses seek distraction and comfort in cloned Aerated Bread Company restaurants. Furthermore, the *ubi sunt* motif undercuts all irony. Despite the speaker's best efforts to convince himself that Pipit is a cooking egg, it is he who sits on the rack. Not like a gun, not going off with a bang, but drooping and whimpering.

Given its use of a persona, its slightly deviating structure, and its prioritisation of the private over the public, it may seem that "A Cooking Egg" stands anomalously among the other quatrains. But its implicit apprehensiveness of the female figure is coterminous with some of the other poems. In a draft version, the speaker admits that "Peace was to have been extended / From the tip of Pipit's tongue" (*IMH* 358). Despite her homeliness, he desires a secular salvation, a reverse Eucharist. It is not the body of Christ that will provide peace, but the body of Pipit. As in Swinburne's *Lucrezia Borgia: The Chronicle of Tibaldeo Tibaldei*, which very likely informs the irreverent tone of the poem, there is sanctification of the profane. The "tip of Pipit's tongue" is sexually suggestive, but also intimates her capacity for intimate communication. Sadly, the speaker is unable to force the matter to its conclusion and chooses to escape into the intellect.

Such moments of failure are common throughout Eliot's work. Prufrock dare not eat a peach; words and insight fail the hyacinth girl's companion; the hollow men supplicate the inanimate but cannot kiss. Nowhere, however, is the gulf between the sexes more vast and terrifying than in "Whispers of Immortality." On one side of the elliptical divide are Webster, Donne and, by extension, Eliot. On the other side is Grishkin. Where the first half of the poem centres on the living dead, the mirroring four stanzas tiptoe around a *femme fatale* whose vivacity is an effective repellent of the Abstract Entities. Grishkin's eye is "underlined for emphasis" (*CPP* 52) because it defiantly distinguishes her from the anonymous and eyeless corpse in stanza one. Her breasts, unrestrained and voluptuous, mock the skeletal figure. Each breath she takes is a reminder of her vitality, a reminder that she is the antithesis of the metaphysician, a being beyond the frigid gaze of philosophy.

What appears to be a neat, programmatic schism between bones and flesh, thought and feeling, is also a complex amalgam of them. "Whispers of Immortality" stands in many ways as a terse exemplum of the poetry Eliot would praise three years later in "The Metaphysical Poets." What Samuel Johnson unflatteringly regarded as verse that forces heterogeneous ideas together Eliot saw as an ideal. The poets of the early seventeenth century possessed a unified sensibility which enabled them to "devour any kind of experience" (*CP2* 380). Donne, for one, had the chimeric capacity to apprehend thought as a sensual experience, to think of a rose and simultaneously appreciate its scent. Subsequently, however, a dissociation set in: the instantaneous and symbiotic commerce between intellect and sensation was lost. Bleak as the diagnosis seemed, Eliot did not issue his declaration without some remedial direction: "The poet must become more and more comprehensive, more allusive, more indirect, in order to force, to dislocate if necessary, language into his meaning" (*CP2* 381).

The violence advocated here is evident in "Whispers of Immortality." Eliot not only coerces language to do his bidding but reappropriates Webster and Donne in ways congenial to his agenda. The former is not cast as an artist bent on portraying moral corruption (his traditional role), but as one who sees death and sex twirling together in a strange dance. At a cursory glance it would seem that both the skull and breastless creatures are aspects of Webster's morbid vision. But only the first image can syntactically be attributed to him. If "Leaning" had been substituted for "Leaned" (*CPP* 52), the present participle would have enveloped the fourth line as an added qualification of the breastless creatures. More significantly, the breastless creatures – like the skull – would have stood as a zeugma in relation to the verb "saw." Lines three and four, then, are an extension not of Webster's but of Eliot's imagination. Webster's concern is death, though not necessarily death bound to sensuality. But the breastless, lipless skeletons are – through their very morphological negations – reminders of death in sex. Ultimately, it is Eliot who is fearful of the flesh since it is he, the poet-speaker, who avers in the first draft that "I must crawl between dry ribs / to keep my metaphysics warm" (*IMH* 365).

Donne, in his turn, is also selectively represented. It is supposed that sense is of prime importance to him. And yet he is an "Expert beyond experience" (*CPP* 52), one who has tried without trial. As with the picture of Webster, there is awkward communion between thought and sense. The language of the third stanza brims with innuendo. But it is a cold concept rather than a warm body that is ravishingly explored. In his 1926 Clark Lectures, Eliot described metaphysical poetry as that which "elevates sense for a moment to regions ordinarily attainable only by abstract thought, or on the other hand clothes the abstract, for a moment, with all the painful delight of flesh" (*CP2* 617). By this definition, "Whispers of Immortality" achieves unity between sense and thought only partially. The first four stanzas drape the abstract in pleasure but do not effect the reverse. Nowhere in the first half of the poem is a sensory experience used as a starting point. Donne and Webster are on show as analysts, not as men who once lived, felt, breathed. Donne, in particular, was perfectly adept at transmuting a physical experience into a metaphysical deliberation, but this quality is excluded from the poem.

Rather than present an alchemical opportunity to reshape sense into abstract thought, Grishkin causes the poet-speaker to sink into a catatonic state. There is observation but no action, promises of sexual bliss but no fulfilment. Almost as soon as her allure is established, we also sense the threat she poses. No metaphor, no metaphysical conceit holds her. She is compared to the carnivorous Brazilian jaguar, but the comparison fails to capture her movement from the exotic recesses of the mind to quotidian existence: the predator, even in its natural, tenebrous dwelling, is not nearly as intimidating as Grishkin in hers. What she represents is not death, but a challenge to the intellectual detachment of the "really serious men" (Eliot's epithet in an earlier draft, *IMH* 368). The fantastical mental image of a smiling corpse now gives way to the dangerous, mundane reality of a drawing room. The poet tries to clutch, seize and penetrate her being, but in the end he can only cautiously "Circumambulate."

Sweeney, of course, stands on no such ceremony. Where Eliot's other anti-heroes petrify in the presence of the female body, he takes violent pleasure in it; where they punctiliously scuttle along sideways, he is bold and unblinking. Undoubtedly, Sweeney is different. But his real mark of distinction has largely gone unnoticed. Critics readily typecast him as a drunken, philandering savage who is only spared complete identification as an animal by the breadth of his stubble. Eliot did endow "apeneck" (*CPP* 56) Sweeney with shades of the beastly, but he also realised in him a character who, though not acquiescent to it, could acknowledge a spiritual reality. His appearances throughout Eliot's oeuvre are all marked by this duality. To start, one might look to the end. *Sweeney Agonistes* supplies a complex picture of a man who has violent and primitive inclinations but weighs moral consequences with a greater measure of sensitivity than his associates. While the other characters in the verse play want to embroil themselves in the details of a murder case, he ponders its eternal implication. He also sees life for what it is ("birth, and copulation, and death," [*CPP* 122]) but is unwilling to divest himself of the pleasures of the flesh and undergo a second birth – even though he is hauntingly pursued by agents of spiritual retribution.

Sweeney might not have the intellectual prowess of Prufrock and others, but he possesses a far greater resolve. In "Sweeney Erect," this determination is carried to perverse lengths. It shows him at his most calculating, for the poem is hardly about the coupling of beasts. Though a hairy primate is discernible in his silhouette, his actions are far from instinctual. Like Theseus, whose absence lurks behind the poem, Sweeney is also a cruel conqueror who deserts his bed mate on the shores of sexual waste. Unlike the Cyclops or Poe's orangutan in "The Murders in Rue Morgue," however, there is nothing considerate or natural in his behaviour. Before Ovid's Polyphemus attempts to woo the object of his desire, he tries to temper his gruff exterior by trimming his hair and beard. In contrast, Sweeney only shaves once he has satisfied his designs. For him it is matter of cleansing and a gesture of abandonment: the day-old stubble on his face symbolises the primal, but with his animal urges sated, Sweeney can absolve himself of its souvenirs. The Poe allusion further adumbrates his conscious cruelty. The orangutan in the short story also shaves, but only because he thinks he is alone; Sweeney performs his morning ablutions in full view of the prostitute, whom he purposely terrorizes by testing the razor on his leg. And where Poe's creature reacts to screaming by wanting to silence it, Sweeney indifferently allows hysteria to run its course. He is not subhuman, but all too human.

It is vital to Eliot's conception of humanity that Sweeney be defined in opposition to unwitting beasts but still preserve a vague kinship with them. However strange it might seem, he is prized by Eliot over figures like *The Waste Land*'s typist and young man carbuncular, the clerks flowing over London Bridge, or even the Hollow Men who are not committed to light or darkness but sway to the whims of a comatose existence. In his essay on Baudelaire, Eliot claims:

> So far as we are human, what we do must be either evil or good; so far as we do evil or good, we are human; and it is better, in a paradoxical way, to do evil than to do nothing: at least, we exist. It is true to say that the glory of man is his capacity for salvation; it is also true to say that his glory is his capacity for damnation. (*CP4* 162–3)

What he indirectly objects to is life in limbo – living without praise or blame – and being unable to acknowledge the indelibility of the line that separates good from evil. Sweeney is gloriously human because his actions are decided rather than automatic and indifferent. That he is satisfied with just a physical birth points to a wilful embrace of the carnal existence, but it does not imply a facile philandering that extirpates sin through sinning. He is aware of the possibility of spiritual regeneration, and his reluctance to allow such a process also signals his awareness of the rigour and pain it may entail. Though cowardly in his stubborn pursuit of the ephemeral, Sweeney's acknowledgement of an outside and eternal code marks him as the antithesis of Emersonian self-reliance. He is concerned neither with the humanist outlook of such "guardians of the faith" (*CPP* 30) nor with the public code of Mrs. Turner's ladies who weigh "taste" and "reputation" over morality.

Accordingly, the last stanza shifts its tone from formal, tense and pompous to plain and grounded. The language sheds vague rhetoric for concrete and simple description, and the inflated abstractions of the preceding two stanzas give way to a gesture both practical and symbolic. In keeping with the satire of *Poems* (1920), Eliot directs his poem away from critique upon provincial etiquette to questions of greater moralistic magnitude. Had the poem ended at stanza ten, the focus upon good and evil would have been lost. Doris, with all the contradicting force a single "But" can summon, refocuses our attention. The stanza introduces a question of consciousness versus oblivion. On a level of mere plot, the sal volatile is intended to rouse the presumably collapsed epileptic; but within the tensile symbolic design of the poem, the pharmaco of smelling salts or alcohol, the option between living or partially living, are presented to Sweeney.

In "Sweeney Among the Nightingales" he also has a chance to heed the supernatural, for he is the custodian of the gate of horn, the mythological gate through which true dreams pass. Neglectful of his duty, however, he is closer to death than redemption. A witting heir to original sin, and one actively indulging in fallenness, he cannot escape its culminating terror. He is forced into an unkind kinship with Agamemnon: between them there is a communal appetite for the carnal, and above them hang the slain king's final words: "Alas, I am struck a mortal blow." The association is a complex one. As "Burbank" might suggest, Eliot is not concerned with tracing a downward spiral from an Edenic past to a degraded present. Rather, he brings Sweeney into closer contact with heroic but flawed figures for two reasons: first, to brand all human existence with universal fallibility; and second, to gesture at Sweeney's tragic vitality. Whatever his shortcomings, Sweeney thwarts the bourgeois impulse and frustrates an existential outlook. If he did not have access to a higher truth (of which the "hornèd gate" is a symbol), his inferred death would be nothing more than the slaughter of an animal; in order for his death to provide any cathartic release, it must be commensurate to a fatal flaw. In Sweeney's rejection of a second birth Eliot finds sufficient pride to condemn his creation to death and sufficient pride to establish a connection with other tragic heroes. Towards the end of "Baudelaire," Eliot writes that the "worst that can be said of most of our malefactors, from statesmen to thieves, is that they are not men enough to be damned" (*CP4* 163). Sweeney does not fall into this category. He is man enough for damnation and meets his fate not like the oblivious souls of *The Waste Land*, but embraces sin with the knowledge that time's winged chariot draws near and that the doors of redemption are swinging shut. Eliot does not praise his debauchery, his misogyny or his obstinacy to undergo a spiritual rebirth, but he does extol the implicit heroism in the acknowledgement of good and evil.

Above all, the quatrains show Eliot driven by a desire for seriousness. Though still nearly a decade away from his conversion to Christianity, he was searching for – if not religious rigidity – moral absolutism. He had since early adolescence been scornful of his family's Unitarian code of things done and not done. Conversely, he found something strangely appealing about the asceticism and suffering of the saints. Even if the final destination was vague and uncertain, it seemed a given to him that the road there should be trying. His two "church" poems, "The Hippopotamus" and "Mr. Eliot's Sunday Morning Service," exhibit an acute distaste for tepidity, and both criticize greed, spiritual aloofness and the untouchability of the institution.

That said, the two poems differ sharply in degree of severity. "The Hippopotamus" can even be said to stand alone among the other quatrains as an easy poem. The delivery is straightforward, the jokes instantly digestible and the satire wide enough to be only mildly shocking. Pitting the weak and meek hippopotamus against the unshakable church, the poem is couched in toothless mirth. As Eliot's earliest Gautier-modelled quatrain, it gives the impression that the poet is trying the form on for size. Still, beneath the laughter one senses the tug of gravity. The epigraph – a truncated verse from Saint Paul – directs the reader's attention towards the lukewarm Laodiceans, but also in the direction of the Colossians. The Pauline epistle (some doubt exists about the authorship) warns particularly against a deceptive philosophy that is taking hold in the community, which later scholarship has shown to be the infiltration of Gnosticism and legalistic Judaism. The former threatened the pernicious development of hierarchies within the early church; the latter implied a dogged adherence to obsolete codes and conventions.

With this backdrop, the poem then inveighs against spiritual pride and ossified practices. If the hippopotamus errs, at least he is moving; the "True Church" remains stagnant and out of touch. To the poet who would later declare that "For us, there is only the trying" (*CPP* 182), the self-sufficiency of the True Church is deplorable. The 'potamus, physically (and even morphologically) limited, cannot help himself to a mango, while its stony counterpart receives refreshment without making any effort. Curiously, the fourth stanza recycles a phrase from a poem written in Eliot's youth, "A Fable for Feasters," whose comical ottava rima deals with "friars merry" indulging in food and drink beyond all restraint. The words "from over sea" (*CPP* 587) occurs in a stanza dealing with the purchase of relics, and is subsequently transposed to the quatrain to suggest the corruption and ease of the church.

The attack, however, is not sustained. As the improbable and bathetic events of the last three stanzas unfold, the seriousness of the poem evaporates. The heaven into which the hippopotamus disappears is as real as the one imagined by the speaker of "A Cooking Egg," and the Church seems based in as much substance as the miasmal mist that surrounds it. When Eliot finally returned to the Church as theme, his gaze was more focused. "Mr. Eliot's Sunday Morning Service" intensifies the concern over spiritual pride, but its ways are more complex, more allusive and more vituperative. As the opening word might suggest, Mr Eliot's sermon takes issue with the obfuscating verbosity that detracts from the Word itself. Origen – exegete, heretic, eunuch – stands as envoy of divisive, sterile, ceaseless theology. Not only is he "enervate" himself; he seeks to diminish the power of the Trinity by arguing that Christ is of a created order and thus inferior to the Father. The phrase "Superfetation of *τὸ ἕν*" suggests that the Word is secondary to the "essential being," that Christ is a product of God rather than consubstantial with him. If the "religious caterpillars" in Marlowe's play produce illegitimate children, the epicene Origen spawns illegitimate ideas.

Fortunately, the unoffending feet of Christ provide an escape. Stanzas three and four, in contrast to the arcane opening, bespeak calm and clarity. For a moment, the ekphrastic description of an unidentified painting provides the poem with stillness and stability. Amid a swirl of words and concepts, the image of the incarnate God anchors the poem in a visual, tangible reality. The speaker's attention is directed away from the simoniac practices of the gloomy clergymen who greedily clench their fists around the profits of absolution. What he sees is the unshod, untainted, humble feet of Christ, which for some reason reminds him of Sweeney. In a gradual stream of consciousness he leaves the arid abstractions of philosophy behind and throws into relief corporeal existence and the water of life. On the one hand is the frail flesh and blood of Sweeney's hams: like the hippopotamus, his physical being must imply humiliation and suffering and sin. On the other hand is the purgatorial water to which the sinner must subject himself if he wishes to be washed with the Blood of the Lamb. Though Sweeney does not undergo a sea-change like Phlebas the Phoenician, he at least seems closer to redemption than the theologians who suppress the facticity of their fallenness through subtle speculation. And though Eliot had not yet fully turned from the turning world, he experienced a deepened hunger for seriousness.

Perhaps nowhere in the pre-1920 poetry is this seriousness as visible as in "Gerontion." Its tone, form and content have led many commentators to see it as the germ from which *The Waste Land* grew, and for good reason. In order to satisfy the minimum page requirement of a book volume, Eliot thought of including "Gerontion" as a prelude to *The Waste Land*. Pound, however, strongly advised against such a move (*L1* 629, 630), and "Gerontion" has since been grouped with the quatrain poems in all collected editions of Eliot's poetry. In part, this editorial decision is guided by chronology. But the position of "Gerontion" as the first poem in *Poems* (1920), might also suggest that Eliot came to see it as the tone-determining work in that collection, a work which would both gesture at the gravity of the quatrain poems and show continuity leading towards *The Waste Land*.

It is true that Eliot was less than pleased about reprinting some of his earlier work. After the appearance of *Poems 1909–1925*, Eliot wrote to Leonard Woolf claiming that "the book gives me no pleasure – and I think *The Waste Land* appears at a disadvantage in the midst of all this other stuff, some of which was not even good enough to reprint. But I regard the book merely as an ejection, a means of getting all that out of the way" (*L2* 802). Of course, one cannot know which "stuff" Eliot had in mind. But his polemical redirection to "Gerontion" via "Lancelot Andrewes" intimates that he still thought the poetry of that period worthy of closer inspection.

The 1926 *TLS* essay on the seventeenth-century bishop is not only a revaluation of a neglected prose stylist or an affirmation of new allegiances; it is also a document of disclosure in which Eliot casts light on past sources and sources in the making. Pointing readers towards the *Seventeen Sermons on the Nativity*, he proceeds to provide samples of Andrewes's memorable prose (though claiming earlier that Andrewes is not readily quotable):

> Phrases such as "Christ is no wild-cat. What talk ye of twelve days?" or "the word within a word, unable to speak a word", do not desert us; nor do the sentences in which, before extracting all the spiritual meaning of a text, Andrewes forces a concrete presence upon us.
>
> Of the wise men from the East:
>
> "It was no summer progress. A cold coming they had of it at this time of the year, just the worst time of the year to take a journey, and specially a long journey in. The ways deep, the weather sharp, the days short, the sun farthest off, *in solstitio brumali*, 'the very dead of winter'." (*CP2* 823–4)

"Journey of the Magi" had not been written by the time of this essay, so this assembly of phrases is not completely disingenuous. But Eliot's assimilation of Andrewes is as much in his mind as are Andrewes's proper words. The snippet from the nativity sermon of 1618 referred to above actually reads "the word *without* a word"; "within" is a substitution or misremembering that occurs in "Gerontion."[7] Though the slip is probably unintentional, Eliot achieves here a return of the expressed, a mirroring of his allusions in the 1919 poem. The sermons of 1618 and 1622 are singled out for special attention and compressed in a fashion comparable to their appearance in "Gerontion."

> Signs are taken for wonders. "We would see a sign!"
> The word within a word, unable to speak a word,
> Swaddled with darkness. In the juvescence of the year
> Came Christ the tiger (*CPP* 37)

A brief summary of the two sermons serves to adumbrate their recurring significance for Eliot. The earlier sermon takes Luke ii.12–14 as its focus and examines the nature of the *sign* of Christ's birth in excruciating detail. Andrewes sees the circumstances surrounding the incarnation not only as the accidents of humility but also as its index. The distinction between "*signum humile, signum humilis*"[8] (humble sign, sign of humility) posits both the nature of the event and the nature which the event seeks to inculcate. It indicates an external, objective reality, while inviting a subjective discovery of that reality. The sign, Andrewes stresses repeatedly, is not merely "the child swaddled, and laid in a cratch"; it is *finding* the child in his modest surroundings: "For what is *natus est* without *invenientis*? Such a one there 'is born.' What shall we be the better, if we 'find' Him not? As good not born, as not known – to us all one ... *Christus inventus* is more than *Christus natus*. Set down *invenientis* then first."[9] So the sign is humble, but the sign also signals humility. There is the humility of Christ, of God become human. There is also the humility of the shepherds: humans approaching the humble sign with the requisite humility to recognize it as the glorious sign. With this emphasis on participation, Andrewes distinguishes between signs and miracles. The Pharisees' plea ("Master, we would fain see a sign," Matt. xii.38) is unequivocal, or at least unilateral, proof of Christ's divinity – hard evidence that requires no analysis or involvement from the witness. What they seek is a "wonder," not a "sign."

Through its exegesis of Matt ii.1–2 the later sermon likewise establishes tension between commitment and complacency. On the one hand it extols the obedience of the magi between whose "seeing" and "doing" there is no wavering; on the other hand it bemoans inaction and ease. Since Christ "is no wild-cat" whose infancy will be lost in the space of a short delay, there is no need for urgency.

> Come such a journey at such a time? No; but fairly have put it off to the spring of the year, till the days longer, and the ways fairer, and the weather

> warmer, till better travelling to Christ. Our Epiphany would sure have fallen in Easter-week at the soonest ... We love to make no very great haste ... Why should we? Christ is no wild-cat. What talk ye of twelve days? And if it be forty days hence, ye shall be sure to find His Mother and Him; she cannot be churched till then. What needs such haste?[10]

Far from implying a contrary view, Eliot's pointed reversal – "Christ the tiger" – undoes the irony to convey the discomfiting, dangerous implications of the advent and the crucifixion. The neologism ("juvescence") allows for a temporal ambiguity that envelopes both the new calendar year and also the vernal renewal of the natural world. In this simultaneity there is no lapse of time between Epiphany and Easter, which explains why the speaker's apprehension about Christ is not achieved through dark divinations ("concitation / Of the backward devils" [*CPP* 38]). Rather, like the magi in Eliot's later poem, he intuits the "Hard and bitter agony" (*CPP* 104) in a birth that necessitates the death of the old self.

For some, however, the threat is empty. Christ may "spring" and "devour"; but in his turn he is also "eaten ... divided ... drunk" (*CPP* 37) by Mr. Silvero and others. It is significant that these figures take the strange Eucharist belatedly. Good Friday tends to fall in April, sometimes in March, but never in May. So, just like the worshippers berated by Andrewes, the cosmopolitan company of "Gerontion" move at their leisure. Though the "whispers" might suggest reverence for the rite of communion, one realises that the hushed atmosphere attends other priorities. Mr. Silvero's hands caress Limoges porcelain; Hakagawa bows enraptured in the art gallery; Madame de Tornquist engages the esoteric.

It takes no great leap of the imagination to recognise in this poem some of the concerns that would manifest in *The Waste Land*: the reluctance to cede numbing comforts, the seduction of vain distractions, the search for something beyond the self. But if "Gerontion" prefigures *The Waste Land*, "Gerontion" is itself prefigured in the quatrain poems. It shares with "A Cooking Egg" and "Whispers of Immortality" the themes of regret and inaction; it channels the tension between spiritual earnestness and spiritual laxity that is dramatized in the two church poems; and its speaker, like Sweeney, is caught between the vision of a terrible truth and the act of awful surrender. This last link is perhaps the most significant of all. It is worth remembering that in the same year Eliot drew attention to the prose of Lancelot Andrewes (and inadvertently his own use of Andrewes's prose in "Gerontion"), he published the first installment of what would become *Sweeney Agonistes*, in which its anti-hero acknowledges the possibility of spiritual rebirth but declines submitting to it ("I've been born, and once is enough" [*CPP* 122]). If, as Eliot claims in the letter to Woolf, he wanted to "liquidate" some of the earlier work and dissociate it from "some new incomplete things," this rupture could hardly implicate *Poems* (1920). Sweeney surfaced for the fifth time in eight years, the ghost of "Gerontion" haunted "Lancelot Andrewes," and the Lancelot Andrewes of "Gerontion" would soon echo in "Journey of the Magi." The investment of emotional and spiritual anguish was simply too great, and the subsequent yield too irrepressible.

The poems in this volume mark an extremely important development in Eliot's career. They do not only represent the concentrated poetic outflow of his most influential theories about art, nor do they merely prepare the ground for *The Waste Land*'s allusive technique. To see them as preliminary is to see them only as a stirring of the backward devils, as faint ghosts of greater achievements to come. But in and of themselves, these poems stand as a landmark in the oeuvre. As clearly as any of his other works, they witness Eliot's capacity to compel disparate materials and experiences into a cohesive poetic and moral vision. And they assert, as E. E. Cummings put it, that "nobody in general and some one in particular is incorrigibly and actually alive" (Brooker 43).

NOTES

1 In a letter of 1916 Eliot told his brother that "I often feel that 'J.A.P' ['The Love Song of J. Alfred Prufrock'] is a swan song ..." (*L1* 165).

2 T. S. Eliot, "The Art of Poetry, I," *Paris Review* 21, 1959. Reprinted in George Plimpton (ed.), *Writers at Work: The Paris Review Interviews, Second Series* (Harmondsworth: Penguin, 1977), p. 95.

3 The title of the volume was erroneously printed as *Ara Vus Prec*. In a letter to Donald Gallup, Eliot explains that it was an error he introduced and which was not picked up by the printers, since neither party knew Provençal. See Gallup, *T. S. Eliot: A Bibliography* (London: Faber and Faber, 1969), pp. 4–5.

4 *The Divine Comedy*, translated by Allen Mandelbaum (New York: Everyman's Library, 1995), p. 340. In one form or another, Arnaut Daniel's words occur in the epigraph to the original draft of "The Love Song of J. Alfred Prufrock," in *The Waste Land*, and in part IV of *Ash-Wednesday*.

5 Marion Strobel, "Perilous Leaping," *Poetry* 16.3 (1920): 159.

6 Ford Madox Ford, *Henry James: A Critical Study* (New York: Octagon, 1972), pp. 140–1.

7 The original phrasing is restored in *Ash-Wednesday*, V.

8 Lancelot Andrewes, *Seventeen Sermons on the Nativity* (London: Griffith Farran Okeden & Welsh, 1887), p. 200.

9 Andrewes, p. 193.

10 Andrewes, pp. 253–4.

5

LAWRENCE RAINEY

With Automatic Hand: *The Waste Land*

Consider the first verse-paragraph that opens *The Waste Land*:

April is the cruellest month, breeding
Lilacs out of the dead land, mixing
Memory and desire, stirring
Dull roots with spring rain.
Winter kept us warm, covering
Earth in forgetful snow, feeding
A little life with dried tubers.
Summer surprised us, coming over the Starnbergersee
With a shower of rain; we stopped in the colonnade,
And went on in sunlight, into the Hofgarten,
And drank coffee, and talked for an hour.
Bin gar keine Russin, stamm' aus Litauen, echt deutsch.
And when we were children, staying at the archduke's,
My cousin's, he took me out on a sled,
And I was frightened. He said, Marie,
Marie, hold on tight. And down we went.
In the mountains, there you feel free.
I read, much of the night, and go south in the winter. (*CPP* 61)

These lines pose an intriguing question: How many people are speaking here? To answer it, we can only scrutinize the text in order to identify the lexical and syntactic patterns that distinguish each individual's speech.

If we begin to do that, we swiftly observe that lines 1–7 are very distinctive. We notice the participial constructions that end many lines: "breeding" (1), "mixing" (2), "stirring" (3), "covering"(5), and "feeding" (6), a pattern that is even repeated once more and reappears at line 8, in "coming over the Starnbergersee." We also can't miss the use of adjective-noun pairings that occur in these lines, usage so insistent that there are seven of them: "cruellest month" (1), "dead land" (2), "dull roots" and "spring rain" (4), "forgetful snow" (6), and "little life" and "dried tubers" (7). Taken together, then, participial constructions and adjective-noun pairing seem to typify a coherent voice, and we can identify that voice for the moment as Zone 1. Further, we can also identify that voice as masculine, oddly, because we have no idea whatsoever who is speaking the poem's first four lines; yet they sound threatening ("cruellest month" and "dead land"), and minatory speech not assigned to any individual or source is conventionally spoken by a masculine voice.

It is fairly easy, as well, to identify a second, distinctive voice in this opening passage. It looms into view with the word "Starnbergersee," in line 8, which is amplified by the word "Hofgarten," in line 10. It is then given further resonance by the entirety of line 12, "Bin gar keine Russin, stamm' aus Litauen, echt deutsch," and finds a final echo in line 13 with the word "archduke." All these words are either German terms ("Starnbergersee" and "Hofgarten," the entirety of line 12) or are associated with a German-speaking area – the former Austro-Hungarian Empire ("archduke," at line 13). We can designate this area Zone 2. But while it is easy enough to see where it begins, at line 8, it is harder to define where it ends: Does it stop at line 13, with the word "archduke," or does it continue all the way to the end of line 18, which would appear to be suggested by the syntax that is carried over from line 14 on?

One way to answer that question might be to look at another distinctive feature, one making its first appearance in line 10 – the use of the conjunction "and" to bind together two independent clauses. That usage becomes very frequent in the lines that follow: it appears twice in line 11 and yet again in lines 13, 15, 16, and 18. In short, it appears seven times in a span of only nine lines, almost once a line. Should we regard this zone as an independent area – call it Zone 3 – that is nestled within much of Zone 2?

Complicating our deliberations is yet another grammatical clue that springs into view already in line 5, the term "us," a pronoun in the first-person plural, which appears for the first time in line 5, "Winter kept us warm." It is echoed and elaborated in lines 8 ("Summer surprised us..."), 9 ("we stopped in the colonnade"), and 13 ("and when we were children") before it gives way to another pronoun, "me," in the first-person singular, which appears for the first time in line 14, and is then echoed by "I" at lines 15 ("And I was frightened") and 18 ("I read, much of the night..."). Yet noting these seven instances of personal pronouns only complicates our quest to identify the number of speakers to be discerned in this passage, for it seems to imply an entire fourth zone, running from line 5 to line 18, in which first-person pronouns, whether singular (I, me) or plural (we, us), predominate and overlap with Zones 1, 2, and 3.

Yet identifying the personal pronouns may also alert us to a potential danger, a source of menace for attempts to endow the poem with the kinds of coherence we expect from more ordinary texts. Consider only the most modest of terms, the personal pronoun "us." It most certainly appears in line 5, in the phrase "Winter kept us warm," and it most certainly reappears in line 8, in the line "Summer surprised us, coming over the Starnbergersee." But are these really the same? Most certainly the same term, "us," is being repeated, and we have a clear case here of a likeness. But the referent in the first usage, in line 5, or "Winter kept us warm," seems to be far more general, more oracular: "us" in this case means something like "everybody" or even "all of us who are dead." But "us" in the second instance, "Summer surprised us, coming over the Starnbergersee," means something rather more limited, something more like "only us two," the two who go on to drink coffee together. In other words, what had first seemed to be a likeness gives way to an illusion, a mere semblance of likeness. Moreover, this dissolution of likeness into illusion is repeated elsewhere in the first verse-paragraph. Consider the term "winter." It plainly occurs in lines 5 and 6: "Winter kept us warm, covering/ Earth in forgetful snow." But is this really identical with the one that occurs in line eighteen, "I read, much of the night, and go south in the winter"? The first is solemn, oracular, gnomic; the second, insipid. But the effect of their conjunction is devastating, for here repetition is functioning not to reinforce semantic likeness, but to eviscerate it. Likeness, again, is giving way to illusion. And a similar movement occurs over the paragraph's entire trajectory, which begins by intoning a pattern of oracular solemnity but ends by reporting empty patter – those final spasms of vacant thought. Instead of building toward a conclusion, we find ourselves confronting an anti-climax. What began with a solemn pattern has ended with distracted patter.

The problem, then, is not in recognizing the syntactic and lexical repetitions that unfold in the opening verse-paragraph. If anything, they are not just discernible but too readily discernible. Let us, for the sake of argument, add them up: six participial constructions, seven adjective-noun pairings, four German-speaking terms or sentences, seven uses of the conjunction "and," and eight uses of first-person pronouns. The result is slightly staggering. If we take these syntactic and lexical features as markers of identity, then we have thirty-two such markers in this passage, all in the space of only eighteen lines. The problem here is not, as so often said, that the poem is "too disconnected" or "fragmentary." It is just the opposite: the poem suffers from an excess of connectedness, it is hyperbolically over-connected. The result is self-cancelling.

Yet despite this surfeit of syntactic and lexical markers of identity, it is by no means clear just how many identifiable speakers the passage contains. Three? Four? More disconcertingly, the gender of these voices has also changed. We began, after all, with a masculine baritone evoking minatory solemnity; but the last six lines (13–18) are quite plainly spoken by a woman, someone named Marie. Where, then, did this change of gender occur? Was it smuggled in during the course of line 12, the line in German, where the speaker says "Bin gar keine Russin," using the feminine gender, rather than the masculine ("Bin gar kein Russe")? Is this a sort of verbal sleight of hand that adopts German to invoke a woman in ways we cannot do in English? (Because English makes no use of grammatical gender, we have only the term "Russian," whereas German distinguishes between "Russe" [Russian man] and "Russin" [Russian woman]). Or did the change take place earlier, concealed within the "us" that occurs in line eight: "Summer surprised us, coming over the Starnbergersee."

Three last points about this opening verse-paragraph deserve mention. First, we would certainly agree that a semantic vein that concerns the seasons flickers across this passage: "April" (1), "spring" (4), "Winter" (5), "Summer" (8), and once again "winter" (18). Yet one may legitimately wonder where is "autumn" in this catalogue of the seasons, if catalogue it be; or why the catalogue follows no discernible order. Second, line 12, the one spoken in German, seems to utter an illogical and contradictory claim: "I am not a Russian woman, I come from Lithuania, a real German." But how can one be a "real German" if one comes "from Lithuania"? Yes, one can provide an answer – of sorts. Colonies of German-speaking nationals were found in all the principal cities of the Baltic states (Lithuania, Latvia, and Estonia) during the 1850–1940 period, but they were numerically quite small. Conceivably, someone from one of these colonies might well say, "I come from Lithuania, a real German," but it would require more explanation to make sense to anybody other than a Baltic German. Of course, we have no idea who speaks this line, nor to whom it is addressed. Or is it merely a line that is overheard while "we" are drinking coffee in the Hofgarten? Third, the very specific site of the Hofgarten, or "Court garden," in Munich, jars against the placeless anti-locale that appears through lines 1–7. Some editions of *The Waste Land* even provide aerial photographs of the entire Hofgarten, together with period photos of the arcade, or "colonnade" (9) that abuts it on one side, and even the Arcade Café just beyond it; but such period photographs cannot lessen the disorientation that results from having the gnomic opening lines bristle against the stark specificity of the Hofgarten.[1]

There are, we have seen, thirty-two instances of syntactic and lexical repetition within the opening verse-paragraph, which occupies only eighteen lines. Their sheer number and obviousness seem to urge their unimportance: it is not here that the poem is doing the real work of offering an account of the world. And that impression is reinforced by another: the assertions of connectedness may be remarkably insistent, but the connectedness itself isn't really vivid. It remains inert and extraneous, like so much scaffolding erected around a building that remains obstinately invisible. Even today, nearly a century after the poem was first published, critics disagree about that building's shape or how many rooms it contains, divided over how many speakers are voicing these lines. As zones of coherence loom into sight and recede, they insinuate that the poem's real reckoning with the world must be happening elsewhere: perhaps in the intersection and overlap of those evanescent zones; or in the interchange of oracular solemnity and cosmopolitan banality, in the overall play of opacity and transparency. Or perhaps somewhere else altogether.

Some critics have not, of course, been slow to respond to that insinuation. After all, one "somewhere else" is quite explicitly indicated in the first note that immediately follows the poem proper: "Not only the title, but the plan and a good deal of the incidental symbolism of the poem were suggested by Miss Jessie L. Weston's book on the Grail legend: *From Ritual to Romance*" (*CPP* 76). But this is just one more dead end, and surely the deadest of them all. *The Waste Land* has as much to do with Grail legends and vegetation rituals as *Ulysses* has to do with the notorious schema that Joyce concocted as he neared the end of his masterpiece, the one he first gave to Valéry Larbaud in late 1921 and that he then allowed Stuart Gilbert to publish in 1931. (Vladimir Nabokov famously thought the entire schema was devised "tongue-in-cheek").[2] Both writers, as publication approached, worried that their works might seem too disordered, too lacking in structure for contemporary readers, and each responded by hinting that his work was governed by an arcane logic that could be readily reconstructed by anyone willing to look for it. But the core of *The Waste Land* is not to be found in the speculations of Arthurian scholar Jessie Weston, or in the pseudo-arcana of vegetation rituals.

Other critics have also been fond of turning the poem into a narrative in which there is a "protagonist" or even (in those accounts most influenced by the medieval Grail legends) a "quester" who, in some mysterious way, moves through the poem's scenes. In this account, the problems that we had with the first verse-paragraph are tidily erased: the numerous and contradictory voices are flattened out into a single voice, the thoughts of an isolated individual. In my view, this erases too much; it replaces the untidiness of poetic texture with the neatness of narrative simplicity. It does, however, respond to another dimension of the poem that deserves further attention: the relationship between the cards that are dealt out by Madame Sosostris at the end of Part I and the title of Part IV. Famously, at line 55, Madame Sosostris tells her listener (who is a figure for the reader): "Fear death by water"

(*CPP* 62). And just as plainly, the title of Part IV is "Death by Water." We have, in other words, a use of repetition, a likeness. As one critic has observed of Madame Sosotris, "She must provide the dots that the rest of the poem must connect into a semblance of plot."[3] This is perceptive, provided that we understand that its key word is really "semblance," to be taken in the strong sense as "An appearance or outward seeming *of* (something which is not actually there or of which the reality is different from its appearance)" (OED 4.a). *The Waste Land* has neither a plot nor narrative coherence, but the semblance of a plot, the likeness of a plot that swiftly dissolves into illusion. For it requires only a moment to recall that Madame Sosostris is a charlatan, or that the drowned Phoenician sailor isn't even a card in the traditional Tarot pack. And when she discloses the drowned Phoenician card ("Here, said she, / Is your card, the drowned Phoenician Sailor"), the text swiftly divorces itself from straightforward narrative, intruding cruelly: "(Those are pearls that were his eyes. Look!) [*CPP* 62]." Phlebas the Phoenician, whose reappearance (read: repetition) at first promises narrative connectedness between the first and later parts of the poems, turns out to be another figure in the poem's grim histrionics of non-relationship. *The Waste Land* doesn't have a narrative; instead, it has the scent of a narrative hovering in the air, like the perfume of a woman who has just left the room.

If there is a single moment in the poem where we can see that grim histrionics of non-relationship enacted, and a moment as well where the conjunction of narrative and repetition is restaged with agonizing ferocity, it is the encounter between the typist and the young man carbuncular, an encounter that takes place in the middle of the poem's Part III, or in the middle of the five-part work. The typist, after all, is repetition personified; her chief task is to transcribe someone else's words, whether dictated aloud or previously transcribed in longhand; while the young man carbuncular is a paradigm of the stranger or intruder whose arrival sparks narrated activity, sets in motion the mechanics of event and plot. Their story is a narrative of repetition, in the sense that their loveless coupling is inferred to be only one in a protracted series of such encounters, while it is also repetition of narrative insofar as it elaborates *topoi* associated with representations of the typist in realist and naturalist fiction of the 1910–22 period. Moreover, a juxtaposition of narrative and repetition structures the presentation of their entire encounter: a laconic story, divided into several scenes or tableaux (lines 215–17, 220–7, 231–42 and 247–8), is punctuated by the stark repetition (three times) that demarcates the presence of the observing "I Tiresias" (lines 218–19, 228–30, 243–6).

Tiresias, we recall, is an ancient Greek seer from the city of Thebes. One day, when he saw snakes coupling and struck them with his stick, he was instantly transformed into a woman; seven years later the same thing happened again and he was turned into a man. Since he had experienced the body in both sexes, he was asked by Jove and Juno to settle their dispute over whether men or women had greater pleasure in making love. Tiresias sides with Jove, who urged that women had more pleasure; as a result, Juno blinds him. To compensate him for this misfortune, Jove endows him with the gifts of prophecy and long life.

In taking up a typist as subject matter in a serious poem, Eliot was doing something unprecedented. Before *The Waste Land*, typists had figured only in light verse that was humorous or satirical.[4] To be sure, typists had long been a subject matter for novels: between 1893 and 1923, sixty-five novels had been published in which the principal protagonist, the heroine, had been a typist. But of these, only eight specifically took up the subject taken up here – a typist who engages in what we would now call premarital consensual sex.[5] Their typical age was twenty-two, and it was a ubiquitous convention of these novels that the typists in them were orphans. They came from middle-class families that had precipitously fallen on hard times. In many cases, the novels elaborated on commonplaces of contemporary journalism about typists, which featured numerous stories about the poor food they consumed, the cramped lodgings they inhabited, which often meant that a bed would double as a divan, or even the threadbare lingerie they wore.

Consider food, a subject taken up by "Frances," an otherwise anonymous journalist whose "Five O'Clock Tea Talk" appeared in the popular British newspaper, *T.P.'s Weekly*. (It reached "an estimated half a million readers, chiefly among the culturally aspiring urban working- and lower-middle-classes").[6] Frances cites Oliver Goldsmith, author of *The Citizen of the World* (1762), whose "inquiring citizen" ambles through London's streets, to validate her view that typists eat poorly at lunchtime:

> Over the quality of that mid-day meal there need not be any contradictions. Goldsmith's inquiring citizen might pursue his way from Broad Street to S. Paul's ... yet have naught to report at his journey's end but "coffee or tea and roll," with the sometimes addendum of "sandwich," or "sausage," or "pastry," or "jam." Can the girl-worker thrive and be happy on such fare, and does it content her?

Typists who still lived with their families, she thought, could survive well enough: "But the girl who has to provide food, lodgings and clothing out of a salary which does not always reach a pound a week, and rarely exceeds thirty shillings [1.5 pounds], more often than not has to make her tea-shop lunch her principal meal. She would rather die than confess it."[7]

Larger firms, such as the Prudential Assurance Company, provided a "bar" on site where secretaries and typists could eat. "At any rate, whether they admitted it or not, it was a distinct advantage to the girls that they were able to get even an indifferent lunch in the office. Anyone, that is to say any woman, who has attempted to get lunch at city restaurants of the cheaper kind will realize the truth of this."[8] When some 1,000 women who had been secretaries or typists in 1919 were asked to recall their experiences, they stressed food again and again. They recalled eating at Lyons or ABC teashops and getting "a boiled egg, ginger pudding with treacle and a cup of tea for 1/3d." But since even that cut into one's pay, "the large majority" took sandwiches. Some firms even paid their women for overtime work with food: "Bread, jam and tea for one hour," and "Scrambled eggs, scones and tea for two hours." Summarizing their recollections, one respondent commented: "It was not unknown for a girl to faint at her work from lack of adequate nourishment."[9]

Small lodgings are omnipresent in novels about typists. "I had one small room, at the top of a dreary old house," says the first-person narrator of Tom Gallon's *The Girl Behind the Keys*.[10] The single room also presented a practical problem for receiving visitors – the bed. When Fred Norman, successful lawyer, goes to visit the home of typist Dorothea Hallowell in *The Grain of Dust*, he seizes on this feature: "It was a small neat room, arranged comfortably and with some taste ... The bed was folded away into a couch – for space and for respectability."[11]

Shabby or threadbare undergarments also recur. The narrator of *The Questing Beast* tells us: "Rachel Cohen, rising twenty, standing barefooted in her meagre cotton nightgown (they can only be got rather meagre for two and eleven three), looked like a very tired child of thirteen years."[12] A more elaborate variant is found in *The Grain of Dust*:

> He went up with her [to her room] and helped her to pack – not a long process, as she had few belongings. He noted that the stockings and underclothes she took from the bureau drawer were in anything but good condition, that the half dozen dresses she took from the closet and folded on the couch were about done for. Presently she said, cheerfully and with no trace of shame: "You see, I'm pretty nearly in rags."[13]

These, then, were *topoi* of contemporary journalism and realistic fiction that treated typists: poor food, a single room with cramped conditions, a bed that doubles as a couch or divan, and threadbare garments or undergarments. Eliot revisits them all very succinctly:

> At the violet hour, the evening hour that strives
> Homeward, and brings the sailor home from sea,

> The typist home at teatime, clears her breakfast, lights
> Her stove, and lays out food in tins.
> Out of the window perilously spread
> Her drying combinations touched by the sun's last rays,
> On the divan are piled (at night her bed)
> Stockings, slippers, camisoles, and stays. (*CPP* 68)

But the passage does more than import realistic details into the poem. For beginning at line 224 ("Out of the window perilously spread"), a quatrain slowly emerges into view, and by its end it lies spread before us as neatly as "Stockings, slippers, camisoles, and stays." Well, perhaps not quite so neatly: for the metre of this passage is marked by deep uncertainty – it shifts uneasily between four and five stresses per line, and ranges between nine and thirteen syllables in length – uncertainty that turns it into a sign of poetry's flimsiness, its fragility in the face of the modern world, or that tacitly asks a question. Can poetry's traditional resources, rhythm and rhyme, suffice for what the modern world can throw in its path: a typist, her room, a scene of urban squalor?

Similar uncertainty is also apparent in the point of view adopted from the moment the typist appears on the scene, at line 215: "At the violet hour, when the eyes and back / Turn upward from the desk, when the human engine waits / Like a taxi throbbing waiting" (*CPP* 68). For what perspective can enable us to see, at the same time, "the eyes and back" of that "human engine," unless a very contorted or abnormal one? And these difficulties in metre and perspective find their counterpart in syntactical complications that require the reader to readjust and reconsider. Consider the passage beginning at line 218:

> I Tiresias, though blind, throbbing between two lives,
> Old man with wrinkled female breasts, can see
> At the violet hour, the evening hour that strives
> Homeward, and brings the sailor home from sea,
> The typist home at teatime, clears her breakfast, lights
> Her stove, and lays out food in tins. (*CPP* 68)

At line 222, the phrase "The typist home at teatime" is made to perform three different grammatical functions. On the one hand, it may be the grammatical object of the verb "see" (line 219); on the other, it may be the grammatical object of the verb "brings" (line 221), which in turn is governed by the noun phrase "the evening hour" (back in line 220): "... the evening hour that strives / Homeward, and brings the sailor home from sea, / The typist home at teatime." At the same time, however, "the typist" is simultaneously not just a grammatical object but also a grammatical subject that governs the verb "clears" in line 222: "The typist home at teatime, clears her breakfast, lights / Her stove, and lays out food in tins." Nor is this case of syntactic uncertainty an isolated aberration. At line 237, the verb "endeavours" (in "Endeavours to engage her in caresses") is lacking any grammatical subject to govern it, and the same thing happens again at line 247 with the verb "bestows" (in the line "Bestows one final patronising kiss"), which again lacks a grammatical subject to govern it.

This accumulation of syntactic, metrical, and perspectival uncertainty makes what happens next still more startling. For when the poem returns to the scene, the principal actress disappears (beginning at line 231):

> He, the young man carbuncular, arrives,
> A small house agent's clerk, with one bold stare,
> One of the low on whom assurance sits
> As a silk hat on a Bradford millionaire.
> The time is now propitious, as he guesses,
> The meal is ended, she is bored and tired,
> Endeavours to engage her in caresses
> Which still are unreproved, if undesired.
> Flushed and decided, he assaults at once;
> Exploring hands encounter no defence;
> His vanity requires no response,
> And makes a welcome of indifference. (*CPP* 68)
> ...
> Bestows one final patronising kiss,
> And gropes his way, finding the stairs unlit... (*CPP* 69)

In this tableau, the typist vanishes entirely as an autonomous agent. She exists only through the thoughts of the young man carbuncular. She is reduced to a present-tense variant of free indirect discourse, as at line 235–6 ("as he guesses ... she is bored and tired") or into the pronominal object of his gropings, as at line 237 ("Endeavours to engage her..."). Further on, she dissolves into a series of negations at once ghastly and ghostly: "unreproved" (238), "undesired" (238), "no defence" (240), "no response" (241), "indifference" (242). Their horror is amplified because four of them occur in the emphatic position of ending a line of verse, reverberating with each other (thus, "no defence" in line 240 rhymes with "indifference" in line 242) or with other rhyme words ("undesired" with "tired" at 238 and 236; or "no response" with "at once," in lines 241 and 239). Words such as "unreproved," "undesired," or "indifference" are said to have privative prefixes, because the prefix "deprives a word of its original force." But the same term appears in the cognate word "privation," and that is certainly what we have here: inexplicable, unbearable privation.

Not only the typist disappears in the course of this central tableau. The young man carbuncular, as soon as he "assaults at once" (line 239), is displaced with synecdoche ("Exploring hands encounter..." in line 240) and then vanishes under personification ("His vanity requires no response" [241]). Even his "final patronising kiss" has nobody and nothing that serves as a grammatical subject to bestow it; we must infer that "bestows" is governed – but is anything being "governed" here? – by the subject of the preceding clause, "His vanity." Vanity is a cognate of the term "vanishing" that we have used to describe the typist's disappearance. Both stem from the Latin *vanus*, meaning "empty," or to cite a fuller definition: "1, *that contains nothing, empty, void, vacant*; 2, *empty* as to purport or result, *idle, null, groundless, unmeaning, fruitless, vain*."[14] But is that all there is at the end? Void and vacant, groundless and unmeaning, fruitless and vain. What should we make of this "sense of universal and hysterical negation"?[15]

That final kiss is horrific, rehearsing a convention of popular fiction, in which a kiss is often the climax of a scene, a chapter, even a whole work. Eliot, instead, turns it into a wilfully gratuitous anti-climax. Then he turns to the coda, the aftermath.

Eliot was not the first author to portray a young woman in the aftermath of a sexual liaison. In the early twentieth century, a growing number of novelists took up secretaries who engage in what we would now call premarital consensual sex, using the occasion to revisit the conventions of the "fallen woman novel" that had been codified in the Victorian period.[16] One such book is *The Questing Beast*, by Ivy Low, a left-wing feminist, first published in 1914. After the heroine, Rachel Cohen, has her first sexual experience, she ponders:

> She wondered if she had not plumbed the limits of disgust. She could not believe that life would ever hold zest for her again. A very plain person, who had never seen his face in a glass and had had to form an opinion of his features from his natural vanity and the features of other people, might have felt, on being suddenly presented with a mirror, something of the shock and horror that Rachel now felt. Exactly the question that this person would most naturally ask was constantly in Rachel's mind: "Am I like *that*?" ... Rachel, hitherto triumphant over other people's weakness, now thought, in her bitter humiliation, that none was so fallen that she was not sister to. Again and again the memory of her pride in being "not that sort of girl" stung her to fresh writhings.[17]

Consider an analogous scene from a novel serialized in numerous newspapers throughout the United States, also belonging to the Hearst news syndicate which boasted some fifty million readers; it was called *Chickie* and appeared just a year after *The Waste Land*'s publication:

> In her mind was a black spot of terror. It grew large – a stark live thing, shaking her pulse with dread. It was the memory of the night.
>
> She shrank from it. It pressed down and seized her heart. It was a dark, heavy beast crouching on her chest. She tried to beat it off. It came nearer and blew warm, sickening breaths in her nostrils. Fighting, she had to draw them down. Again and again…
>
> She hid from it – oh, she would get away – push off this thing of horror weighing so heavily on her breast. Be free – be light again.
>
> She hated herself.[18]

Both books were written by feminists who were tacitly urging a more tolerant approach to premarital consensual sex. But the guilty histrionics in which they indulge are double-edged; they make it seem as if their heroines have participated in something truly sordid, something that genuinely merits condemnation if only because the heroine herself has issued such a judgment: disgust, shock, horror, bitter humiliation, terror, dread, memories that sting, seize the heart, or weigh heavily. Here is the lexicon of the contemporary, popular novel when treating a post-coital scene.

The text of *The Waste Land* is far more restrained:

> She turns and looks a moment in the glass,
> Hardly aware of her departed lover;
> Her brain allows one half-formed thought to pass:
> "Well now that's done: and I'm glad it's over."
> When lovely woman stoops to folly and
> Paces about her room again, alone,
> She smoothes her hair with automatic hand,
> And puts a record on the gramophone. (*CPP* 69)

More than any other passage in the poem, this one attracted the ire of conservative critics, who damned it for desecrating a song in Oliver Goldsmith's *The Vicar of Wakefield*:

> When lovely woman stoops to folly
> And finds too late that men betray,
> What charm can sooth her melancholy,
> What art can wash her guilt away?[19]

Eliot's aesthetic, by contrast, is cold, aloof, austere, evincing icy neutrality. He shuns both the easy moralizing of Goldsmith and the guilty histrionics of the contemporary novel, replacing them with the mute, yet eloquent, gesture of playing a popular song to fill the silent void: *empty* as to purport or result, *idle*, *null*, *groundless*, *unmeaning*, *fruitless*, *vain*.

Two points in the concluding lines to this final quatrain are arresting. One is that "automatic hand." For in Western philosophy from Aristotle to Heidegger, the hand has been invoked to signal the critical difference between the human and the animal, at once the instrument of reason and its material counterpart.[20] Yet the typist's gesture blurs precisely that boundary between wilful human action and the helplessness of automatism. At the same time it also invokes what might be called a lyrical temporality and effect: for it interrupts, shocks, and freezes the scene. Gesture, here, is being summoned to substitute for speech, assigned a total expressivity. Tellingly, Eliot himself urges that the hand performs an analogous function in the Jacobean play, *The Duchess of Malfi* (1623). Reviewing a recent performance of it in 1920, he singles out the notorious scene in which the Duchess, trapped in a darkened chamber, is deceived into kissing a severed hand, one she is told is that of her lover Antonio. It was "extraordinarily fine," Eliot says, for "the actors were held in check by violent situations which nothing in their previous repertory could teach." What Eliot calls "the scene of the severed hand" has an uncanny effect: it prevents the actors from acting. The dead hand, contracted in the clutch of rigor mortis, dispenses with all mediation, which can only "distort," and is transformed into an eerie paradox: it is a trope of not troping and, at the same time, is pure, unmediated communication. "Here," writes Eliot, "the play itself got through, magnificently, unique" (*CP2* 171).

Another resides in the name of the machine that the typist cranks up: rhyming with "alone," it is the gramophone. It comes with an etymology that Eliot knew well: the first part of the word, "gramo-", derives from the ancient Greek word *gramma*, meaning a "letter" or an "inscription"; while the second part, "-phone," is the ancient Greek for "voice." Inscribing voices is of course just what *The Waste Land* has been doing, both in its lavish use of quotation and its brisk modulations through numerous voices. It has become a machine for replaying them, a species of dictaphone. And that, after all, is one of the fundamental activities performed by a typist in this period, taking dictation, inscribing the voice of someone else onto paper. Her final action is a microcosm of the poem – and is all the more haunting for just that reason.

In the long scene that occupies the middle of the poem, competing rhetorics reach an impasse. The trope of repetition, uttered insistently by Tiresias, is cancelled out by the shards of narrative that culminate only in still more repetition – an "automatic hand," a "record on the gramophone." The two rhetorical modes restage a grim histrionics of non-relationship, itself a recapitulation of the grisly puppet show that is the encounter between the typist and the young man carbuncular.

Ironically, the final lines that conclude the entire poem might easily be titled: "He smoothes his hair with automatic hand / and puts a record on the gramophone." The poem concludes with a final, antic swirl of quotations:

> London Bridge is falling down falling down falling down
>
> *Poi s'ascose nel foco che gli affina*
> *Quando fiam uti chelidon* – O swallow swallow
> *Le Prince d'Aquitaine à la tour abolie*
> These fragments I have shored against my ruins
> Why then Ile fit you. Hieronymo's mad againe.
> Datta. Dayadhvam. Damyata.
>
> Shantih shantih shantih (*CPP* 74–75)

It begins with the refrain of a common nursery rhyme, though we cannot be certain which version is being cited. Or does that make no difference? Is the nursery rhyme simply meant to signal a childish lack of consequence? Or are we to supply the line that follows the ones cited here, "my fair lady," construing these words as a last pointer to the many female figures in the poem, including the typist? It is followed by a line from Dante's *Purgatorio*: "Then he vanished into the fire that refines them" (XXVI: 148). "He," in this passage, refers to Arnaut Daniel (fl. 1180–1200), a Provençal poet known through only sixteen extant lyrics; "them," instead, refers to the other spirits who, together with him, occupy the seventh circle of purgatory, spirits guilty of acting lustfully. Are we to view his disappearance "into the fire" ("nel foco") as a signal that the fitful "I" who has intermittently appeared in *The Waste Land* is also about to disappear? After all, the line from Dante brings Canto XXVI of the *Purgatorio* to a close; does its presence here signal that *The Waste Land*, similarly, is drawing to a close? Or are we to read it thematically, as indicating that the tragicomedy of human lust can, with grace, be refined or purified? Readers who share Eliot's post-1927 religious views will stress the purifying effects of grace or the fire; others, instead, will emphasize the hint of forthcoming closure. And a third group will call attention to the verb in the original Italian, *s'ascose*, translated here as "he vanished"; but a more literal translation would be "he hid himself," suggesting the elusive nature of the poem's "I."

These two lines are followed by a third: "*Quando fiam uti chelidon*," Latin for "when shall I become like the swallow?" Here, again, the question arises of whether a reader should supply the words that immediately follow in the Latin original, "*ut tacere desinam*," or "that I cease being silent?" It would seem that one should, if only because Eliot's note to this line urges the reader: "Cf. [i.e., compare] Philomela in Parts II and III" (*CPP* 80). The note is slapdash about detail, insofar as Philomela doesn't appear in Part III at all. But its essential point remains: one should indeed supply the missing words, "that I cease being silent," and correlate them with the tale of Philomela. She, we recall, is raped by Tereus, who then cuts out her tongue to prevent her recounting the event. Later, she is turned into a swallow while fleeing from Tereus, and so ceases "being silent." Moreover, when Tereus asks for his son, Itys, and Philomela, with vengeful joy, hurls the child's dissevered head into his face:

> *... nec tempore maluit ullo*
> *Posse loqui et meritis testari gaudia dictis.*
>
> ... and never more than then did she desire
> To be able to speak and fittingly express her joy.

But is the vengeful joy that Philomela wants to express really the same as the simple wish for the faculty of speech that is voiced by the first-person speaker in the *Pervigilium Veneris* (The Vigil of Venus)?

We begin with a nursery rhyme in English, move to a quotation from Dante in Italian, advance to a line from a late-ancient poem in Latin. We next turn to a line from the poet Gérard de Nerval, in French: "*Le Prince d'Aquitaine à la tour abolie.*" It can be translated as "The Prince of Aquitaine, his tower (or castle) in ruins." It reinforces the sense of menacing decay invoked by "London Bridge is falling down." Alternatively, one can argue that this view gives too much weight to the second half of the line, slighting the first. But attending to the first entails knotty problems. Gérard de Nerval was the pen name adopted by Gérard Labrunie and Nerval, drawing on his real family name in many writings, identified himself as a "poor and obscure descendant of a chatelain in the Perigord region," or in the modern French department of Dordogne, one of the five making up Aquitaine, itself one of the twenty-seven regions in modern France.[21] In short, Nerval drew on his real name to affiliate himself with a family of nobility prominent in the Middle Ages, affiliation further aggrandized here by styling himself "the prince of Aquitaine." But it is very unlikely that Eliot was familiar with the biographical minutiae of Nerval, and so unlikely that he was stressing the first half of the line ("*Le Prince d'Aquitaine*") rather than the second ("*à la tour abolie*"). And the emphasis on the line's second half ("his tower in ruins") is reinforced by the next line, the only one actually penned by Eliot in this closing verse-paragraph: "These fragments I have shored against my ruins."

"Why then Ile fit you," is how the character Hieronymo, in Thomas Kyd's play *The Spanish Tragedy* (1592), responds to the request of Balthazar that he prepare a "show," or play, to entertain the king. The verb "fit" is best understood in the sense of "to supply with what is needed." But Hieronymo's assent is also a ruse; his real plan is to turn the play into a vehicle for revenging the death of his son, Horatio, death that has also provoked the suicide of his wife, Isabella. Yet can we ascribe such motivations to the labile "I" of the poem? Or are we, instead, to read the "you" (in "Why then Ile fit you") as being addressed to the poem's reader? "I will supply you with what is needed, with mere show." Does it comment obliquely on the status of the poem's conclusion, implying that its final swirl of quotations is not an organic outcome stemming from what has preceded, more a semblance of an ending, much like the brittle "death by water" that tenuously links the speech of Madame Sosostris with the title of Part IV? Do we find, approaching the poem's ending, a passage that is less a swelling diapason, more a mechanical murmur of repetitions only obliquely related to one another?

And what should one make of the next grammatical unit: "Hieronymo's mad againe." It constitutes a subtitle that was appended to *The Spanish Tragedy* beginning with the edition of 1615, though not found in any earlier edition (1592, 1594, 1599, and 1602). Are we to emphasize its belated, feeble attempt to summarize the play, urging that the conclusion to *The Waste Land* is equally factitious? Or should we, instead, emphasize the identification drawn between Hieronymo and the poem's "I," so viewing the statement as an act of playful self-deprecation? And if we do, how can we reconcile playful self-deprecation with the desire for vengeful speech that rages in Philomela and Hieronymo? Or has our unstable "I" finally come to sense so intensely the burden of living that he desires revenge for the curse of having to carry on? Has he at last assimilated the power of the Cumean Sybil's wish, voiced in the epigraph "ἀποθανεῖν θέλω" (*CPP* 59), which translated from the ancient Greek means "I want to die"?

The final two lines are quotations (repetitions) from Sanskrit. The first, "Datta. Dayadhvam. Damyata.", repeats words seen earlier in Part V (lines 401, 411, 418), while the second, "Shantih shantih shantih," is a purely formal conclusion to an Upanishad, any of a group of ancient Sanskrit commentaries. Seven of the poem's eight final lines are quotations, or repetitions of somebody else's words. Repetition is perhaps the simplest form of language. In everyday speech, we repeat something when there has been a communicative failure: the other person hasn't heard us, or a sudden noise has drowned out our words. Repetition enables us to reiterate the point. But in literary usage, repetition functions differently, for it entails a compelling paradox. To be identified as instances of repetition, words or phrases must be discernibly the same; yet at the same time, the second appearance of a word or phrase differs from the first, insofar as it is no longer performing the same communicative function it at first did. Repetition must be doing something more, something different, however difficult it proves to say precisely what that "more" consists of. Or is it the case that literary repetition is only a test case for the minimum conditions necessary to restaging the production of the aesthetic? And is that what *The Waste Land* does in its conclusion?

> He smoothes his hair with automatic hand
> And puts a record on the gramophone.

NOTES

1 For these photos, see Lawrence Rainey (ed.), *The Annotated Waste Land with Eliot's Contemporary Prose* (New Haven: Yale University Press, 2005), figs. 1–3, following p. 74.

2 "One bore, a man called Stuart Gilbert, misled by a tongue-in-cheek list compiled by Joyce himself, found in every chapter the domination of one particular organ – the ear, the eye, the stomach, etc. – but we shall ignore that dull nonsense too." Vladimir Nabokov, *Lectures on Literature* (New York: Harcourt, 1980), p. 288.

3 Calvin Bedient, *He Do the Police in Different Voices: "The Waste Land" and Its Protagonist* (Chicago: University of Chicago Press, 1986), p. 56.

4 Examples include T. W. H. Crosland, "To the American Invader," in his *Outlook Odes* (London: At the Unicorn, 1902), pp. 30–2; Enoch Miner, *Our Phonographic Poets: Written by Stenographers and Typists upon Subjects Pertaining to their Arts, Compiled by "Topsy Typist"* (New York: Popular Publishing, 1904); Samuel Ellsworth Kiser, *Love Sonnets of an Office Boy* (Chicago: Forbes, 1907), twenty-eight sonnets addressed to the office typewriter girl; Andrew Lang, "Matrimony," in *The Poetical Works of Andrew Lang*, Volume 3, Leonora Lance Lang (ed.), (London: Longmans, 1923), pp. 179–80. A serious, and hence rare, poem about a typist is "Interlude: Eurydice," by Arthur Henry Adams, in his *London Streets* (London: T. N. Flouris, 1906), pp. 34–6.

5 Four of the eight novels are British: Ernest Temple Thurston, *Sally Bishop: A Romance* (London: Chapman & Hall, 1908); Ivy Low, *The Questing Beast* (London: Martin Secker, 1914); Marjorie Grant, *Latchkey Ladies* (London: William Heinemann, 1921); and Arnold Bennett, *Lilian* (London: Cassell, 1922). For a discussion of these, see Lawrence Rainey, "From the Fallen Woman to the Fallen Typist," *English Literature in Transition, 1880–1920* 52.3 (2009): 273–297. Four are American: Elizabeth Dejeans, *The Winning Chance* (Philadelphia: J. B. Lippincott, 1909); Pearl Doles Bell, *Gloria Gray, Love Pirate* (Chicago: Robert & Co., 1914); Winston Churchill, *The Dwelling-Place of Light* (New York: Macmillan, 1917); and Elenore Meherin, *Chickie: A Hidden, Tragic Chapter from the Life of a Girl of this Strange "Today"* (New York: Grosset & Dunlap, 1925). This latter edition was published as a movie tie-in; the book's real first edition was its serial publication in all the newspapers belonging to the legendary Hearst empire, from November 26, 1923, to February 28, 1924.

6 Peter D. McDonald, *British Literary Culture and Publishing Practice, 1880–1914* (Cambridge: Cambridge University Press, 1997), p. 96.

7 "Frances," "Five O'Clock Tea Talk: A Woman's Restaurant," *T. P.'s Weekly* (December 11, 1902), p. 918.

8 Low, *The Questing Beast*. Low herself worked for the Prudential Assurance Company, which is turned into the New Insurance Company in her novel.

9 Anonymous, "Suffragette Secretaries: A Report on Office Life 60 Years Ago," *Survey of Secretarial and Clerical Salaries: Alfred Marks Bureau, Statistical Services Division* (October 1979): pp. 19–29.

10 Tom Gallon, *The Girl Behind the Keys* (London: Hutchinson, 1903), p. 5.

11 David Graham Phillips, *The Grain of Dust* (New York: D. Appleton, 1911), p. 300.

12 Low, *The Questing Beast*, p. 9.

13 Phillips, *The Grain of Dust*, p. 326.

14 Charlton Lewis and Charles Short, *A Latin Dictionary* (Oxford: Oxford University Press, 1980), s.v. *vanus*.

15 Matei Calinescu, *Faces of Modernity: Avant-garde, Decadence, Kitsch* (Bloomington: Indiana University Press, 1977), p. 140.

16 For the eight novels, see note 5. The category of the "fallen woman" conflated three forms of sexual activity that to later observers seem quite distinct: premarital consensual sex, extramarital sex, and prostitution. The best overviews of Victorian sexuality remain Michael Mason's two volumes, *The Making of Victorian Sexual Attitudes* (Oxford: Oxford University Press, 1994) and *The Making of Victorian Sexuality* (Oxford: Oxford University Press, 1994). On the fallen woman, with reference only to prostitution, see Amanda Anderson, *Tainted Souls and Painted Faces: The Rhetoric of Fallenness in Victorian Culture* (Ithaca: Cornell University Press, 1993). On the theme in the English novel, see George Watt, *The Fallen Woman in the Nineteenth-Century English Novel* (Croon Helm; Totowa: Barnes & Noble, 1984). On the theme in drama, see Sos Eltis, "The Fallen Woman on Stage: Maidens, Magdalens, and the Emancipated Female," in Kerry Powell (ed.), *The Cambridge Companion to Victorian and Edwardian Theatre* (Cambridge: Cambridge University Press, 2004), pp. 222–36.

17 Low, *The Questing Beast*, p. 157.

18 Meherin, *Chickie*, pp. 272–3. On this novel and its adaptation into a film, see Lawrence Rainey, "Popular Literature, Silent Film, and the Perils of Genre: *Chickie* (1923–1925)," *Literature/Film Quarterly* 38.4 (2010): 277–88.

19 Oliver Goldsmith, *The Vicar of Wakefield* (London: Sammels and Ritchie, 1792), p. 147.

20 See Jonathan Barnes (ed.), *The Complete Works of Aristotle* (Princeton: Princeton University Press, 1983), vol. 1, "Parts of Animals," 1071–2; for Heidegger, see the terms "presence-at-hand" and "ready-to-hand," which recur throughout his *Being and Time*, trans. John Macquarrie and Edward Robinson (New York: Harper and Row, 1961).

21 Jean-Luc Steinmetz, note 2 to "El Desdichado," in Gérard de Nerval, *Oeuvres complètes* in Jean Guillaume and Claude Pichois (eds.), vol. 3 (Paris: Gallimard, 1993), p. 1277.

6

SARAH KENNEDY

"Let These Words Answer": *Ash-Wednesday* and the Ariel Poems

"A thin, firm minor music, of ceremonious intricacy, dissolving the world of Tiresias, Hamlet, and Mrs. Equitone"; "a visionary precision"; "a wholly transparent network of allusions, tacitly nourished"; "a religious poem which contains no slovenly phrase, no borrowed zeal, no formulated piety."[1] This is Hugh Kenner's description of the poem he identified as marking a departure from the conversational rhythms and "gritty substantiality" of Eliot's earlier writing. *Ash-Wednesday* (1930) marks a shift in Eliot's poetics away from the urbanity and Laforguean disaffection of his youth toward the lyrical assurance and meditative transcendence of *Four Quartets*. A religious poem devoid of dogma, *Ash-Wednesday* enacts the renunciatory suffering of the supplicant as the poetic consciousness strains to turn inward, forsaking the sensual life of memory and desire. It is a poem fundamentally concerned with alterations in state, with the painful processes of becoming, and with the subtle permutations of the changed and changing self. In seeking for an altered means of expression for his religious impulse, Eliot created a new language of spiritual lucency that becomes a form of metaphysical aspiration. In its wavering between personal and impersonal, in its subtle dream-like ellipses and sudden shifts in register, and in its syntactical involutions and recursions, *Ash-Wednesday* engenders a spiritual process in which poem and experience are often indistinguishable.

In the Christian calendar Ash Wednesday is a day of introspection and penitence. It marks the commencement of Lent, a liturgical period of forty days of prayer and abstinence that recalls the fasting and temptation of Jesus in the wilderness. The title *Ash-Wednesday* might therefore be expected to proclaim a public, ceremonial role for the poem in keeping with its uses of the Anglican Liturgy and the sermons of seventeenth-century Bishop Lancelot Andrewes, who preached before the court of King James I. Yet the poem eschews an explicitly ecclesiastical context and its recourse to liturgy only commences at the conclusion of the opening section ("Pray for us sinners now and at the hour of our death / Pray for us now and at the hour of our death" [*CPP* 90]). The voices of the Hebrew prophets Ezekiel, Jeremiah, and Micah toll through the poem's other, stranger musics: Catholic prayers interwoven with Dante, eighteenth-century fairy tale, Elizabethan verse, and Symbolist aestheticism in a characteristically eclectic assemblage of fragments.

Denis Donoghue discerns three fields of diction in *Ash-Wednesday*: religious texts (rituals, sermons, prayers, and meditations), literary material (Dante, Shakespeare, Cavalcanti, Baudelaire), and a generalised "common worldly language."[2] The poem's semantic strength and strangeness derives from its negotiations between these fields and their attendant aural structures. What might otherwise be startling leaps in register are held in fine tensity by filaments of image and idiom that reconcile the mind to the poem's indeterminacy, creating a feeling of amplitude. So, for example, the shift from Part I's submission of the will and ritual invocation of the *Angelus* into Part II's high-Symbolist narrative is bridged by the vocative use of "Lady." The incantatory song of the bones ("Lady of silences" [*CPP* 91]) – itself tracing the antiphonal dynamics of the Litany of the Blessed Virgin Mary – is enclosed by the narrative addressed to the Lady and suffused with Old Testament imagery. In "The Music of Poetry" (1942) Eliot says that "the germ of a poem may be quickened" in the concert room, and refers to the "possibilities of contrapuntal arrangement of subject-matter" (*OPP* 38). *Ash-Wednesday* borrows from the structural vocabulary of Baroque music an oblique contrapuntal motion in which rhythm and image operate in separate spheres yet come together to create an harmonic interdependency (like the juxtaposed movements of wings flying seaward above shore-bound waves). Progressions such as "Not on the sea or on the islands, not / On the mainland, in the desert or the rain land" (*CPP* 96), in addition to a tightly packed internal symmetry, provide a melodic presentiment of "the granite shore / The white sails still fly seaward, seaward flying" (*CPP* 98) so that each line relies on the plangency of the others for its full resonance. The repeated assonance of "between," "dream," and "redeem" builds a cumulative metaphysical sympathy played out across the poem's contingencies of tone and rhythm.

In this respect, the elliptical consciousness of *Ash-Wednesday* operates in a microcosmic relation with the mind of the poet. In his source-hunter's guide to Eliot, B. C. Southam records "the composite nature" of *Ash-Wednesday*, quoting the poet's 1959 statement that the poem "originated out of separate poems": "gradually I came to see it as a sequence. That's one way in which my mind does seem to have worked throughout the years poetically – doing things separately and then seeing the possibility of fusing them together, altering them, and making a kind of a whole of them."[3]

As with many of Eliot's lengthier compositions, *Ash-Wednesday* emerged gradually as floating fragments later assembled into their final form. The composition history of the fragments that became Parts I, II, and III is particularly interwoven with two other poems, "Journey of the Magi" (1927) and "A Song for Simeon" (1928), commissioned by Faber for their Ariel Poems series.[4]

There is permeability between these works in their apprehension, remote from time, of spiritual significations lying hidden in a landscape of chronic latency. Bishop Andrewes's wonder, in his Nativity Sermons, at the infant Christ, *Verbum infans*, "the Word and not able to speak a word"[5] charge "Journey of the Magi," "A Song for Simeon," and "Gerontion" (1920) – "We would see a sign!" (*CPP* 37) – with what energy they contain. Together with "Animula" (1929) and "Marina" (1930), each poem is situated somewhere within the "brief transit where the dreams cross / The dreamcrossed twilight between birth and dying" (*CPP* 98). "Journey of the Magi" presents a consciousness transformed by what it has seen, but, unable to locate the precise moment and purpose of the transformation, the poem slips between the "Hard and bitter agony" of its witness and the superannuated folly of the "old dispensation," ending in confusion ("Birth or Death? ... "I had seen birth and death, / But had thought they were different") (*CPP* 104). "A Song for Simeon" edges closer to revelation: its sphere of action is more immediate than the events of "Journey of the Magi." Simeon has kept faith with the prophesied "still unspeaking and unspoken Word," but his spirit is stretched thin by waiting ("My life is light, waiting for the death wind, / Like a feather on the back of my hand."). Denied participation in a future he cannot conceive, his partial vision encompasses the suffering of "scourges and lamentation" (*CPP* 105) but fails to envisage *Ash-Wednesday*'s "Garden / Where all love ends" (*CPP* 92). Both "A Song for Simeon" and "Animula" strain toward silence, but their imaginative powers terminate in the peaceful emptiness of exhalation. The imaginative trajectories of Eliot's later poems (*Ash-Wednesday*, "Marina," *Four Quartets*) reach beyond this eschatological limitation into silences heavy with expectation of the "Word of no speech."[6]

The beginning of *Ash-Wednesday* inherits a sense of incompletion from the shivering inchoate voice of "The Hollow Men" (1925) – "For Thine is / Life is / For Thine is the" (*CPP* 86) – evidence in that poem of a spiritual affliction from which only the "Desiccation of the world of sense" (*CPP* 174) of *Four Quartets* might redeem. Evolving out of the legacy of these fractured exhalations, *Ash-Wednesday*'s opening exudes a subtle cyclic cohesion, its rhythm established early by the insistent anaphora ("Because ... Because ... Because," "And ... And ... And"), which seems to supervene upon some pre-existing meditation. The repetition of conjunctions at the beginning of multiple lines provides rhythmic propulsion beyond the line endings, while the literal turning back of each phrase enacts the ambivalence of its spiritual endeavour. Circumambulation is a peculiarly encompassing form of movement-in-stasis, which might easily lapse into the enervated catechism of "The Hollow Men" ("*Here we go round the prickly pear*" [*CPP* 85]). Yet *Ash-Wednesday* is also a poem innately aware of its own being (this is evident in its artful borrowing from Shakespeare's Sonnet 29, as well as in the self-consciousness of lines like "These matters that with myself I too much discuss" [*CPP* 89]). Etymologically, a "verse" is both a turning and a wavering between (as in "versus"). The poem acknowledges this by undercutting the potentially stifling symmetry of its spiralling rhythm with sudden syncopation ("place is always and only place," "Against the Word the unstilled world still whirled" [*CPP* 89, 96]). The self-correcting stammer of "what is actual is actual only for one time" (*CPP* 89) and "fly seaward, seaward flying" creates, in Kenner's phrase, "a vertigo of assonances" as it skims from moment to moment.[7]

The poem also makes exquisite use of silence, in the form of pauses and caesurae, to allow the ear to rest and to give a metrical grounding in sequences that are otherwise rhythmically destabilising. An exemplary instance of this occurs at the end of the second stanza:

> There, where trees flower, and springs flow, for there is nothing
> again (*CPP* 89)

With its emphatic "There" the poem seems to make a momentary approach to the concrete, only to fall away into the quiet between subordinate clauses ("where trees flower, and springs flow"). These silences sap the continuity of the imagery, which dissipates into a "nothing" saved from nihilism by the enjambed "again" that returns the poem to the open-ended terms of the first line: in neither case is there any concluding punctuation to give the reassurance of finality. This is an exquisitely compacted version of the momentary revelation of the heart of light in *Four Quartets* ("Then a cloud passed, and the pool was empty" [*CPP* 172]), but where in the latter poem the moment is inhabited, here it is only glancingly – and intermittently – apprehended.

The poetic consciousness of *Ash-Wednesday* strains toward asceticism ("Teach us to care and not to care / Teach us to sit still" [*CPP* 90]), but its renunciatory impulse is complicated by its awareness of the emotional affinities between moments of lived and divine experience. There is an acute consciousness, too, of the metaphysical resemblance between opposing spiritual states (an awareness developed in the image in *Four Quartets* of the "live and the dead nettle" [*CPP* 195]). In *Murder in the Cathedral* (1935) a mere hair's-breadth separates Becket's holy submission to martyrdom from the deathly sin of seeking it out. Hugh Kenner describes this "knife-edge between annihilation and self-surrender" as Eliot's overarching "moral dialectic."[8] A preoccupation with the temptation of spiritual pride is deeply ingrained in Eliot's 1930 description of a mystical approach to God by way of negation as requiring "the most terrible concentration and askesis ... men like the forest sages, and the desert sages ... Only those have the right to talk of discipline who have looked into the Abyss" (*CP4* 39).

This may be one reason Eliot removed *Ash-Wednesday*'s original section titles, substituting the numerical system that appears in the present poem. The titles (which appeared in an unpublished typescript of five of the poem's six final sections, as well as on the three sections of the poem earlier published in fragmentary form) aligned the poem more strongly with Dante's journey through the *Purgatorio* and into the *Paradiso*.[9] Section III, for instance, bore the title "som de L'Escalina" ("to the summit of the stair"), a phrase addressed to Dante as, "guided by virtue," he ascends the third staircase from the Mount of Purgatory to the Earthly Paradise. The poem's ascent, as it struggles with "the devil of the stairs" (*CPP* 93), also echoes the progress of the sixteenth-century mystic St. John of the Cross in his allegorical *Ascent of Mount Carmel*. But such echoes are tempered by coexistence with others in a landscape stripped of all consistency or particularity of time and place. Rather than presuming to chart an immersion in aphotic deprivation, the poem offers only a single glimpse of the dark night of the soul on which the ascetic path is predicated (Part III's "There were no more faces and the stair was dark" [*CPP* 93]). The spiritual migrations of those, like John of the Cross, "who walk in darkness, who chose thee" (*CPP* 96), are acknowledged with penitential awe, but the poem rightly abjures any attempt at participation.

Instead, what *Ash-Wednesday* pursues is the diminutive questing of the ordinary penitent (undifferentiated amongst the many "children at the gate" [*CPP* 96]) who must turn his eyes upward without hope. The poem's confessional tone is ritualized into abstraction: never in *Ash-Wednesday* do we find a catalogue of spiritual traps and vices as specific even as in "Marina": "Those who glitter with the glory of the hummingbird" (*CPP* 109). It studiously avoids the self-dramatizing presences of earlier works, characters like Prufrock and Gerontion, each of whom (in Eliot's self-revealing description of Othello) "sees himself in a dramatic light" (*CP2* 90). The poem's first-person articulation is accordingly emptied of individualized passion, its rare moments of apparent self-regard ("the agéd eagle" with its wings "no longer wings to fly" [*CPP* 89, 90]) evade the lure of self-pity through their unflinching self-mockery. It is these subtle discriminations that give

Ash-Wednesday a greater complexity and resonance than either "Journey of the Magi" or "A Song for Simeon," both of which dramatize individual spiritual states and thus lack the scrupulous tension of *Ash-Wednesday* in its navigations of the spaces "between." Its most fundamental poetic kinship is not with the vacuity of "Gerontion," the metamorphic strangeness of "Mr. Apollinax," nor the enervated despair of "The Hollow Men" (although all these are at times present), but with the delicate attenuation of "Marina."

Ash-Wednesday establishes an internal logic of distances, founded on syntactical and narrative layering and reinforced by the intricate internal dynamics of the poem's six-part structure. F. R. Leavis found in the ritualized rhythms of *Ash-Wednesday* a "frame-effect," a dissociation from the ordinary world of language and things into "a special order of experience, dedicated to spiritual exercises."[10] Denis Donoghue similarly points to the syntactical "displacement of attention" that arises from the prevalence of conjunctions, prepositions, and participles and the commensurate deferral of main verbs ("hope to turn," "strive to strive," "hope to know") that make *Ash-Wednesday* feel "as if it were written within parentheses or seen under glass."[11] Such critical images of frames are apt not only because dissociations and displacements are key elements of the poem's overall effect, but because frames can also be porous in their delineations: like the "slotted window bellied like the fig's fruit" (*CPP* 93) they allow for the interpenetration of "here" and "beyond." The defining feature of *Ash-Wednesday* – and one that distinguishes it from Eliot's earlier writing – is its submission to an overarching principle of adjacency, established here and used again in "Marina," "Landscapes," and *Four Quartets*. As Hugh Kenner notes with characteristic succinctness, "the most arresting images now *recede*."[12] The quiescent presence of the white leopards in Part II displaces the savagery of their imputed actions into an indeterminate space between past and present, much as the "Lady is withdrawn / In a white gown, to contemplation" (*CPP* 91), a spiritual reagent whose presence-in-absence is one of the poem's most vivid and discomforting elements. Even the Dantean dream-vision of "jewelled unicorns" (*CPP* 94) sits uncomfortably within the traditional framework of the beast's chivalric and Christian iconography. The elusive, paralleled syntax ("While jewelled unicorns draw by the gilded hearse") transposes the pageantry out of both time and space. Glimpsed sideways, the creatures recall Rilke's unicorn in the *Duino Elegies*, existing only by its absence.

Leavis suggested that *Ash-Wednesday*'s "compensations, resolutions, residuums and convergences" function as a form of spiritual irony, a "self-admonition against the subtle treasons" of the ego. He saw the poem's "attainment of a difficult sincerity" as its greatest achievement, writing that "it is impossible not to see in it a process of self-scrutiny, of self-exploration; or not to feel that the poetical problem at any point was a spiritual problem."[13] The poem's overwhelming impulse is of course penitential, but its religious questing is configured in uneasy relation to the poet's powers of creation. If every poem is an epitaph (as *Four Quartets* suggests), how then can the supplicant-poet meaningfully surrender the will and "Proffer my deeds to oblivion" (*CPP* 91)? Eliot was acutely aware of the subtleties of ego involved in the transactions between "the man who suffers and the mind which creates" (*CP2* 109) and the poem mines various literary seams in exploration of its responses.

Shortly after the publication of *Ash-Wednesday*, Eliot wrote to his friend Paul Elmer More that the poem was "a first attempt at a sketchy application of the philosophy of the *Vita Nuova* to modern life" (*L5* 209). This authorial description directs attention to the poem's drive to transmute personal passion into a poetry of transcendence. Charged with the self-conscious tension of not wholly achievable renunciation, *Ash-Wednesday* irresistibly turns back toward the ghostly presence of the desired, like Orpheus upon the stair. It cannot help but caressingly recall: "Blown hair is sweet, brown hair over the mouth blown, Lilac and brown hair" (*CPP* 93). There is no horror here, as in earlier poems, of the "salt savour" (*CPP* 98) of the sensual. This is perhaps what I. A. Richards meant when he declared *Ash-Wednesday* "better poetry than even the best sections of *The Waste Land*" by reason of its effusing "less dread of the unknown depths."[14] In its plangent recollection of the "lost lilac and the lost sea voices" (*CPP* 98) the poem immerses itself in those elements most destructive and fertile.

Yet Eliot's statement also lays bare another instinct altogether at odds with the poem's ostensible aims ("I no longer strive to strive towards such things" [*CPP* 89]). Placed by its author in the tradition of Dante's *Vita Nuova*, *Ash-Wednesday* is at least as much an act of poetic self-construction as it is an act of spiritual self-abnegation. Writing on *Ash-Wednesday* and Shakespeare, Neil Corcoran comments that "allusion willingly runs the risk of defacement: and the willingness is a measure of ambition at least as much as a register of admiration."[15] The poem begins by translating the opening of Cavalcanti's "*Perch'io non spero di tornar già mai*" ("Because I do not hope to turn again" [*CPP* 89]), an allusion that, even as it renounces the world, stakes a claim to literary tradition that assumes an ongoing posterity of its own. The alteration of Shakespeare's Sonnet 29 (substituting "this man's *gift* and that man's scope" for "this man's *art* and that man's scope" [italics added]) seems again to confound the renunciatory objective by referencing the Shakespearean desire to be "like to one more rich in hope, / Featured like him, like him with friends possessed." The poem's recessional dynamics cloak, but do not efface, its sublimated ambition: it is able to risk its borrowings and incorporations only because it itself is a form of being-in-absence that mimics the function of allusion. The poem's evasions – those compensations and residuums Leavis found so salutary – allow the poem precisely "to strive towards such things." This phrase recurs, tellingly, in Eliot's 1933 description of his ambition to attain an artistic transparency *beyond poetry*, to express that which "the forty of fifty original lines I have written strive towards" (*CP4* 848).

Edmund Wilson heard in *Ash-Wednesday* "the faltering accents of the supplicant," but the poem's ever-present sense of revision also serves to enliven the verse with the quality of thought (in the poem's own phrase, the "stops and steps of the mind" [*CPP* 93]).[16] May Sinclair suggested that by avoiding the "logical stages and majestic roundings of the full literary curve" Eliot's poems moved "as live thoughts move in live brains" (Brooker 12). The recursive syntax and repetitive rhythmic contours create patterns of likeness and maintain a centrifugal momentum that contains the poem's weight of spiritual and creative tensions. The poem acts upon the imagination by a process of embodiment that necessarily confounds its renunciatory objectives. To do this, *Ash-Wednesday* repeatedly exploits the slippage in English between the transitive and intransitive, testing to the limits the capacity of language to integrate the dynamics of thought. As is suggested by its Latin root "*transire*" ("to go across"), transitivity implies the bridging between action and object by which most relations are made. The poem is dense with verbs ("hope," "know," "think," "strive," "drink," "mourn," "pray," "walk") whose intensity of vertical repetition forms the weft across which the lines are woven. Yet by effacing their putative objects, the poem unmoors these verbs from their epistemological relation with experience: it is not without import that the two verbs most resolutely resistant to this impulse are "teach" and "suffer." This is the sense in which the syntax is forced to perform a ritual function ("Let these words answer / For what is done, not to be done again" [*CPP* 90]). The effect is to produce a ghostly architecture, whose suggestive absences grant a poignant immediacy to the poem's seeking for grace.

Ash-Wednesday articulates the burden and paradox of its self-conscious constructivism, in lines concerned with the mind's awareness of its own deceptions: "Because I cannot hope to turn again / Consequently I rejoice, having to construct something / Upon which to rejoice" (*CPP* 89). These lines draw on a Coleridgean model, taking up and turning the phrase "We in ourselves rejoice!" from Coleridge's "Dejection, An Ode" (1802). Yet it is the later "Constancy to an Ideal Object" (written in 1804) that provides the truer antecedent of *Ash-Wednesday*'s syntactical involutions:

> And art thou nothing? Such thou art, as when
> The woodman winding westward up the glen
> ...
> Sees full before him, gliding without tread,
> An image with a glory round its head;
> The enamoured rustic worships its fair hues,
> Nor knows he makes the shadow, he pursues![17]

The woodman's unwitting act of creation is transposed in *Ash-Wednesday* onto the poetic consciousness so that – in spite of its injunction "Suffer us not to mock ourselves with falsehood" (*CPP* 98) – the poem knowingly exploits the "treasons of the ego" for its own purposes. And yet, this construction is undertaken in an atmosphere of such stringent renunciation that it seems almost a metaphysical necessity. Maintaining what Hugh Kenner calls its "tension of implicit delusion,"[18] the poem returns to the shadows of its own casting amid the sweeping resonance of Part VI, where "the blind eye creates / The empty forms between the ivory gates / And smell renews the salt savour of the sandy earth" (*CPP* 98). Karl Shapiro recognized the tension of the poem's poise when he wrote of *Ash-Wednesday* that "in a hundred years no poem / Has sung itself so exquisitely well."[19]

The poem makes a persistent undersong of its own enactment, caught up by and involved in its processes of creative thought and afterthought. In Part II *Ash-Wednesday* plays with subtleties of semantics to subvert the biblical "burden of the grasshopper" (*CPP* 91). In *Ecclesiastes* (12:5) even the tiny weight of the grasshopper oppresses the weak and deathly. Here, the grasshopper's burden attunes to the chirping song of the bones. The act of singing something into being is played out in the passage's many references to Ezekiel and the valley of bones ("Thus saith the Lord God unto these bones; Behold, I will cause breath to enter into you, and ye shall live ... Come from the four winds, O breath, and breathe upon these slain, that they may live" 37:9) and to the vivid folkloric tropes that attend it. Donoghue sees in the passage's invocation of Grimm's fairy tales "The Juniper Tree" and "The Singing Bone" a reminder of the barbaric, with its incursion of "strangely imperturbable presences."[20] Such critical focus on the violence of the allusions occludes their true purpose: to effect a retrieval of lost and forestalled voices in the poetic equivalent of the grace that "made strong the fountains and made fresh the springs" (*CPP* 94). They are of a piece with *The Waste Land*'s conjuration of Philomel, speechless victim of King Tereus given "inviolable voice" (*CPP* 64) in her avian transfiguration, although the pared narrative here is without the Baroque richness of the earlier tableau. "The Juniper Tree," in which the bones of a murdered child are reconstituted in the figure of a singing bird, is one of many such reclamations that lie behind *Ash-Wednesday*'s ritualized, shamanistic recovery of the dry bones that, though dissembled, may yet sing. The work of the poet is to be alive to the scattered songs of "that which had been contained / In the bones" (*CPP* 91) and to let these shades breathe music again.

Ash-Wednesday is, then, a poem of encounter: in this it prefigures *Little Gidding*. Its polyvocalism and self-recursive mirroring are more subtly spectral than the latter poem's "familiar compound ghost" (*CPP* 193), its emotional effect more diffuse. Yet *Ash-Wednesday* brims with the insubstantial. The figure of the Holy Ghost is hinted at here, but the poem eschews the overtly pentecostal or incarnational in favour of something less doctrinally uncanny. Delmore Schwartz was moved by Eliot's 1953 description of "The Three Voices of Poetry" to comment that Eliot's poems are equally "often dominated by a listening to other voices – the voices of other poets, in other centuries and countries."[21] A 1935 letter to Stephen Spender expresses the intensity of association between the literary and the spiritual in Eliot's oeuvre through its religious vocabulary of surrender and revelation:

> You don't really criticise an author to whom you have never surrendered yourself. Even just the bewildering minute counts; you have to give yourself up, and then recover yourself, and the third moment is having something to say, before you have wholly forgotten both surrender and recovery. Of course the self recovered is never the same as the self before it was given.[22]

From its earliest utterances *Ash-Wednesday* implicates multiple figures in a ghostly conversation. The first line's allusion to "*Perch'io non spero* ..." invokes the literary relationship between Dante and Cavalcanti (the dedicatee of the *Vita Nuova*). Their thirteenth-century literary friendship, conducted via an epistolary poetic conversation, is reimagined in *Ash-Wednesday* as the poem reconvenes the emotional force of Cavalcanti's self-preoccupied poem of exile in dialogue with what Eliot called Dante's "Catholic philosophy of disillusion" (*CP3* 733).

Canto XXIV of Dante's *Paradiso* borrows from the opening of the letter to the Hebrews (11:1), rendered in the King James Version as "Now faith is the substance of things hoped for, the evidence of things not seen." This elaborate *rime de correspondenza* is woven obliquely throughout *Ash-Wednesday*, yet the poem's full effect derives in large part from its operation. It is a repeat instance of Eliot's having something to say in response to the bewilderment of encounter with a literary progenitor. In his 1929 essay "Dante" (written at the same time as *Ash-Wednesday*) Eliot writes:

> The experience of a poem is the experience both of a moment and of a lifetime. It is very much like our intenser experiences of other human beings. There is a first, or an early moment which is unique, of shock and surprise,

> even of terror (*Ego Dominus Tuus*); a moment which can never be forgotten, but which is never repeated integrally; and yet which would become destitute of significance if it did not survive in a larger whole of experience; which survives inside a deeper and a calmer feeling. The majority of poems one outgrows and outlives, as one outgrows and outlives the majority of human passions: Dante's is one of those which one can only just hope to grow up to at the end of life. (*CP3* 711)

Eliot's reference to *Ego Dominus Tuus* (Latin for "I am your master") deftly expresses the interplay between spiritual surrender and literary mastery, and indeed Yeats's meditation on the self-reflexive deceits and half-creations of poetic endeavour forms an allusive undercurrent in *Ash-Wednesday*. In Yeats's poem "Ego Dominus Tuus," Dante is forced "To climb that stair and eat that bitter bread"; he too has "A hunger for the apple on the bough." Yeats's "Hic" is poignantly naked in his desire ("I would find myself and not an image"), while "Ille" worries, in the act of literary excavation, at what is being resurrected ("and is that spectral image / The man that Lapo and that Guido knew?").[23]

Seamus Heaney observes of Yeats's tortured Dante that "when poets turn to the great masters of the past, they turn to an image of their own creation, one which is likely to be a reflection of their own imaginative needs, their own artistic inclinations and procedures."[24] As images of struggle and ciphers of literary ambition, literary antecedents are ambiguous figurations of the ghosts of the poet's former selves, the lost-but-sought-for, and the renounced-but-recurring. Harold Bloom, who uses the term *apophrades* in relation to the resurgence of the literary dead, writes that "apophrades, when managed by the capable imagination, by the strong poet who has persisted in his strength, becomes not so much a return of the dead as a celebration of the return of the early self-exaltation that first made poetry possible." He notes that Eliot "became a master at reversing the apophrades."[25]

If we accept the full flight of Bloom's argument, that in invoking the dead poets Eliot meets and exalts his poetic self, then it is a strange and lacerating form of exaltation. The equivocal presence that presides over and negotiates the perilous dynamics of encounter – in *Ash-Wednesday* as elsewhere – is the touchstone figure of Arnaut Daniel, the twelfth-century Occitan troubadour praised by Dante as his *miglior fabbro* or "better craftsman" even as he consigned Daniel to eternal purgation for lustfulness in the *Purgatorio*. Daniel is intricately entwined in Eliot's recurrent spiritual and creative convulsions. Eliot undertook a walking tour in the Dordogne with Pound in the summer of 1919. While visiting sites associated with Daniel in Périgueux, Eliot had a spiritual crisis that seems to have combined sexual horror, artistic paralysis, and existential despair. He later wrote in a letter to Reverend

William Force Stead: "This sense of dispossession by the dead I have known twice, at Marlow and at Perigueux" (*L5* 287). The residue of these experiences became concentrated, for Eliot, in Daniel's four-line plea to Dante in Canto XXVI (145–8):

> *"Ara vos prec, per aquella valor*
> *"que vos guida al som de l'escalina,*
> *"sovegna vos a temps de ma dolor."*
> *Poi s'ascose nel foco che gli affina.*

["And so I pray you, by that Virtue which leads you to the topmost of the stair – be mindful in due time of my pain." Then dived he back into that fire which refines them.] (Eliot's translation, *CP3* 716)

The Waste Land uses line 148 ("Poi s'ascose...") as one of the fragments that conclude the poem in "What the Thunder said." Eliot titled his second volume of poetry "Ara Vus Prec" (1920), in a mis-transliteration of the Provençal that now seems peculiarly fitting. The compound ghost in *Four Quartets* returns to the medium of Daniel's refining fire after his encounter with the speaker-poet. The scene's veiled irruption in *Ash-Wednesday* Part IV, "sovegna vos" ("be mindful"), is phantasmal and suggestive, both plea and admonition.

Massimo Bacigalupo describes Daniel as "*the* Eliot persona," although it may be more accurate to characterise the troubadour as Eliot's poetic psycho-pomp.[26] Daniel appears in Eliot's poetry as an apparition whose exhalations make whisper music, tolling faint bells of recrudescence and discovery. Daniel's appearance signals a subtle progress, faring forward even as it urges reminiscence in "the time of tension between dying and birth" (*CPP* 98). "Sovegna vos" is accorded the status of a precept, hived off from the rest of the stanza as if emanating from a different source. There is a syntactical symmetry between this phrase and the phrase concluding the second stanza of Part VI, "Unbroken wings." Donald Davie writes with imaginative conviction that "if all poems are born as rhythms, then some, it seems, may be born as rhythms of ideas, that is, as patterns of syntax rather than patterns of sound."[27] The softly rhythmic insufflation of the w's ("From the wide window towards the granite shore") and the lapping, recursive sibilants ("The white sails still fly seaward") embody the swooping progress of Eliot's "Unbroken wings" (*CPP* 98) borne upon a seaward wind.

Following the trajectory of the drifting voices from the yew-tree away from "The place of solitude where three dreams cross" (*CPP* 98), the aerial advance of the final section seems to slip free of the poem's confines. The final "cry" importunes the "spirit of the river, spirit of the sea" (*CPP* 99) across a breadth of space beyond the poem's conclusion, from the "granite shore" of *Ash-Wednesday* toward the "granite islands" (*CPP* 110) of "Marina." There is consanguinity between these poems, subject as they are to very different pressures. "Marina" is unmoored and indeterminate in a way that *Ash-Wednesday* is not. The plangent music of the former allows for a drifting not possible within the constraints of *Ash-Wednesday*'s syntactical nets. "Marina" is softer, more deliquescent – notwithstanding its assimilation of Seneca's *Hercules Furens* – because it gathers the pulsating motion of ocean and antiphon into the very systole and diastole of itself while also inhabiting an expansive landscape whose blurred contours mirror the gentle indeterminacy of the poem's search for grace. Between "Marina" and *Ash-Wednesday*, the subtle shift of emphasis calls to mind the words of the Shepherd of Shakespeare's *The Winter's Tale*, "thou mettest with things dying, I with things new-born" (III.iii). Shriven of the pain of sin, its ghostings trace the forms of things not dissembled, but made. The "images return," not through resurrection, but recognition (as in *Pericles* V.i, suggested by the poem's title) and prolepsis: "The awakened, lips parted, the hope, the new ships" (*CPP* 109, 110). "Marina" completes the circumvolution of perspective from the line "I am tired with my own life and the lives of those after me" in "A Song for Simeon" (*CPP* 106) to:

> Living to live in a world of time beyond me; let me
> Resign my life for this life, my speech for that unspoken (*CPP* 110)

This is the contingent, modest grace that the poetry achieves.

NOTES

1 Hugh Kenner, *T. S. Eliot: The Invisible Poet* (London: Methuen, 1965), p. 224.

2 Denis Donoghue, *Words Alone: The Poet T. S. Eliot* (New Haven: Yale University Press, 2000), p. 153.

3 B. C. Southam, *A Student's Guide to the Selected Poems of T.S. Eliot* (London: Faber, 1968), p. 134. Quoting T. S. Eliot, "The Art of Poetry" (Interview with Donald Hall), *The Paris Review* 21 (Spring/Summer 1959).

4 "Journey of the Magi" was written in August 1927, followed by "Salutation" (later Part II of *Ash-Wednesday*) in December 1927. "Perch'io no spero" (*Ash-Wednesday*, Part I) followed in the spring of 1928. "A Song for Simeon" was written in September 1928, then "Som de l'escalina" (*Ash-Wednesday*, Part III) in the autumn of 1929. Then followed "Animula" (October 1929), *Ash-Wednesday* (March 1930), and "Marina" (1930).

5 Lancelot Andrewes, *Seventeen Sermons on the Nativity* (London: Griffith Farran Okeden & Welsh, 1887), p. 200.

6 Steven Matthews writes illuminatingly on the anxieties present in both Andrewes's and Eliot's texts that the Word may remain unheard. See *T. S. Eliot and Early Modern Literature* (Oxford: Oxford University Press, 2013) pp. 141–2.

7 Kenner, *The Invisible Poet*, p. 227.
8 Hugh Kenner, "Eliot's Moral Dialectic," *The Hudson Review* 2.3 (Autumn, 1949): 429, 432.
9 For a detailed description of the material history of the poem, see Southam, *A Student's Guide to the Selected Poems of T.S. Eliot*, "Appendix," pp. 133–6.
10 F. R. Leavis, *New Bearings in English Poetry* (Harmondsworth: Penguin, 1972), p. 89.
11 Donoghue, *Words Alone*, p. 149.
12 Kenner, *The Invisible Poet*, p. 225.
13 See Leavis, *New Bearings*, pp. 89–98.
14 I. A. Richards, *Science and Poetry* (London: Routledge, 1935), p. 71.
15 Neil Corcoran, *Shakespeare and the Modern Poet* (Cambridge: Cambridge University Press, 2010), p. 91.
16 Edmund Wilson, *Axel's Castle: A Study in the Imaginative Literature of 1870–1930* (New York: Charles Scribner's, 1931), p. 130.
17 *Selected Poems of Samuel Taylor Coleridge*, ed. James Reeves (London: Heinemann, 1959), p. 112.
18 Kenner, *The Invisible Poet*, p. 227
19 Karl Shapiro, *Essay on Rime* (New York: Raynor and Hitchcock, 1945), p. 17.
20 Donoghue, *Words Alone*, p. 158.
21 Delmore Schwartz, "T. S. Eliot's Voice and His Voices: III," *Poetry* 85.4 (1955): 233.
22 Stephen Spender, "Remembering Eliot," *T. S. Eliot: The Man and His Work*, ed. Allen Tate (London: Chatto & Windus, 1967), pp. 55–6.
23 *Yeats's Poems*, ed. A. Norman Jeffares (London: Macmillan, 1989), pp. 264–6.
24 Seamus Heaney, "Envies and Identifications: Dante and the Modern Poet" in Peter S. Hawkins and Rachel Jacoff (eds.), *The Poets' Dante* (New York: Farrar, Straus, Giroux, 2002), p. 239.
25 Harold Bloom, *The Anxiety of Influence: A Theory of Poetry* (Oxford: Oxford University Press, 1997), pp. 147, 142.
26 Massimo Bacigalupo, "Dante" in *T. S. Eliot in Context*, ed. Jason Harding (Cambridge: Cambridge University Press, 2011), p. 180.
27 See Donald Davie, *Purity of Diction in English Verse and Articulate Energy* (Harmondsworth: Penguin, 1992), p. 278.

7

STEVE ELLIS

Four Quartets

Four Quartets is in many ways a work of purification and purgation, linguistically and morally, and one which strives to "dispossess" itself of the world and its "distractions" in its quest for the absolute. The more severe and homogeneous diction of Eliot's later style, heralded in the 1929 essay on Dante – "one has learned from the *Inferno* that the greatest poetry can be written with the greatest economy of words, and with the greatest austerity in the use of metaphor, simile, verbal beauty, and elegance" (*CP3* 712) – means that the multiple discourse of the earlier work – the quotations in foreign languages, the presence of dialect, jazz idiom, nursery rhyme, all *The Waste Land*'s different voices, as well as its multifarious personae – has disappeared. What we rather have in *Four Quartets* is the "I" persona in a state of prolonged spiritual self-communing within a pronounced doctrinal context, with a good deal of iteration of some of the poem's key points: "You say I am repeating / Something I have said before. I shall say it again" (*CPP* 181). If this suggests that *Four Quartets* remains primarily the preserve of the religious interpreter, a significant amount of recent criticism has emphasised historical contexts and occasions, focussing on the poem as a document of the Second World War, and indeed the later three Quartets, *East Coker*, *The Dry Salvages* and *Little Gidding*, published in 1940, 1941 and 1942, respectively, are heavily imbued with wartime experience. But whatever the social, political or "patriotic" interventions *Four Quartets* can be seen as making, these cannot be divorced from religious positions that heavily inflect the topical commentary the poem has to offer, and to neglect such positions precisely obscures the insistent dialogue between religion and "history" that takes place throughout. In Jed Esty's words, *Four Quartets* is not "a retreat from history into religion" but a "confrontation" between the two.[1] I will return to this issue at the end of this chapter, pursuing in the meantime the poem's religious narrative particularly in relation to its abiding consciousness that, as *Little Gidding* puts it, "History may be servitude, / History may be freedom" (*CPP* 195).

The opening Quartet, *Burnt Norton*, published in 1936 as the final item in Eliot's *Collected Poems 1909–1935*, records an autumnal visit to a manor-house of that name in rural Gloucestershire when the garden seemed to be transformed from something "dry" and full of dead leaves into a higher reality, with an entrance like Dante's in the *Paradiso* into the "heart of light" (*CPP* 172), but this is only a momentary vision. The poem ends in a kind of impasse (which might anticipate Eliot's subsequent extension of the narrative through further Quartets: it was only in writing *East Coker* he noted, that he "began to see the *Quartets* as a set of four"),[2] with the protagonist trapped in the earthly realm of dust and desire, but still able to intuit the sunlight and children's laughter in the garden representing the eternal world he is excluded from. This world is "always present" but always out of reach, on the other side of the "ridiculous" temporal barrier – "Quick now, here, now, always" (*CPP* 176). Thus the children's laughter, expressive of the joy and innocence of humanity's original paradisal state, also functions as a mockery and ridicule of those tantalised by its simultaneous presence and absence during their earthly lives. When the line "Quick now, here, now, always" (*CPP* 198) is repeated near the end of the final Quartet, *Little Gidding*, the experience it represents now bears an accumulated weight of significance provided by the entire sequence. *Four Quartets* is among many things a journey, or a process of exploration that ends where it began:

> We shall not cease from exploration
> And the end of all our exploring
> Will be to arrive where we started
> And know the place for the first time. (*CPP* 197)

"The place" is once again represented in part by "children in the apple-tree," signifying the realm of the timeless beyond the temporal, but the means of access to it has changed substantially by the end of *Four Quartets*, so that the initial visionary experience in the rose-garden of *Burnt Norton* can only now be properly understood. In the third Quartet, *The Dry Salvages*, we are presented with moments of "sudden illumination" where "We had the experience but missed the meaning" (*CPP* 186), and the "meaning" of what happened in the garden of *Burnt Norton* can only be approached through the later Quartets as its explicit Christian significance unfolds.

At the end of the first section of *Burnt Norton* the unnamed protagonists are ushered out of the visionary garden in a re-enactment of the Fall, and the rest of the Quartet is a meditation on the relationship between what is seen as this transcendental order of "reality," which is always ghosting our earthly lives, and the crippling and thwarting dimension of time in which those lives have to be lived. This latter life in time is represented as unreal, a continuation indeed of the time-bound "Unreal City" (*CPP* 62) of *The Waste Land*, and as in the earlier poem life on earth is portrayed as a state of death or non-being. Thus in the garden scene it is "we," rather than the "they" who "were behind us, reflected in the pool" (CPP 172), who are the reflections, the shadows of the higher order, indeed the true ghosts. "In spite of which we like to think / That we are sound, substantial flesh and blood" (CPP 182), *East Coker* later notes, having already summarised in a series of paradoxes the relation between temporal and eternal life, to conclude with "And where you are is where you are not" (*CPP* 181). Where you are (on earth) is where you do *not* exist; conversely, where you (truly) *are* (that is, in the next life) is where at present, being in this life, you have no place.

If *Burnt Norton* ends with a frustrated lament at the exclusion from "reality," the later three Quartets realise there can be no simple and direct return to the garden, but that the journey back to it has to be a circuitous one, taking on board rather than rejecting time and history as the medium through which the final destination has to be won. The disappointments and disillusions of time are in fact necessary stages in the journey, strengthening the desire for transcendence through the repeated experiences of life's insufficiency which they bring. In particular, the idea that growing old brings any kind of fruition, wisdom or genuine achievement is repeatedly undermined in the poem; central to *East Coker*, this theme culminates in the encounter with the revenant in *Little Gidding* II with his sardonic account of "the gifts reserved for age / To set a crown upon your lifetime's effort" (*CPP* 194). Part of the identity of the "familiar compound ghost" who speaks here is undoubtedly the poet W. B. Yeats, who had recently died (in 1939) and whom Eliot regarded in his commemorative lecture given the following year as both a stylistic forerunner, in the common quest to "purify the dialect of the tribe" (*CPP* 194), and himself the poet of troubled old age in poems like "Vacillation." But the "compound ghost" is also Eliot's own double, and the so-called "dialogue" with him is really a monologue, continuing a series of declarations that earlier stages of the poem had already made evident. There is only one authentic "crown" to be won, referenced by "the crowned knot of fire" (*CPP* 198) in *Little Gidding*'s penultimate line, a heavenly rather than earthly consummation.

There can thus be no complacency in age, no resting on one's laurels: "Old men ought to be explorers" (*CPP* 182) as *East Coker* concludes. The exploration theme then carries over into the following Quartet, *The Dry Salvages*, where the experience of religious doubt is encountered and probed, doubt that for Eliot was an integral part of religious faith, and which, in being overcome, strengthened that faith.[3] This doubt is staged in a post-Victorian mode with the protagonist's facing the oceanic "fury" as it tosses up on the beach the losses and skeletons of time, suggesting that humankind may merely be one in a succession of life-forms, and that existence is in the governance of elemental, rather than divine, powers. Life's voyage across the ocean of doubt (allegorically, "In a drifting boat with a slow leakage," *CPP* 186) does, however, manage to reach port at the end of *The Dry Salvages* in the "significant [that is sanctified] soil" of the churchyard, "Not too far from the yew-tree." After the trial by water of this Quartet comes one final obstacle to the return to the garden, the trial by fire of *Little Gidding*. Here, the destructive element of fire is embodied in the wartime air bombardment which Europe undergoes while Eliot is writing, but this is understood as part of the divine purpose – "Who then devised the torment? Love" (*CPP* 196) – in again confirming the realm of time in its unending cycle of destruction and transience, where, to pick up on the opening from *East Coker*, "Houses live and die" (*CPP* 177). There is, however, the option of a better fire, so to speak – this is "the choice of pyre or pyre" (*CPP* 196) – the "refining fire" of Purgatory where after death the spirit will be restored; as with Dante, the paradisal garden is in effect circled by a ring of fire (*Purgatorio*, cantos 25–27) which has to be submitted to. "To arrive where we started" by the end of *Four Quartets* has meant therefore not a turning back "Towards the door we never opened" (*CPP* 171) of *Burnt Norton*, but a considerable detour through the exacting lessons our personal and political history has to teach.

On this strenuous and difficult journey we have various spiritual aids. *Burnt Norton* had talked of the earthly exile in terms that drew on very little explicit Christian imagery, although by 1936 Eliot had long been a committed and practising Christian, and in a sense the first Quartet approaches the idea that "To be conscious is not to be in time" (*CPP* 173) outside of any obvious doctrinal context. One might say that the matter of the poem could be relevant to many different "out-of-body" experiences. By *East Coker*, however, with its Book of Ecclesiastes–inspired opening sequence (Ecclesiastes 1. 1–11, 3. 1–8), its reference to the Christian virtues of faith, hope and charity in section III and above all its allegorical depiction of the Fall and Redemption in section IV, the Christian note has become much more prominent. *The Dry Salvages* extends this with the prayer to the Virgin in section IV as a haven from the perilous oceanic voyage and its featuring of the Incarnation in section V. Here the poem once more recapitulates the rose-garden experience of *Burnt Norton*, "the moment in and out of time, / The distraction fit, lost in a shaft of sunlight" (*CPP* 190), but the previous intersection of the two dimensions is now seen to be dependent on and validated by the only "intersection" of any real significance, when God took on human form; all the other visionary "moments" are "only hints and guesses" (*CPP* 190) that lead us back to this as the original guarantee.

The Incarnation theme is pursued into the opening of *Little Gidding* – the later three Quartets being more clearly linked as parts of a deliberate series – with its scene of "Midwinter spring" and the fierce light that appears in "the dark time of the year" (*CPP* 191). By now the journey of exploration has become a pilgrimage: this is the only Quartet set in a religious location, the Anglican settlement of Little Gidding in the English county of Huntingdonshire, founded by Nicholas Ferrar in 1625. This is a locale at "the world's end" in that attention there is predominantly focussed on the hereafter, and the visit to it of the "broken king" (*CPP* 191) Charles I, seeking refuge during the English Civil War, indicates the subordination of the temporal to the eternal power, as well as indicating again the fragility of earthly crowns. The Nativity-inspired opening of the Quartet reminds us of the original royal journey of this type undertaken by the Magi, an event Eliot commemorates in his Ariel Poem of 1927, "Journey of the Magi," but the theme is completed in *Little Gidding* by the events of Pentecost, referred to below, Incarnation and Pentecost being the key occasions of "the dove descending" (*CPP* 196) when the Holy Spirit came down to earth.

In outlining the poem's basic religious narrative we should bear in mind Eliot's lifelong insistence that "poetry is not ... religion or an equivalent of religion" (*CP3* 414). We should also note his frequent attacks on nineteenth-century English poetry for becoming essentially a vehicle for moral instruction or philosophising ("Tennyson and Browning ruminated" *CP2* 381). In the "Dante" essay of 1929 he maintains this emphasis on "the integrity of poetry" by insisting that the non-Christian reader can get as much pleasure from the *Divine Comedy* as the Christian one, and that sharing Dante's beliefs is irrelevant in any appreciation of the poetry. And yet, in thinking this position through, Eliot does come to contradict himself: "Actually, one probably has more pleasure in the poetry when one shares the beliefs of the poet" (*CP3* 729–30). The problematic relation between poetry and belief became acute for Eliot after his entry into the Anglican Church in 1927, and the explicit Christian moralising of works like *After Strange Gods*, the pageant-play *The Rock* (both 1934) and *Murder in the Cathedral* (1935) is a consequence. But although, as Eliot noted in his interview with John Lehmann, *Burnt Norton* grew out of some lines that were cut from *Murder in the Cathedral*, this poem is much more indirect in its approach to the Christian story, and although, as we have seen, its religious narrative is hardly ignorable, *Four Quartets* remains more circumspect as an example of religious discourse. For example, there is no mention throughout the poem of Jesus by name, nor is the garden explicitly referred to as Eden, nor is Adam identified, though all are present under allegorical cover in section IV of *East Coker*. Likewise, the Nativity is figured as a seasonal rather than Biblical phenomenon at the opening of *Little Gidding*: England in the early 1940s, like all times and places, can at any instant become the Holy Land given that "all is always now" (*CPP* 175). And Eliot stresses this universalist dimension by occasionally incorporating symbols and references from other religions into the poem, such as the lotus in *Burnt Norton* I, or the words of Krishna in *The Dry Salvages* III.[4]

The encounter with "history" is most marked in the final Quartet, *Little Gidding*, with its famous scene of fire-watching during the Blitz in section II. But the poem is extremely mindful of previous history too: published in 1942, it not only features the English Civil War, but is in effect a tercentenary poem commemorating its opening. "History may be servitude, / History may be freedom" (*CPP* 195) *Little Gidding* declares, as noted above; it becomes "freedom" if we can apprehend, as the poem later puts it, what the true events of history are: "history is a pattern / Of timeless moments" (*CPP* 197). Thus what the English Civil War has to teach is nothing to do with political or constitutional outcomes as normally understood, but that

These men, and those who opposed them
And those whom they opposed
Accept the constitution of silence
And are folded in a single party. (*CPP* 196)

The "symbol" which the protagonists of that earlier war "had to leave us" is only "perfected in death"; in other words, the divisions and dissensions of the world are transient, but unity and order lie beyond the grave. The word "folded" here is resumed in the last lines of *Little Gidding*, when the poem's journey is completed:

All manner of thing shall be well
When the tongues of flame are in-folded
Into the crowned knot of fire
And the fire and the rose are one. (*CPP* 198)

The "tongues of flame" which descended on the apostles at Pentecost, enabling them to preach the Christian message in all the various languages of the earth (see Acts 2: 1–4), will be folded back together; nations and the enmity between them will cease, the chastisement and the moments of happiness which are two manifestations of the divine presence *Four Quartets* has featured throughout will likewise be subsumed into the final unity. The most significant term here is arguably the poem's final word, "one," and the most affirmative for a Europe torn apart by wartime hostilities. The ultimate state will be "A condition of complete simplicity" as *Little Gidding* labels it seven lines before the end, following the complete cessation of the world and its desires, "Costing not less than everything" (*CPP* 198).

This response to "the world" is enabled in *Little Gidding* by the pronounced apocalyptic atmosphere of this Quartet and its wartime scenario, with the bombs falling from the sky and the fire raging everywhere – in every sense we are at "the world's end" (*CPP* 192), and the opening three verses of section II picture the death of the very elements after they themselves have been the agents of civilisation's destruction through flood and fire and so forth. The previous three Quartets, however, feature the provisional nature of temporality and the frustrations experienced within it in a rather different manner. "Time" and its discontents are, as we have seen, one of the main themes of the *Quartets*. We have noted the cumulative adjectival onslaught at the end of *Burnt Norton*, where time is "ridiculous," "waste" and "sad" (*CPP* 176), the dimension of earthly exile. Elsewhere in that Quartet time is categorised in terms of constraint and imprisonment, an "enchainment" (*CPP* 173), the harsh taskmaster of the "time-ridden faces" (*CPP* 174) of the urban crowd, and more generally a dimension of unconsciousness and death, "the form of limitation / Between un-being and being" (*CPP* 175), that is an interval between pre-existence and the reality of the afterlife. The best that can be said of it is that it yet permits the "moments" of consciousness when we can pass beyond it. In the later Quartets it is the hateful medium of ageing, as we have seen, of experience the value of which is illusory, and it further threatens, in *The Dry Salvages*, to be "never ending" and therefore, appallingly, the ultimate truth. It is, further, a realm of mockery and malice, offering resources and aid to a degree, but not at the times these are needed: "one has only learnt to get the better of words / For the thing one no longer has to say" (*CPP* 182); "time is no healer: the patient is no longer here" (*CPP* 187). (This verdict is anticipated as early as Eliot's 1920 poem "Gerontion," where time and history are explicitly seen as a female torturer preying on her postlapsarian victims). And even if it is not solely a realm of destruction – "Time the destroyer is time the preserver" – what time preserves is often discomfiting, the "rock" of past agony on which faith could shipwreck (*CPP* 187), or the shameful moments from our past which are always subject to the "rending pain of re-enactment" (*CPP* 194).

The poem does, however, feature moments when "time is conquered," moments of visitation from the eternal world as we have seen, the "intersection of the timeless / With time." These moments are often imaged as an interval, or pause, in our habitual lives: on a journey, for example, "between the hither and the farther shore / While time is withdrawn" (*CPP* 188), or "when an underground train, in the tube, stops too long between stations," even if "the dwellers in cities" in particular have lost the ability to respond to such spiritual possibilities in any other than a numbed or evasive way: in the scenario of the halted tube-train "you see behind every face the mental emptiness deepen / Leaving only the growing terror of nothing to think about" (*CPP* 180). In *Burnt Norton* this tube civilisation – running on "its metalled ways / Of time past and time future" (*CPP* 174) – had already been used to represent the "horizontal" axis of temporality, while the vertical axis of the spirit that there intersects it moves upwards into the light or down into a state of darkness and deprivation – which is expanded upon in *East Coker* as "the darkness of God" (*CPP* 180) – where the individual can cast off the allurements of the world and the pretensions of the self as a necessary preface to salvation ("In order to possess what you do not possess / You must go by the way of dispossession" [*CPP* 181]). As with Dante, and as with the opening section of Eliot's *Ash-Wednesday* (1930), you first have to go to the bottom of Hell before the upward journey can begin. Indeed, as the second epigraph to the *Quartets* declares (in translation), "the way up and down is one and the same." Eliot's emphasis on access to God via the so-called "dark night," rather than in a more "positive" manner – rejoicing in the beauty of the natural world, for example – is indebted to the writings of the sixteenth-century Spanish mystic St John of the Cross, including his poem and commentary of that name.[5]

"The world," rejecting the vertical axis, moves as we have seen "In appetency, on its metalled ways / Of time past and time future." "Appetency": always searching for something, relating to ambition, appetite, something seen to lie in the future or the past, but in this search always "clinging" to the wrong dimension, ignoring the luminous "now" where the eternal order might intervene at any time – "the time of death is every moment" (*CPP* 188), as *The Dry Salvages* later puts it in a line heavy with ambiguity. "Metalled ways" suggests the narrow confinement of the journey that is merely horizontal. Moreover, any conventional understanding that such a journey is actually going anywhere, in terms of personal or evolutionary "development," or that it has any stable "sequence" that can be categorised into past, present and future, is repeatedly undermined in the poem, as announced in the very opening lines of *Burnt Norton* and *East Coker*. The future is always present in the past, and vice versa: "In my beginning is my end" (*CPP* 177), as the opening line of the latter Quartet puts it, in the sense that the moment of birth is the beginning of the approach of death, while, as we have seen, past events and their meaning are always being reformulated in the light of successive understanding. (Only divinity can comfortably inhabit these sequential conundrums, as when the Virgin Mary is addressed in *The Dry Salvages* IV in Dante's paradoxical phrase "*Figlia del tuo figlio*" ("Daughter of your son"; *Paradiso* XXXIII.1). Add to this the importance of heredity and more impersonal racial and biological strains in our present make-up, as featured in the middle two Quartets, and the past is inescapable. Any notion of progression is inevitably disappointed: again with reference to Dante's political and moral travails at the opening of the *Divine Comedy*, we are "In the middle, not only in the middle of the way / But all the way" (*CPP* 179). The visionary or meditative moments of "freedom / From past and future" (*CPP* 190), from the snares and toils of temporality, are linked as *Four Quartets* develops to particular virtues and qualities foreign to competitive "appetency": humility in *East Coker* – significantly described as "endless" – "right action" (and its associates "prayer, observance, discipline, thought" [*CPP* 190]) in *The Dry Salvages*, and, most important of all, in the final Quartet, love, which becomes, in "expanding / ... beyond desire ... liberation / From the future as well as the past" (*CPP* 195). The conclusion of *Burnt Norton* had already indicated that "desire" (that is, for something) is the aspect love takes when caught in the limitation of time; "love" is rather the perfection of desire as the heavenly beneficence lying at "the end of all our exploring" and calling us on: "With the drawing of this Love and the voice of this Calling" (*CPP* 197).

Another way in which time can be if not conquered then at least allayed is through art and its formal properties, as announced in the final section of *Burnt Norton*:

> Only by the form, the pattern,
> Can words or music reach
> The stillness, as a Chinese jar still
> Moves perpetually in its stillness. (*CPP* 175)

Four Quartets, as its title suggests, is emphatically akin to music, in that its themes and phrases are continually repeated, often with carefully planned variation, across its four parts. Readers are constantly being invited to return to earlier parts of the poem – the meaning of which now becomes modified, just as *Burnt Norton,* originally an end in itself, later became a beginning – through the recapitulation of these themes, so that the meaning of the whole lies not solely in a sequential narrative, but in "the pattern," the ever-present totality of all the parts in synchronic dialogue, the "co-existence" in which "all is always now" (*CPP* 175). In this sense art and its permanence gestures towards the eternal "now." At the same time, art is not eternal: the material it is made from is perishable – "last year's words belong to last year's language" (*CPP* 194); words "Decay with imprecision" (*CPP* 175) – and intractable, involving the "intolerable wrestle / With words and meanings" which always results, for the poet, in "a different kind of failure" even if ultimately "the poetry does not matter" (*CPP* 179, 182). If poetic form can impose some order and harmony on the unstable medium of language, as the final part of *Little Gidding* announces, where "every phrase / And sentence ... is right ... every word is at home / ... The complete consort dancing together," this sense of completion also enshrines the inevitable limitations of time and place pertinent to that medium, so that "Every poem [is] an epitaph" (*CPP* 197). *Four Quartets* is, unavoidably, written in the English of the 1930s and 1940s, and largely set in the England of that period, though it is haunted by the visions it aspires to communicate of the timeless, placeless, and so to speak English-less state where "the tongues of flame" will finally be "in-folded / Into the crowned knot of fire" (*CPP* 198).

Through poetic ordering words might, therefore, "reach / The stillness," but when *Burnt Norton* later confesses that words "Will not stay still" the struggle between stillness and motion is admitted into the poem as one of its major elements. "After the kingfisher's wing / Has answered light to light, and is silent, the light is still / At the still point of the turning world" (*CPP* 175), the little end-of-day vignette of *Burnt Norton* announces, suggesting the contrast between the divine and unchanging "stillness" and the mere intervals we have on earth. Any stillness here can only be a pseudo-stillness, so to speak; it is a condition of temporality that, as *East Coker* puts it, "We must be still and still moving" (*CPP* 183): attending indeed to the stillness of the spirit, but needing to constantly refine and strengthen our search for it, recognising that any stopping on the journey could only be complacency and what *Burnt Norton* calls "fixity" (*CPP* 173). The same applies to the poem as a creation of time, and in essays written around the period of *Four Quartets*, principally "What is a Classic?" (1944), Eliot recognises the need for art to aspire to the finality and the various perfection of what he calls the "classic" whilst recognising that any such achievement could only mean, given a temporality where change cannot be arrested, the petrifaction and exhaustion of the language. He points to Virgil's *Aeneid* as a case where "the classic" cast just such an impoverishing shadow over future Latin writers and the language they used. The mobility of language might be a frustration, but it is inevitable, and Eliot accepts that even language's "deterioration" must be "accepted by the poet and made the best of" (*OPP* 37). If words will never lie "still," that mobility can yet be formally ordered as the poetic "dance." And it may be that linguistic change on some occasions yields a bonus: the dismissal of "this twittering world" (*CPP* 174) in *Burnt Norton* certainly takes on an added resonance in today's social networking context.

The boundaries of time and place that beset a given language in its attempts to communicate universality can also be transcended, to a degree, by stylistic choices. In the "Dante" essay of 1929, Eliot drew attention to the easier translatability of Dante into other languages compared with the difficulties of translating the complex opacities of Shakespeare's style. Dante, Eliot argues, uses a relatively simple diction – "The thought may be obscure, but the word is lucid, or rather translucent" (*CP3* 702) – while his Italian remains closely rooted in the international language of medieval Latin. *Four Quartets* too combines lines of linguistic (though not conceptual) simplicity – "All is always now," "In my beginning is my end" – with recurrent Latinate terms – "eructation," "inoperancy," "appetency," "haruspication," "conciliation," "communication" and many more – that gesture towards the common heritage of the classical European tradition, a deliberate counter-insistence to a European war that was for Eliot another civil war, given his repeated insistence on "The Unity of European Culture," the title of a talk he published in 1946. Eliot had long insisted on the poet's necessary piety towards "the mind of Europe" (*CP2* 107), but whereas his earlier poetry had acknowledged through quotation a range of European writers and languages, *Four Quartets* does not work in this way. There is one German word in *Burnt Norton,* and one French and Italian phrase in *East Coker* and *The Dry Salvages* respectively, before we return "home" to England in the final Quartet, or rather to "England and nowhere" (*CPP* 192), which further emphasises the nation's provisional status.

We are thus reminded that *Four Quartets*, for all its insistence on the unsatisfactory nature of secular existence, on the unreality and ridiculousness of life in time, by no means washes its hands of the political and historical situation. The very act of writing the poem implies a commitment of sorts to the temporal even if Eliot's fundamental allegiance lay elsewhere, and, returning to points made at the start of this essay, all sorts of debates are being conducted within *Four Quartets* which connect with the public intervention amply evidenced in Eliot's prose writings of the time. Eliot did indeed remark that "the last three of my quartets are primarily patriotic poems," but his "patriotism" lies precisely in challenging a narrow jingoism held by others and reminding readers of what the European nations share together.[6] Likewise, the anti-urbanism of *Four Quartets*, the depiction indebted to canto V of Dante's *Inferno* of the "unhealthy souls ... Driven on the wind that sweeps the gloomy hills of London" (*CPP* 174), can be linked with Eliot's desires (and those of many others) at this time for rural and agricultural renewal, as formulated in his *The Idea of a Christian Society* of 1939 and elsewhere. This social thinking is present in *East Coker* in its contrasting the urban crowd of *Burnt Norton* with the erstwhile rustic community and their "country mirth." Here we have a group linked to the organic cycle, fertile in death as in life, "long since under earth / Nourishing the corn" (*CPP* 178). At the same time, however, the limitations of such a way of life if divorced from Christian culture are clearly apparent in the *Quartets* as a reproof to what Eliot saw as contemporary pagan philosophies – the "blood and soil" ideology of Nazism, the "nature-worship" of many back-to-the-land proponents in this country.[7]

Four Quartets is always concerned, in short, to keep "nature" in its subordinate place. In *The Idea of a Christian Society* Eliot argues that "a wrong attitude towards nature implies, somewhere, a wrong attitude towards God" (*ICS* 62), and such an attitude can be as much over-valuing nature as exploiting and desecrating it "for commercial profit" (the discussion here about the relation between "religious fear" and "religious hope" provides an invaluable commentary on *The Dry Salvages* in particular). Thus the actual country settings of *Four Quartets* – the dry concrete garden of *Burnt Norton*, the sultry light of *East Coker*, the path "behind the pig-sty to the dull façade" (*CPP* 191) of the church in *Little Gidding* – allow for no scenic indulgence on the part of the reader – "Wordsworthian" the poem is not. The truly "significant soil" is delayed till the churchyard reference in the final line of *The Dry Salvages*, and this has to be distinguished from the mere "Dung and death" (*CPP* 178) of the Somerset village labourers, however much this is in turn preferable to the insentient life of the city dwellers of *Burnt Norton*. Here the *Quartets* sequentially develops an incremental set of meanings, leading to the truly authentic scene of "fertility" at the opening of *Little Gidding* – the "crowning" Quartet – with the apprehension of the Nativity in the very dead of winter, when there is "no earth smell / Or smell of living thing" (*CPP* 191). It is important, of course, for a nation, especially in wartime, to produce and nourish its corn, but ultimately, as *East Coker* stresses, our "only food" is "the bloody flesh," and "The dripping blood our only drink" (*CPP* 182).

As John Xiros Cooper argues, it is unlikely that the readers of the thousands of copies of the poem that were printed both singly and as a foursome in the early 1940s were especially interested in following the poet on his path "towards God."[8] Readers might rather take from the poem a more generalised stoicism – "all shall be well and / All manner of thing shall be well" (*CPP* 198) – or embrace the patriotic uplift that surges through lines like "History is now and England" (*CPP* 197), even though the poem severely qualifies any such positions. But beyond this Cooper persuasively argues that the poem's elite or "mandarin" readership found comfort and consolation in *Four Quartets* in the aesthetic and psychological "refuge" it offered from a world in ruins, and with it the ruins of the political activism many writers in the 1930s had embraced. The poem encourages an inwardness and self-communing perfectly suited to the recoil from social and political engagement we see among many intellectuals in the more cautious Cold War climate of the late 1940s and 1950s, according to Cooper, becoming indeed a kind of foundational document of post-war quietism at a time when Eliot's reputation as the leading poet and critic of his age was at its peak. "In these sheepish reversals, a whole generation learned how to read *Four Quartets*," says Cooper, and no doubt the poem will continue to minister to readers "in need of escape and consolation."[9] But if, thanks to Cooper and others, we now have a much fuller understanding of how to historicise Eliot's own encounter with history, the religious thinking of the poem remains the key element in that encounter, and cannot be marginalised or dismissed.

NOTES

1 Jed Esty, *A Shrinking Island: Modernism and National Culture in England* (Princeton: Princeton University Press, 2004), p. 140.
2 See Eliot's interview with John Lehmann for the *New York Times Book Review* (29 November 1953), reprinted in Bernard Bergonzi (ed.), *T. S. Eliot: "Four Quartets": A Casebook* (Basingstoke: Macmillan, 1969), p. 23.
3 See Eliot's discussion of Tennyson's *In Memoriam* as "not religious because of the quality of its faith, but because of the quality of its doubt" (*SE* 336).
4 On this subject see Paul Foster, *The Golden Lotus: Buddhist Influence in T. S. Eliot's "Four Quartets"* (Sussex: The Book Guild, 1998) and Cleo McNelly Kearns, *T. S. Eliot and Indic Traditions: a Study in Poetry and Belief* (Cambridge, Cambridge University Press, 1987).
5 "The Dark Night," in St John of the Cross, *Selected Writings*, ed. Kieran Kavanaugh (New York: Paulist Press, 1987), pp. 155–209.
6 Eliot's (cancelled) remark is in the first draft of his essay "The Three Voices of Poetry"; quoted in A. D. Moody, *Thomas Stearns Eliot: Poet* (Cambridge: Cambridge University Press, 1979), p. 203.
7 For more on Eliot's response to this aspect of Nazism, see chapter 1 of Steve Ellis, *British Writers and the Approach of World War II* (Cambridge: Cambridge University Press, 2014).
8 John Xiros Cooper, *T. S. Eliot and the Ideology of "Four Quartets"* (Cambridge: Cambridge University Press, 1995), p. 136.
9 Ibid., pp. 141, 167.

8

ANTHONY CUDA

"A Precise Way of Thinking and Feeling": Eliot and Verse Drama

Though his fame rests upon his poetry, T. S. Eliot spent a significant portion of his career writing about drama and composing plays. Before he was the author of *The Waste Land* or the editor of the *Criterion*, before he converted to Anglicanism or won the Nobel Prize for literature, Eliot was a critic and theorist of the stage, profoundly concerned with the state of contemporary theatre and determined to change its direction. His productions eventually drew the best actors from Hollywood and London and won him great commercial success. This chapter seeks to emphasize Eliot's lifelong commitment to the theatre and especially to plays composed in verse rather than in prose. He regarded drama as a genre of poetry, like lyric or epic, rather than as a distinct form. And he believed, like many of his contemporaries, that naturalistic prose plays had severely limited its range and expressiveness. "The prose play," he frequently insists, offers "only a part of what the theatre can give," adding that "the verse play is capable of something much more intense and exciting."[1]

Eliot found examples of that intensity and excitement in ancient Greek and Renaissance English sources: Aeschylus and Sophocles, Marlowe and Jonson. But the form also flourished in the nineteenth century, as he recognized: "Nearly all the greater poets of the last century," he admits, "tried their hands at verse plays" (*OPP* 27). Though frequently critical toward them in his essays, Eliot was influenced by the verse plays of Byron, Shelley, Browning, and Tennyson. He was drawn to the tragedies of Swinburne, especially *Atalanta in Calydon* (1865); and he admired Rostand's *Cyrano de Bergerac* (1897) and Hardy's *The Dynasts* (1904–8). Of course he found a stalwart ally in W. B. Yeats, whose ritualistic, abstract play *At the Hawk's Well* (1916) he attended when it opened. And he promoted the theatrical experiments of W. H. Auden, whose *Paid on Both Sides: A Charade* (1930) first appeared in the *Criterion* and whose collaborations with Christopher Isherwood were indebted to Eliot's own work, especially to the many essays and reviews in which he had begun to elaborate his theories of dramaturgy.

Theories of Verse Drama

Eliot began to write extensively about drama early in the 1920s, and he pursued the topic avidly in essay after essay from this period. A survey of his voluminous prose during these years and shortly afterward reveals the emergence of three major ideas that became, over time, permanent aspects of his writing about stagecraft and of the principles underwriting his own verse plays. First, like many modernist playwrights, Eliot argues that the dominance of realistic plays in prose since the mid-nineteenth century had corrupted drama by leading it away from artifice and toward mimesis. Drama needs a new set of formal conventions, he asserts: "A dramatic poet needs to have some *kind* of dramatic form given to him as the condition of his time, a form … which permits an artist to fashion it into a work of art" (*CP2* 241). A dramatic form includes rhythm and various stage conventions, but it also involves widely accepted thematic commonplaces that are "capable of indefinite refinement" (*CP2* 242) by the artist, such as the irreversibility of "fate" in Greek drama, or the insistence on death and physical decay on the Elizabethan stage. A form offers "a precise way of thinking and feeling" (*CP2* 280) and thus frees the playwright to experiment elsewhere.

Eliot's conviction about the need for dramatic form arises in part from a theory that had gained acceptance in his day, namely that drama originated as ritual in connection with primitive fertility cults. From his study of cultural anthropology at Harvard, and especially of the Cambridge Ritualists, Eliot drew the assumption that drama bears a fundamental relationship to the basic human needs and desires that ritual satisfies, and it loses power as it ignores this relationship and simply imitates life: "For the stage – not only in its remote origins, but always – is a ritual, and the failure of the contemporary stage to satisfy the craving for ritual is one of the reasons why it is not a living art" (*CP2* 435). The further drama drifts away from ritual and liturgy, the more realistic it becomes, and the less effectively it engages its audience. As Eliot puts it 1926: "Dramatic form may occur at various points along a line, the termini of which are liturgy and realism; at one extreme the arrow-dance of the Todas and at the other Sir Arthur Pinero" (*CP2* 773). It is essential to recognize the persistence and pervasiveness of these anthropological interests in the ritual origins of literary forms: by way of Frazer and Weston, they influenced the substructure of *The Waste Land*, and by way of Cambridge Ritualists like F. M. Cornford, they influenced nearly every play that Eliot composed.

Another central element of Eliot's theatrical writing is his conviction that verse drama could appeal to a wide audience and exert as invigorating an effect as more "popular" entertainment. Why should revivals of old-verse plays suggest "virtue, vegetarianism, and a headache," he asks, whereas the best performances of the ballet or the music hall have an "intense" and "immediate" effect on their audiences? (*CP2* 173) The new dramatic form must find ways to attract contemporary audiences, and one of Eliot's ideal models for this prospect was the music hall, a variety entertainment program featuring live singing and performances by musicians and comedians. The music hall is often a point of reference in his critical prose, but especially so in the series of "London Letters" that he wrote for the *Dial* in 1921 and 1922, in which he repeatedly aligns the virtues of the theatre with those of the music hall. He adored the grotesque and often outrageous comedy of music hall performers, and in the enjoyment of their audiences he recognized a power and vitality missing from contemporary theatre.

One final topic that frequently absorbed Eliot's attention is the theory of dramatic "planes" or levels of meaning, what he calls "a kind of doubleness in the action, as if it took place on two planes at once" (*SE* 229). He suggests that poetic drama, because of its rhythmic aspects, is particularly suited to operating on two planes: the superficial one involving character and plot, and a deeper, more universal one pertaining to spiritual realities and often associated with the poet's own perspective. His theory of dramatic levels develops somewhat later than the others; he formulates it most fully in his essay "John Marston" (1934), suggesting that verse drama should possess an "under-pattern, less manifest than the theatrical one," "a pattern behind the pattern," that hints at "some other plane of reality … some world that we cannot perceive" (*SE* 229, 232). In one sense, this is a nuanced version of the "mythical method"; nearly every one of Eliot's verse plays takes its underlying model from ancient Greek drama. But the theory of dramatic levels affects the action of the play still more directly. Discussing George Chapman, he explains: "Here and there the actors in his drama appear as if following another train of thought … and acting out another scene than that visible upon the stage" (*CP2* 695). This "double pattern" can be accomplished via symbols and tone, but Eliot frequently argues that it depends primarily upon rhythm. Rhythm accelerates "the pulse of our emotion," he writes in "Poetry and Drama" (1951), until "we are lifted for a moment beyond character" (*OPP* 81).

While he was formulating these ideas, Eliot was immersing himself in the world of independent and experimental theatre in London. He joined the board of the independent theatre group, The Phoenix Society, and publicly defended its productions of Elizabethan and Restoration plays against attacks by champions of realism such as William Archer. He inveighed against the distorting influence of the popular translations of Greek plays by Gilbert Murray. He lectured to theatre societies and wrote front-page essays in the *TLS* about dramatic blank verse. He reviewed and supported Gordon Craig's radical theories about puppetry in the theatre; he sought the counsel of Alfred Kreymborg, whom he asked about building his own marionettes. He regularly attended the stunningly experimental productions of the *Ballets Russes*, cultivating relationships with director Sergei Diaghilev and applauding dancer Leonide Massine as a model of theatrical performance. This powerful fusion of avant-garde theatre and traditional stage convention soon prompted Eliot to attempt, after years of preparation, his own first verse drama.

Sweeney Agonistes

Eliot began thinking about his first play as early as 1920. Fragments of it appeared in the *Criterion* six years later, but *Sweeney Agonistes: Fragments of an Aristophanic Melodrama* was not performed until 1933 at Vassar College in New York and then in 1934 in London. The unusually long gestation meant that it became a crucible for Eliot's nascent dramatic ideas and a powerful creative catalyst during the formative years of his thinking about the stage. The first part features two women, Doris and Dusty, who banter, draw tarot cards, and entertain several boorish male guests. Sweeney enters later in the second part (during the same party); he engages Doris in a quick-witted exchange about missionaries and cannibalism and then captivates the guests with the macabre, mystery-novel tale of a murderer (who is perhaps Sweeney himself) who kept his victim's corpse hidden in a bath of Lysol. A chorus concludes by warning about the coming of the menacing "hoo-ha's," Eliot's darkly comic version of the Greek Furies. The play's humour is ferociously moral, aimed at portraying the protagonist's nightmarish vision of irrevocable guilt and violent purgation.

The verse of *Sweeney Agonistes* is clipped and rhythmic, blending jazz rhythms, minstrel show songs, and "backchat" to keep the surface buzzing with chatter, sexual innuendo, and playfulness while the play's darker elements – including cannibalism, sacrifice, and murder – begin to emerge. In terms of prosody, the hemistich lines and alternations combine the influence of Seneca's Latin verse and contemporary jazz syncopation. Eliot told his American director, Hallie Flanagan, that he based the play heavily upon the theories that F. M. Cornford sets out in *The Origin of Attic Comedy* to explain the origins of Aristophanic drama in the rituals of primitive fertility cults. Cornford identifies specific plot-formulae, including series of fixed incidents such as entrances and exits, all deriving from ceremonies aimed at ensuring the fertility of the land; the original plan for *Sweeney Agonistes* adopted these categories in detail. Madame Sosostris's tarot cards reappear with a tone that, just as in *The Waste Land*, is parodic yet gravely serious:

DORIS: What comes next. It's the six.
DUSTY: 'A quarrel. An estrangement. Separation of friends'.
DORIS: Here's the two of spades.
DUSTY: The *two of spades*!
THAT'S THE COFFIN!!
DORIS: THAT'S THE COFFIN?
Oh good heavens what'll I do?
Just before a party too! (*CPP* 117)

Such casual fortune telling is a parody of the formalized, predictive rituals of fertility cults, and instead of fecundity and rebirth, these cards foretell degeneration and death. Likewise the Lysol bath is a hideously literal parody of baptismal rites.

Most of the supporting characters in *Sweeney Agonistes* are deliberately flat and interchangeable, modelled on the "polished veneer" of Ben Jonson's comedies (*CP2* 151). To intensify this effect, Eliot envisioned them in masks, speaking with minimal inflection and accompanied by light drum taps. Flanagan describes her innovative staging of the play in *Dynamo* (1942); an account of Rupert Doone's London version appears in Michael Sidnell's *Dances of Death: The Group Theatre of London in the Thirties* (1984). The Group Theatre's performance in particular boosted Eliot's standing as a dramatist, earning him an enthusiastic response from Bertolt Brecht and a compelling BBC broadcast review by Desmond MacCarthy. In the text, Sweeney himself is dimensional and complex, markedly different from his appearances in earlier poems like "Sweeney Erect" and "Sweeney Among the Nightingales."[2] Like Orestes, who appears in the play's first epigraph, he is haunted; and like Prufrock and Gerontion, he seems to penetrate to a deeper, more tragic vision of reality than the social farce in which he nonetheless participates. The contrast between him and the others emphasizes his unique moral burden, which arises from a frequent scenario in Eliot's work: the belated recognition of a violent, irreversible crime and the guilt that results. Though it is universalized by Sweeney's tone and sensationalized by the mystery-novel-like treatment, this Dostoevskian moral ordeal was sharply personal for Eliot; it came to bear a dark kinship to his deteriorating marriage, and it persisted in various forms, as Lyndall Gordon and others have demonstrated, for the much of his career.

The Rock and *Murder in the Cathedral*

Eliot's next two stage productions were undertaken in explicitly religious contexts and for audiences very different from either *Sweeney Agonistes* or the later plays. In this regard, his beginnings in the theatre corroborated his early dramatic theories: both plays were undertaken in liturgical contexts and both benefited from a framework of predictable audience expectations. *The Rock: A Pageant Play* (premiere 1934) was part of a massive project to fund the construction of forty-five new churches in the Anglican diocese of London. The director E. Martin Browne had been commissioned to stage the pageant and he asked Eliot to write the words for his scenario and provide the choral segments that would unify the sprawling production, which featured some 330 characters played by amateur actors in more than 20 different scenes, each presented as a moment in the construction of the historical church. Eliot's work with Browne on this project proved so successful that they collaborated on every play that he wrote thereafter.

The most significant and underestimated aspect of Eliot's involvement with *The Rock* is the fact it was modelled on popular Cochran-like revue forms, which meant that he could finally put his love for the music hall "turn" to use in the theatre, where he had long envisioned it. He felt most comfortable, though, composing for the chorus, which laments and rebukes modern secular society in Biblical and prophetic tones. Visually, Eliot conceived of the chorus as coldly impersonal and abstract, dressed in "half-masks and stiff robes which allied them to the rock-foundation on which the church was being built."[3] These haunting, inhuman figures are surprising echoes of the masked actors and the hoo-ha's in *Sweeney Agonistes*, and they reappear in unexpected disguises – as Tempters, Eumenides, and even the "guardians" – in several subsequent plays. The chorus served Eliot in multiple ways: it gave him a way to preserve a direct link to his Greek models; it justified lyric speech and was deliberately conventional, unrealistic; and it appealed to admirers of his poetry. One reviewer called it "the most vital part of the performance" (Brooker 304). As Malamud writes, the coordination of these elements with the massive cast and scene changes, while resulting in "a haphazard range of dramaturgy running from the ridiculous to the sublime," nonetheless gave Eliot a "basic background, an apprenticeship in conventional theatrical matters."[4]

In the audience for *The Rock* was the Bishop of Chichester, George Bell, who asked Eliot to collaborate again with Browne on an original work for the Canterbury Festival. The result was *Murder in the Cathedral* (premiere 1935), a play about the assassination of twelfth-century archbishop Thomas Becket by the knights of King Henry II. In the first part, Thomas returns from abroad to confront the king's authority, and he is visited by four Tempters who test his determination and purpose. After the interlude – an abstract, seemingly impersonal prose sermon delivered by Becket on the Christmas morning of 1170 – the second part portrays the archbishop's assassination at the hands of the king's knights, who conclude the play by pleading the rectitude of their actions before the audience.

Once again, Eliot implemented a chorus to heighten the dramatic artifice and unrealistic elements of the play. Now, however, he had gained a clearer sense of its function as intermediary between the characters and the audience: the chorus "intensifies the action by projecting its emotional consequences, so that we as the audience see it doubly, by seeing its effect on other people."[5] The chorus of Canterbury women adopt a tone of dread and anxiety familiar to readers of *The Waste Land* and "The Hollow Men":

> Now I fear disturbance of the quiet seasons:
> Winter shall come bringing death from the sea,
> Ruinous spring shall beat at our doors,
> Root and shoot shall eat our eyes and our ears,
> Disastrous summer burn up the beds of our streams (*CPP* 240)

Unlike the persistent despair of those earlier poems, however, the women of Canterbury experience dramatic changes and moral realizations as the play progresses. Becket himself re-enacts the exilic condition of Eliot's recent poetry, retracing, as Hugh Kenner observes, "in specific terms the zone traversed by *Ash-Wednesday*."[6] Both the poem and the play focus upon the solitary man, his spiritual election, and his struggle to find a point of certainty amid the chaos of external demands and inward turmoil. The speaker of *Ash-Wednesday* strives for stillness beyond the "unstilled world"; later, in *Burnt Norton* (1936), Eliot refines the same theme, imagining "the still point of the turning world" (*CPP* 96, 175). Some of Becket's most memorable lines incorporate this trope: "Only / The fool, fixed in his folly, may think / He can turn the wheel on which he turns" (*CPP* 247). But even more compelling in terms of Eliot's maturation as a dramatist is how he stages the theatrical equivalent of the "still point," when the knights approach Thomas and, as Carol Smith describes, "circle around him with outstretched swords, visually forming for the audience a wheel with Thomas as the still point."[7]

Readers are quick to assume that Eliot's insights into Becket's inward struggle were solely the result of his own religious conversion in 1927. But the personal upheavals that he was experiencing at the time seem to have been equally influential in this regard. He was deeply conflicted about separating from Vivien and reuniting with Emily Hale during the years before the play premiered; Becket's vicious self-doubts and his convictions about the irrevocability of the past are charged with Eliot's personal struggles as well as his spiritual meditations. One such passage that was cut from *Murder in the Cathedral* became the first lines of his next poem, *Burnt Norton*, which reflects upon the choice between shared intimacy and an ascetic, solitary life. Ultimately, though, the speaker of *Burnt Norton* fails to resolve the conflict meaningfully and a year later Eliot returned to the stage to envision an alternate path.

The Family Reunion

To many audiences and reviewers, Eliot's next work seemed to take a step backward. A realistic drawing-room play set in a modern-day English country home, *The Family Reunion* clings "to naturalism of surface" (Brooker 379) as one reviewer put it. Even Browne admits to having responded to a first reading with dubious silence.[8] Nearly two decades earlier, Eliot had complained of "the impotence of contemporary drama" and the lack of audience; now he came to recognize that there was "less resistance to verse as a dramatic medium than was formerly supposed" and that the public for verse plays "could be enlarged almost indefinitely" given the right circumstances.[9] A drawing-room play, he now suspected – realistic but incorporating elements of ritual and stylized convention – might succeed at creating those circumstances.

In the play, Harry, Lord Monchensey returns to his family's ancestral home at Wishwood, where he confesses his fear that he has killed his wife (by pushing her overboard at sea) and claims that the Furies are hunting him. The play describes his attempt to purge himself of the guilt associated with his wife, whom he did not actually murder, and ultimately of a familial curse. It also describes the renewal and interruption of his intimacy with Mary, whose comfort he foreswears for the solitary path of spiritual purgation. Eliot's first non-commissioned, commercial production, *The Family Reunion* essentially rewrites *Sweeney Agonistes* in a language accessible to a broader audience and without the fragmentation, the influence of the music hall, or jazz syncopation. Like *Sweeney Agonistes*, it is based on Aeschylus's *Oresteia*, with a modernized set of Eumenides (dressed in suits and ties in one production) replacing the comical hoo-ha's. Harry's apparently drowned wife supplants the Lysol-bath corpse, both of which are cast in terms that Eliot also used to describe the cycles of estrangement and emotional detachment that characterized his own marriage. "I have deliberately killed my senses," Eliot confided to John Middleton Murry in 1925, "in order to endure, in order not to feel – *but it has killed* V[ivien]" (*L2* 627). *The Family Reunion* is autobiographical in other ways, with Harry's return to Wishwood doubling for Eliot's own return to New England after decades away. "Harry's ghosts are Eliot's," Malamud suggests.[10]

The surface realism is frequently disrupted by the chorus, a fluid group composed of the play's minor characters who slip in and out of their individual and communal roles. This choral experiment – which Gareth Lloyd Evans calls "choric ritualism" – extends to the major characters as well, who often drift from dialogue into brief, lyrical interludes or duets.[11] The realism is also complicated by Eliot's decision to allow his protagonists to dimly recognize when they have been speaking "beyond character." They emerge from enunciating the stylized lyric passages as if from a trance:

MARY: And what of the terrified spirit
Compelled to be reborn
To rise toward the violent sun
Wet wings into the rain cloud
Harefoot over the moon?

HARRY: What have we been saying? I think I was saying
That it seemed as if I had always been here
And you were someone who had come from a long distance.
(*CPP* 310)

Such moments are subtly meta-theatrical, with characters themselves vaguely calling attention to the play's conventions. This self-consciousness allows them brief access to a significance deeper than they themselves can express, but it also involves a deliberate self-dramatization that Eliot believed was powerfully true to life, though not realistic. "In plays of realism," he writes, "we often find parts which are never allowed to be consciously dramatic, for fear, perhaps, of their appearing less real. But ... in many of those situations in actual life which we enjoy consciously and keenly, we are at times aware of ourselves in this way" (*CP2* 90).

In the years following *The Family Reunion*, Eliot turned his attention back to lyric poetry and the series that would become *Four Quartets*. With remarkable continuity, *East Coker* picks up where the play leaves off, reformulating Harry's path of pilgrimage and purgation: "O dark dark dark. They all go into the dark, / ... / In order to possess what you do not possess / You must go by the way of dispossession" (*CPP* 180, 181). Despite his break from playwriting while he was composing *Four Quartets*, Eliot maintained close contact with Browne, who undertook a very important revival of *The Family Reunion* late in 1946. With the war over and the West End enjoying a popular resurgence, the new production was lauded by critics who had formerly professed uncertainty. "After a second European war, and much beside," one reviewer wrote, "I have seen the play again. This time there was no shadow of doubt; it is incomparably the best modern play now running in London."[12] Eliot was uncertain about his accomplishment in *The Family Reunion*, but the widespread success of the 1946 revival bolstered his confidence; just over a year later, he sent Browne the first drafts of his next play.

The Cocktail Party: A Comedy

In nearly all respects, *The Cocktail Party* (premiere 1949) represents an extension and enlargement of Eliot's theatrical achievements; critics and scholars have written about it more than any of his other productions, and it won him the greatest commercial success. It is also the topic of the first book-length study of a play by Eliot, Virginia Phelan's *Two Ways of Life and Death: "Alcestis" and "The Cocktail Party"* (1990). The play opened at the Edinburgh Festival and had great success thereafter in New York and the West End, thanks in part to the newfound assistance of the savvy theatre manager and producer Henry Sherek, whose efforts at casting and publicity were crucial in the international fame that Eliot enjoyed as a playwright during these later years.[13]

Unlike the focus of his previous plays on the solitary struggles of a central character, *The Cocktail Party* features a complex intersection of storylines, including the separation and reunion of the long-married Edward and Lavinia Chamberlayne, the frustrated love and adultery of Peter Quilpe and Celia Coplestone, and the covert ministrations of the three characters identified as spiritual "Guardians," including the charismatic psychologist and spiritual doctor figure, Sir Henry Harcourt-Reilly. Through a series of contrived encounters, the Guardians help Edward abandon his affair with Celia and reunite with his wife, whom he discovers has had an affair with Peter. The Guardians lead Peter away from his unrequited love for Celia, and Celia away from her tortured solitude, toward a mission of spiritual service and, ultimately, to a gruesome martyrdom.

This complex morality tale is also a narrative brimming with comedy and wit. In the years since his previous play, Eliot had honed his sense of pacing and stagecraft, so that the characters' lucid, colloquial lines are intricately coordinated with their rapid entrances and exits, their quick and comic interruptions and interjections; there are telephones ringing, eggs burning on the stove, doorbells sounding, and characters coming on and off stage as if through a revolving door. One actress remarked upon the sophisticated integration of verse and action that Eliot's script required, recalling that "even an ordinary piece of stage-business such as the opening of a door is taken into account in the writing and covered by words between beats": "There is never any question of any of us easing up on the mental concentration demanded by our parts."[14] Eliot's deepening grasp of staging is matched by his increased use of meta-theatrical elements: the technical agility of the script is mirrored in the way the Guardians meticulously arrange the arrivals, departures, and realizations of their unknowing charges. He had once claimed that a play, "like a religious service, should be a stimulant to make life more tolerable and augment our ability to live" (*CP2* 774). And the tremendous character of Harcourt-Reilly – part psychologist, part priest, part music-hall comedian – embodies precisely this ritualistic, therapeutic value of the theatre. As in his previous plays, there are deeply personal elements submerged beneath the literary models. Eliot based his plot on *Alcestis* by Euripides, a play that involves a murdered and resurrected wife; two years before *The Cocktail Party* premiered, his estranged wife, Vivien, had died in the sanatorium where she had been kept for nearly a decade.

In an address delivered in the year *The Cocktail Party* opened, Eliot professed his desire to abandon verbal archaisms and unrealistic conventions, to write a play in verse dealing solely with "a plot of contemporary people, such as the men and women we know."[15] On the one hand, this is a drastic reversal of his earlier proposal for playwrights to "adopt a literal untruth, a thorough-going convention" (*CP2* 435). On the other hand, it represents Eliot's desire to distinguish more sharply between the planes or levels of the play: "What I want is something superficially at least purely realistic," he clarified to Browne.[16] The "inner" or invisible drama involves dispossession, humiliation, and renewal as a process of spiritual growth, but the superficies must remain entirely secular, comical, and mundane. This widening divergence reveals a paradox at the heart of Eliot's technique that becomes even clearer in his final two plays, namely the movement of his realism toward the unreality of the spiritual fable.

The Confidential Clerk and *The Elder Statesman*

Eliot's last plays have received less critical attention for a number of reasons, including the simple fact that they were written after he oversaw the collected edition of his poems and plays in 1952. Some reviewers found in them "consummate clarity" of language and purpose; others sensed "snobbery," "melodrama," and "sermonising."[17] Most agree that the author of *The Waste Land* had simplified his vision, but not about whether this simplification resulted in lucidity and "melancholy beauty" or "simplicity's half-wit brother, banality."[18]

The Confidential Clerk (premiere 1953) is a comedy of manners with an improbable case of mistaken parentage at its centre. Questions abound: Is the protagonist, Colby Simpkins, the illegitimate son of successful financier

Sir Claude Mulhammer? Or is he actually the son of Sir Claude's wife by a previous lover? These and similarly puzzling and farcical plot tangles are resolved only by the unlikely arrival in Act III of Mrs. Guzzard, the Dickensian nurse who raised Colby and was entrusted with the illegitimate children of both Sir Claude and his present wife. Even through such a maze of surface twists and relations one can discern Eliot's characteristic focus on breaking relationships apart and then reuniting them in more meaningful ways. Unlike the great reconciliations of traditional comedy, in which identities are disclosed and every disappointed lover finds a partner, the revelations that conclude *The Confidential Clerk* deliberately leave the protagonist alone, both anxious and free to determine his own identity. The play presents no course of harrowing spiritual challenge or purgation; its interwoven plot-lines essentially retrace Eliot's long-standing debates with himself about personality and change, a theme prominent in *The Dry Salvages* ("You are not the same people who left that station / Or who will arrive at any terminus" [*CPP* 188]) and in *The Cocktail Party*, "we die to each other daily" (*CPP* 384). Sir Claude, however, articulates the problem in much simpler terms:

> There's always something one's ignorant of
> About anyone, however well one knows them;
> And that may be something of the greatest importance.
> It's when you're sure you understand a person
> That you're liable to make the worst mistake about him.
>
> (*CPP* 449–50)

The limpid verse is shaped by Eliot's insistence on realism and colloquial speech; it results in a diction as realistic as the plot. Raymond Williams calls it "mannered slackness," a surrender to "the inertia of a convention he had begun by attacking."[19] But other scholars, including Helen Gardner and Denis Donoghue, believe that the simplification lends the play a vigour and unity greater than his previous productions. Donoghue even proposes that Eliot's mature plays attain "a greater range of expressiveness, greater precision" and "finer adjustment of verbal weight" than in any of his previous work.[20]

Lord Claverton is the protagonist of Eliot's final play, *The Elder Statesman* (premiere 1958), which focuses on an aging man's relationships with his two grown children, and on his ultimately successful attempt to repent of his wrongdoings, escape the demons of his past, and reconcile himself to death. *The Elder Statesman* takes *Oedipus at Colonus* as its model, integrating the mysticism and pessimism of Sophocles' late masterpiece with the sense of resolution and surrender that Eliot had long admired in Shakespeare's *The Tempest*. Like so many of Eliot's earlier protagonists, Claverton is haunted by ghosts from his past. In fact, he is a version of the protagonist in *The Family Reunion*; while working on the earlier play, Eliot told Browne that "Harry's career needs to be completed" by a play like *Oedipus at Colonus*.[21] But this time, the ghosts visit him in person, with secrets about his mistakes and misdeeds rather than vague yet heinous crimes. Claverton finally recognizes them for what they are:

> They've always been with me
> Though it was not till lately that I found the living persons
> Whose ghosts tormented me, to be only human beings,
> Malicious, petty, and I see myself emerging
> From my spectral existence into something like reality. (*CPP* 569)

Claverton's recognition, in fact, is analogous to Eliot's own progressive demystification of on-stage ghosts, his determination to eliminate the hoo-ha's, Tempters, and Eumenides of his early plays and maintain fidelity to a naturalistic surface; he is Eliot's Prospero. A corollary to the concern with shifting identities in the previous play is Eliot's long-standing preoccupation with false-masks and social postures, with how we "prepare a face to meet the faces that you meet" (*CPP* 14). The inability to liberate themselves from such inauthentic social masks had always plunged Eliot's speakers and protagonists into inner turmoil. Claverton seems to risk a similar fate: "There'll always be some sort of part for you," one of his persecutors says, "Right to the end. You'll still be playing a part / In your obituary" (*CPP* 552). *The Elder Statesman*, however, deals with them with surprising sobriety and straightforwardness, as Claverton confronts his enemies, reveals his secrets, and faces the liberating nothingness beneath the masks. "I've been freed from the self that pretends to be someone," he declares just before his death, "And in becoming no one, I begin to live" (*CPP* 582). As critics have shown, Claverton's encounter recapitulates the struggles of not only Sweeney but Prufrock and Gerontion; the "haunting loss and limitation" that he accepts is a theme that Eliot confronted for the entirety of his career.[22]

Eliot's last plays were controversial, but for reasons far different from those that ignited such debate over his early work. The avant-garde experiments in form and fragmentation that made *The Waste Land* so revolutionary did, in fact, inform the composition of *Sweeney Agonistes*, but they did not extend to his mature writing for the stage. As one scholar puts it, "On a scale of bangs and whimpers, T. S. Eliot's late plays have been regarded as inclining toward the less explosive end."[23] While playwrights like Brecht, Artaud, and Beckett were relentlessly challenging theatrical conventions and staging, Eliot was finding increasingly subtle ways to integrate verse into dramatic action and to use naturalistic conventions to arrive at deeply anti-naturalistic conclusions about human nature, spirituality, and the inner life.[24] The fascinating paradox that arises from this process is nowhere more evident than in these final works. The more realistic Eliot attempts to make his plays – the more he rejects ritual, artifice, and abstraction – the less real, the more ghostly and insubstantial, they seem to become. More than one scholar has suggested that the plots of these late plays, in fact, resemble fables, elaborately decorated facades of actions and circumstances always on the verge of crumbling away to reveal the invisible, internal drama. Carol Smith finds Christian sub-narratives of renunciation and sacrifice always unfolding beneath the "dramatic fable" or "transparent mask" of the surface action.[25] Hugh Kenner suggests similarly that "the plot provides, almost playfully, external and stageable points of reference" for what he calls "the invisible drama of volition and vocation."[26] This perspective risks, however, underestimating Eliot's commitment to fully realized characters, what he refers to as "the Theatre of Character": "the essential poetic play," he writes, "should be made with human beings rather than with ideas."[27] More recent scholars – including Julia Daniel and Sarah Bey-Cheng – have returned our attention to the "surfaces" of the plays by examining their staging and meta-theatricality in great detail.[28] The paradoxical relationship between surface and depth is, of course, a theme that reaches back to Eliot's early verse and that spans his career in poetry, from Prufrock's masks and unutterable questions to the illegible stones and half-heard whispers of *Four Quartets*. Discerning the corresponding persistence of this and the other themes in his plays is a significant step toward recognizing the vital continuity of Eliot's poetry and his verse drama, and toward regarding them as the unfolding of an unpredictable and yet startlingly unified imaginative vision.

NOTES

1 "The Need for Poetic Drama," *Listener* 16 (25 November 1936): 994.

2 Christine Buttram offers a compelling explanation of the difference in "*Sweeney Agonistes:* A Sensational Snarl," in David Chinitz (ed.), *A Companion to T. S. Eliot* (Oxford: Wiley-Blackwell, 2009), pp. 179–90.

3 E. Martin Browne, *The Making of T. S. Eliot's Plays* (Cambridge: Cambridge University Press, 1969), p. 18.

4 Randy Malamud, *Where the Words Are Valid: T. S. Eliot's Communities of Drama* (Westport: Greenwood Press, 1994), p. 41.

5 "The Need for Poetic Drama," *Listener*, p. 995.

6 Hugh Kenner, *The Invisible Poet: T. S. Eliot* (New York: Harcourt Brace, 1959), p. 276.

7 Carol Smith, *T. S. Eliot's Dramatic Theory and Practice: From "Sweeney Agonistes" to "The Elder Statesman"* (Princeton: Princeton University Press, 1973), p. 100.

8 Browne, *The Making of T. S. Eliot's Plays*, p. 90.
9 "The Poetic Drama," p. 635; "The Future of Poetic Drama," *Drama (Journal of the British Drama League)* 17 (October 1938): 3.
10 Malamud, *Where the Words Are Valid*, p. 100.
11 Gareth Lloyd Evans, *The Language of Modern Drama* (London: Dent, 1977), p. 161; Eliot refers to them as "lyrical duets" (*OPP* 88).
12 Leila Davies, "Views and Reviews: *Family Reunion* Revisited," *New English Weekly* 30 (January 1947): 149.
13 For details, see Henry Sherek, *Not in Front of the Children* (London: Heinemann, 1959).
14 Margaret Leighton's interview with Eric Johns, "Creating a T. S. Eliot Role," *Theatre World* 46 (July 1950): 34.
15 *The Aims of Poetic Drama: The Presidential Address to the Poets' Theatre Guild* (London: Poets' Theatre Guild, 1949), p. 5.
16 Browne, *The Making of T. S. Eliot's Plays*, p. 232.
17 Philip Mairet, "The Confidential Clerk," *New Republic* 129 (21 September 1953): 17–18 (Brooker 553); Alan Brien, "Review," *Spectator* 201 (5 September 1958) 305–6; reprinted in Gareth and Barbara Lloyd Evans (eds), *Plays in Review 1956–1980: British Drama and the Critics* (New York: Methuen), p. 76.
18 Russell Kirk, "Two Plays of Resignation," *Month* 10 (October 1953), 223–5 (Brooker 554); Kenneth Tynan, "Review," *Observer* (31 August 1958) n.p.; reprinted in *Plays in Review*, p. 74.
19 Raymond Williams, *Drama from Ibsen to Brecht* (New York: Oxford University Press, 1969), pp. 196–7.
20 Dennis Donoghue, *The Third Voice: Modern British and American Verse Drama* (Princeton: Princeton University Press, 1959), p. 140.
21 Browne, *The Making of T. S. Eliot's Plays*, p. 107.
22 Michael Goldman offers an account of this theme in "Fear in the Way: The Design of Eliot's Drama" in A. Walton Litz (ed.), *Eliot in His Time* (Princeton: Princeton University Press, 1973), p. 161.
23 Michael Simpson, "Oedipus, Suez, and Hungary: T. S. Eliot's Tradition and *The Elder Statesman*," *Comparative Drama* 44–45 (Winter 2010/Spring 2011): 509.
24 Kirsten E. Shepherd-Barr, "Staging Modernism: A New Drama," in Peter Brooker et al. (eds.), *The Oxford Handbook of Modernisms* (Oxford: Oxford University Press), p. 124.
25 Smith, *T. S. Eliot's Dramatic Theory and Practice*, p. 215.
26 Kenner, *Invisible Poet*, p. 337.
27 "Comments on T. S. Eliot's New Play, *The Cocktail Party*," *World Review* (November 1949): 22.
28 Julia Daniel, "'Or it Might Be You': Audiences in and of T. S. Eliot's *Sweeney Agonistes*," *Modern Drama* 54 (Winter 2011): 435–54; Sarah Bey-Cheng, "Reality and Its Double in T. S. Eliot's *The Cocktail Party*," *Yeats Eliot Review* 22 (Winter 2005): 2–14. Others notable studies include James Matthew Wilson, "*The Rock* Against Shakespeare: Stoicism and Community in T. S. Eliot," *Religion and Literature* 43 (Autumn 2011): 49–81 and Patrick Query, *Ritual and the Idea of Europe in Interwar Writing* (Burlington: Ashgate, 2012).

9

HELEN THAVENTHIRAN

T. S. Eliot as Literary Critic

Who can doubt that Criticism, as well as Poetry, can have wings?

This epigraph is not by T. S. Eliot, nor is it something he could have written. Nor, for all the imaginative brilliance of his work in both forms, criticism and poetry, is it a phrase we would be likely to encounter about Eliot. It is instead the epigraph to J. E. Spingarn's *Creative Criticism*, which Eliot reviewed for the *TLS* in 1926.[1] Eliot, whose critical eye was often drawn to fragmentary forms such as epigraphs, quotes these words, enjoying the borrowed flight of whimsy, but then adds a stern coda. Spingarn's criticism, he writes, undeniably does have "wings"; alas, "like the fabulous bird of paradise, it has wings but no feet, and can never settle" (*CP2* 805). Literary criticism, for Eliot, might launch, then soar. Nonetheless, it should have firm foundations: tradition, order, precision, and criteria. In the year of this review, Eliot had just emerged from the pseudonym, Crites, champion of the ancients, under which he had written his regular editorial "Commentaries" for the *Criterion*.[2] Spingarn's fancifulness earns him a place in the ranks of the "Imperfect Critics" that Eliot began to assemble from his earliest ventures into literary judgment, granting this title to the second chapter of *The Sacred Wood: Essays on Poetry and Criticism* (1920). His first chapter in this book addresses the more singular (perhaps, by implication, near-mythical) case of "The Perfect Critic": the quest both to delineate and to become this figure gives form to Eliot's prose.

To begin with unattributed words that do not belong to their apparent subject – in fact, that illustrate something that their subject would not have said – was one of the most characteristic tactics of Eliot's own criticism. Lecturing on Matthew Arnold, for example, in the series *The Use of Poetry and The Use of Criticism* (1933), Eliot opens with a long quotation from an authoritative nineteenth-century voice, urging "a new discipline of suffering to fit men for the new conditions." Arnold's vision for civilization, the audience might presume, only to be told: "these words are *not only not* Arnold's, but we know at once that they could not have been written by him" (*CP4* 654, italics added). Eliot's epistemic confidence ("we know at once") hinges on a single word, "suffering." By remarking that Arnold could not have used this (he would have used "culture"), Eliot gives, with the immediacy of a practical discovery, an outline of what he finds typical of the preoccupations and voice of one of the critical predecessors who most concerned him. Arnold is presented with several degrees of indirection, yet Eliot leaves his audience with little doubt about the authority of his verdict or the precision of his critical ear.

Versions of this Eliotic swerve (for which the typical grammar reads, "not only not...") occur across his critical prose. It gives shape, for example, to Eliot's early essay, "Swinburne as Poet" (1920), in which a series of initially anonymous quotations, which the reader might reasonably expect to come from the critic's subject, Swinburne, are followed by explanatory tags such as this:

> This is Campion, and an example of the kind of music that is not to be found in Swinburne. [...]
>
> I quote from Shelley, because Shelley is supposed to be the master of Swinburne; and because his song, like that of Campion, has what Swinburne has not – a beauty of music and a beauty of content. (*CP2* 182–3)

The quotations are orchestrated so that the reader is encouraged to hear them as Swinburne's, only to discover afterwards that they are not: not only are the quotations not from Swinburne, they are examples of what Swinburne, according to Eliot, could not do. In such quiet but emphatic ways, Eliot's literary-critical style unsettles the arrangement of quotation alongside comment expected within discursive prose and the associated relations of authority and reticence between reader and critic. The veneer of Eliot's prose barely shows signs of disturbance, yet the cumulative effect of such subtle tactics is to produce a modernist disruption of critical form. From these controlled explosions, these immaculately conjured moments of surprise or dissonance between expectation and judgement, emerges one of the twentieth century's most distinctive critical manners.

Is it, however, still possible to be surprised by Eliot, almost a century after his critical innovations? His role as critic may remain shadowed by the brightness of his poetic reputation ("Poetry lies at the centre of Eliot's achievement," reads one typical formulation, "[b]ut he was also a literary critic of originality and penetration"),[3] yet many of its facets do now seem clear. As the champion of Donne, the scourge of Walter Pater, and the awkward descendent of Arnold, as the advocate of the metaphysicals and the adversary of the romantics, Eliot has formed our canons, both literary and critical. His prose has populated critical language with new or revised terms, concepts and measures: the objective correlative, tradition, impersonality, the dissociation of sensibility. The architecture of modern critical judgments and ideas also owes much to Eliot's essays, in particular to pieces such as "Tradition and the Individual Talent," which has gathered notably high praise: "a major landmark in the development of modern literary criticism," "the most resonant and widely discussed critical statement of twentieth-century Anglo-American literary theory."[4] For such reasons, Eliot holds a firm place in English literary-critical history as one of the most resonant voices within and beyond modernism. The story of how Eliot arrived at this position can be narrated with the facility of caricature, including Eliot's own. "I can divide my own critical writing roughly into three periods" (*TCC* 17), he commented, summarizing thus: first, the time of experimental pieces in modernist little magazines such as the *Egoist*; then the years as a key literary and cultural commentator for established publications such as the *TLS* and for the journal under his own editorship, the *Criterion*; finally, from his position as "the Pope of Russell Square," an established cultural figure and Faber editor, there was a period "of public lectures and addresses rather than articles and reviews" (*TCC* 17), which broadened in their scope beyond literary criticism to social, political and religious matters. From the early critical iconoclast, to the established reviewer-critic, to the "oracular"[5] public intellectual, Eliot's trajectory as literary critic is a well-told tale.

Equally familiar is the balance sheet of Eliot's critical qualities and flaws and in both cases, they bear an intriguing relation to his appraisals of others. Typical encomia notice how, across his varied prose, Eliot appears as a critic of "sensitiveness, erudition, sense of fact and sense of history, and generalizing power"; "the critical consciousness of a generation," who could "supply the conscious formulas of a sensibility in process of formation" – all qualities Eliot admired in others; the phrases here are borrowed from his own terms of praise, in this instance, for Remy de Gourmont (*CP2* 269). Eliot is, however, just as notorious for his idiosyncrasies and frustrations – for his awkward balance of authority and irony, of dogmatic assertion and corrosive insinuation, of scholarly precision and obdurate misquotation. His infuriating prose and politics have, throughout his critical career, earned scorn. His fellow critic experimenter, I. A. Richards, gave early expression to the sense that "one has to forgive T. S. E. a great deal per page of his prose." Nearly all of Eliot's *Homage to John Dryden* (1924), Richards concluded in the margins of his copy, is "an amusing trail of logically incompetent manipulations of bogus information."[6] F. R. Leavis concurred and delivered a more public excoriation of that "major landmark," "Tradition and the Individual Talent," for "its ambiguities, its logical inconsequences, its pseudo-precisions, its fallaciousness, and the aplomb of its equivocations and its specious cogency."[7] Such traits in Eliot's criticism are a particular provocation because Eliot directs much of his critical animus against imprecision in others, against suggestion where there should be statement, while continuing, in his own prose, to exercise "the tactical power of imprecision."[8] If Eliot could seem exasperatingly elusive, still worse was his tendency not to be sufficiently so; the commitments of his later criticism in particular provoke distaste. The university wit of the early essays, known for his sharp aperçus and bold revaluations, rapidly adopts the mask of the critical authority and lends to the history of Eliot's prose the cadence of disappointment.

Eliot is, thus, all-too familiar, both as a disconcertingly "Perfect Critic," and a highly "Imperfect Critic." As with his own model for the "Perfect Critic," Aristotle, this familiarity carries its own difficulties. "One must be firmly distrustful of accepting Aristotle in a canonical spirit;" Eliot writes, "this is to lose the whole living force of him" (*CP2* 267). So, too, with Eliot. So successful was he in managing "to capture the central ideological ground of an entire literary period,"[9] such is "the tentacular persistence of his ideas in later literary theory,"[10] that it can be difficult to obtain sufficient critical distance. It is still unclear, in the words of William Empson's uneasy joke, "how much of our minds he has invented."[11] The profound movements of irony through Eliot's critical prose also challenge his readers; it has proved difficult not to counter his choreographed ambivalences with over-statement. "While the poetry is cryptic, allusive and ambiguous, the prose is lucid, oracular, loftily self-assured,"[12] one critic writes; another divides Eliot into "a critic who insists on wholeness, on classicism, on tradition, and a poet whose work is strikingly modern, avant-garde, fragmented."[13] The canonical Eliot, then, is too often an Eliot of caricature and, once again, Eliot is one of our best spurs to criticism here. We might remember, for example, his sharp sense of comic timing in identifying how Christopher Marlowe's success owes to a style "which secures its emphasis by always hesitating on the edge of caricature at the right moment" (*CP2* 101). A similar hesitation in the case of Eliot's own prose can allow us to trace some of the main movements of his literary criticism in clear outline, while pulling back from the type of exaggeration that dulls "the whole living force of him."

This hesitation should first accompany the terms that seem simplest, including "criticism" itself. In Eliot's view, the meaning was rarely self-evident: "there is not even any large part of the reading public which knows what the word 'critic' means" (*CP1* 649), Eliot laments in a 1918 essay about Henry James. The proportion of his prose that worries at the problem implies that Eliot himself is less secure in this knowledge than he might wish – perhaps because, as he explores the categories, varieties, and functions of criticism, he also conducts a continual work of self-criticism. Even Eliot's grammar around this key term is tentative, with its profusion of unexpected articles ("*a* criticism," "*the* uncritical," "*The* criticism proper") and, in the early writings, the outgrowth of distancing quotation marks. *The Sacred Wood* begins by announcing that, despite the promise of its title, there has yet been virtually no criticism: Arnold almost achieved the form, no one else has since. Implicit here is a bold rhetorical definition of "critic"; this is a laudatory term, of which the use should be sparing. Yet, with one of Eliot's characteristic cross-winds of inconsistency, the subsequent chapters of the book then present a "gallery of critics" (*CP2* 286), some perspicuous and some flawed. In other writings, Eliot asserts that criticism does not suffer from insufficiency so much as from excess: "the number of ways in which the problems of criticism are approached was never before so great or so confusing" (*CP4* 588), he worries, alongside a proliferation of possible terms for varieties of the critic. Some of these he dismisses as too narrow to deserve fully the title: "the purely 'technical' critic," for example, or "the academic critic," who is in haste to offer the panacea of explanatory notes. Some other types Eliot finds too broad; of "the monumental and encyclopaedic critic," for example, we should be wary, "for the monument is sometimes constructed either by indifference to literature or by indifference to life" (*CP4* 393). Yet some measure of "indifference to life" was, Eliot would argue, desirable insofar as it could preserve the critic from his urge to "take leave of the data of criticism" (*CP2* 268), whether for metaphysics or ideas, for etiolated or suppressed creation, or even for "life" itself. ("'Criticism of life' is a facile phrase" [*CP2* 289], Eliot chides, in his fierce concern not to agree with Arnold as to what they both termed the "function" of criticism). Eliot's "Perfect Critic" remains focused on the detailed criticism of particular poems and plays – novels concerned Eliot much less – and is neither indifferent to nor satisfied by the vagaries of "life" above literature.

In *To Criticize the Critic*, Eliot delivers one of his most comprehensive sets of categories by which to distinguish "between the several types of literary critic," ranging across the Professional Critic, the Critic with Gusto, the Academic and the Theoretical varieties of critic, and, in passing, "the Critic as Moralist" (*TCC* 12). Only at the end of this list does Eliot reach the main type with which both he and his own readers are concerned, yet for which there is no neat label: "And finally we come to the critic whose criticism may be said to be a by-product of his creative activity. Particularly, the critic who is also a poet. Shall we say, the poet who has written some literary criticism?" (*TCC* 13). After this slight stutter of definition, Eliot is prompt to fill his category with exemplars – "Samuel Johnson, and Coleridge; and Dryden and Racine in their prefaces; and Matthew Arnold with reservations" – and to seek a place there: "it is into this company that I must shyly intrude." He returns to this category of "criticism of poetry by a poet, or what I have called workshop criticism" (*OPP* 107) repeatedly, asserting that "the nearest we get to pure literary criticism is the criticism of artists writing about their own art" (*TCC* 26). Here, we seem close to reaching the nub of what Eliot means by "literary criticism" and to how we might think of his own activities as critic. But Eliot's restless sense of irony can anticipate any such move towards definition: it is also his conviction that "an important work of literary criticism can alter and expand the content of the term 'literary criticism' itself" (*OPP* 104). Criticism is, it would seem, as a term and concept, rather like Eliot's bird of paradise – it can never settle.

Working from this unsettled sense of "criticism," it becomes possible to see some more surprising sides to Eliot as a literary critic. Take, for example, this succinct judgment: "If Auden is the satirist of this poetical renascence, Spender is its lyric poet." This appears as a blurb introducing Stephen Spender's first poetry collection for Faber.[14] "Whoever was allowed to write it knew nothing about poetry," expostulated F. R. Leavis.[15] This time, the figure behind these anonymous words *is* Eliot, who Leavis, for all his scorn for the logical vagaries of Eliot's prose, hardly held guilty of ignorance of poetry.[16] On closer inspection the blurb does follow some of Eliot's characteristic critical forms; the neat contrastive swing between two exemplary cases, which is emphatic yet still falls within the careful parenthesis of a hypothetical grammar that refuses to insist on its pronouncement. Such "ephemera" around Eliot's main body of criticism do matter: they exemplify the fact that he was in many ways a very *practical* critic, performing the varied tasks of an active man of letters; editor, journalist, copy-editor. With this in mind, it becomes clearer that Eliot's critical occasions were much more diverse and immediate than we might, from the safe vantage of literary history, assume. Eliot's rhetoric is not, for example, just that of a literary critic but also sometimes that of a literary journalist, writing for a range of publications, from little magazines (the first installment of "Tradition and the Individual Talent" went to the *Egoist*'s select readership of around 400) to periodicals or papers with wide circulation (Eliot's contributions to the *New Statesman* were circulated to around 6,000).[17] Eliot's literary criticism should, then, be considered within the frames of responsive, miscellaneous, occasional prose. Across his career, Eliot's critical occasions became increasingly diverse. To take one sharp contrast, in 1926, we find him adopting some facets of a scholarly tone and apparatus to deliver the Clark Lectures to a select gathering at Trinity College, Cambridge. Three decades later, in 1956, Eliot was required to speak in quite a different voice to deliver "The

Frontiers of Criticism" to an audience of 14,000 in a basketball arena in Minnesota. It is not surprising that some critics have referred to multiple Eliots. There were, according to E. M. Forster, at least three. "There is T. S. Eliot who is a poet, and there are also two Mr. Eliots who write criticism":[18] in brief, the Eliot who writes for "sophisticated and highly educated people" and the Eliot who writes for "popular audiences."

Although Eliot would have contested Forster's caricatured distinction, he was certainly conscious of various critical selves, describing himself as a writer "conditioned by ... the occasion of each essay" (*TCC* 16). Sometimes Eliot's refinements to this self-description were characterized by bathos, drawing attention to the role of pragmatic limitations; financial imperatives, perhaps ("I happen to want just now any money that I can get by journalism" [*L2* 227], he admitted to Wyndham Lewis in October 1923), or even the nature of his intellect ("My mind is too heavy and concrete for any flight of abstruse reasoning" [*CP4* 631]). Sometimes Eliot elevates the occasional nature of his writing to a principle: "I have no general theory of my own" (*CP4* 685), he declares in the concluding lecture of the series, *The Use of Poetry and The Use of Criticism*, confident in the virtues of not being a system-builder or philosopher. Graham Hough gives expression to this anti-theoretical impetus when he writes, with regard to Eliot's early work, that to read these pieces is "to see him in process of defining himself, not according to a predetermined programme, but as the result of chance encounters, appreciations and revulsions."[19] For example, Eliot's essay on "The Perfect Critic" appears to spring in part from the publication by his former tutor, Irving Babbitt, of *Rousseau and Romanticism* (1919) and his subsequent critical tussle, with Middleton Murry among others, over the terms "Romanticism" and "Classicism" owes much to the interest, which grew from his response to Babbitt's book, in taking Aristotle as a model for intellectual inquiry.[20] Critics too often talk "as if I had, at the outset of my career as a literary critic, sketched out the design for a massive critical structure, and spent the rest of my life filling in the details" (*TCC* 14), Eliot exclaimed, urging a sense of the untheoretical, even scrappy nature of much of his prose.

Visions of "a massive critical structure" did, however, have their appeal to Eliot, who was "temperamentally too drawn to metaphysical and theological construction ever to be indifferent to the claims of the principled and systematic."[21] In part, this was a legacy from his early philosophical training, whatever the ambivalence of its direct effects on his thought. The student of Bradley, Aristotle and Bergson, while ready to relinquish his philosophical studies, was more reluctant to cede an interest in the architecture of abstract thought. For all the modesty of his critical manner,

Eliot often displays monumental ambitions. For a gathering of reviews and miscellaneous prose, *The Sacred Wood* puts up a good disguise as a crafted book: title, ordering and gnomic prefatory material all suggest considerable coherence of vision. The result of such discrepancies is that there is, particularly in Eliot's paratexts, a thread of disappointment that almost extends to a sub-genre within his work: the unfulfilled pledge; the announcement of, or the apology for, a grander book or scheme of writing that never takes place. "This," Eliot promised of a lecture on Chapman, "is one chapter in a whole book of Prolegomena to Elizabethan Literature which is still unwritten" (*CP2* 548) – and unwritten it remained. Similarly, in publishing *Homage to John Dryden*, which merely reprints three of his past essays from the *TLS* ("John Dryden," "The Metaphysical Poets" and "Andrew Marvell"), Eliot adds a prefatory note that explains why these essays fail to comprise the intended larger book. Had he sufficient time for his subject, he avers, then "[t]his forbidden fruit of impossible leisure might have filled two volumes." Of the rather more modest work that he has just issued he gives this uncomfortable defence: "I hope that these papers may in spite of and partly because of their defects preserve in cryptogram certain notions which, if expressed directly, would be destined to immediate obloquy, followed by perpetual oblivion" (*CP2* 546). Such rhetoric suggests that Eliot was, in many ways, a much less programmatic critic than he aspired to be.

Eliot's critical papers could, then, be considered a cryptogram without cipher: no full theoretical code lies behind their puzzles, only disappointed theoretical hopes and "cross-winds and inconsistencies, disconcerting to those who think of criticism as philosophical argument."[22] Many have been disconcerted, or, at least, amused, by this dimension to Eliot's criticism and "almost every writer who has ever discussed his criticism has caught him in contradictions."[23] One of the sharpest anatomists of this feature of Eliot's prose, Yvor Winters, offers this diagnosis: "at any given time he can speak with equal firmness and dignity on both sides of almost any question, and with no realization of the difficulties in which he is involved."[24] Alongside evident frustration there tends to run a certain delight in discovering this side to Eliot, against the grain of his apparently magisterial sense of critical criteria, ideas and tactics. There is, for example, mischievous pleasure to be found in the neatness with which Eliot's description of Arnold, whom Eliot would prefer to think of as what he once termed an "anti-mask," also fits his own case. Arnold, Eliot avers, "had little gift for consistency or for definition. Nor had he the power of connected reasoning at any length ... Nothing in his prose work, therefore, will stand very close analysis" (*CP4* 176). Here, Eliot and Arnold seem to be close critical companions.

Eliot's unselfconscious phrase "very close analysis" offers a particularly powerful gauge by which to measure his criticism and its place in literary-critical history. As well as something Eliot clearly wished prose to withstand, such analysis has been regarded as one of Eliot's main legacies. Eliot sought, in principle, to restore to the discussion of literature what he described as "that minute and scrupulous examination of felicity and blemish, line by line, which is conspicuously absent from the criticism of our time" (*CP4* 586). At first glance, it would seem that his critical essays achieve that. It is, it has been argued, in his "brilliant responses to such particular instances, rather than in his apprehensions of philosophical or theological wholeness," that he is found to be "at his most impressive as a critic."[25] The appearance of his essays bears a striking visual difference to the prose of many of his predecessors by virtue of the substantial amount of "line by line" quotation Eliot holds up for scrutiny. Yet what happens if we subject this supposedly "very close analysis" to some "scrupulous examination" in its turn? If Eliot's metaphysics or prose logic will not stand such careful attention, then will his "very close analysis" of literature?

There is a line of poetry Eliot quotes three times in his prose – an apparent focusing of the critical microscope. The line, from John Donne's "The Relique," is this: "A bracelet of bright hair about the bone." In 1917, on the first occasion Eliot quotes this line, he gives it a gloss that is a modernist reworking of a famous phrase from Arnold. "Donne," Eliot writes, "sees the thing *as it is*": the hair *as* hair, rather than as a "ghostly or moralistic" (*CP1* 574) vehicle of meaning. Donne's line then returns in Eliot's essay, "The Metaphysical Poets," where he writes this: "some of Donne's most successful and characteristic effects are secured by brief words and sudden contrasts: 'A bracelet of bright hair about the bone,' where the most powerful effect is produced by the sudden contrast of associations of 'bright hair' and of 'bone' " (*CP2* 376). As critical commentary, this is rudimentary and repetitive, both of the line's key words (bright hair, bone) and of itself ("sudden contrast" comes round twice in a single sentence); nor does Eliot say anything particularly helpful about verse, semantics, history or even sense. In spite of having virtually nothing to say about this line, Eliot returns to it a third time, in his Clark Lectures of 1926: "The associations are perfect: those of 'bracelet,' the brightness of the hair, after years of dissolution, and the final emphasis of 'bone,' could not be improved upon" (*CP2* 674). Why, a reader might question, is Eliot being so coy? On the strength of these repetitions, these brief and basic marginalia around Donne's line, it would be easy to say, as Geoffrey Hartman does, that it is a mistake to think of Eliot as one of the twentieth-century's foremost close readers; in fact, "Eliot quotes closely rather than reads closely … his discriminating taste seeks the approval of the educated reader without excessive demonstration."[26] Certainly, in the above instance, a reader interested in Donne would have to turn elsewhere. Even a reader whose primary interest was in Eliot might also feel disappointed. Yet Eliot's manner of working around the line – the lapidary judgments, the restrained rhetoric – practises a version of the minimalism that characterizes his "perfect critic" and which he defines in reference to Aristotle, who "looked solely and steadfastly at the object" (*CP2* 267). Critical perfection is, for Eliot, synonymous with what he calls "intelligent saturation" (*CP2* 151) in the work of the critic's subject, however undramatic this may appear on the surface of the prose response. So, here, Eliot has highlighted a line that matters and has traced its contours in undemonstrative comments, producing an experience of quiet certitude, of the poet's knowledge of when, with the emphatic sense of a closing box, it can be said that words work.

In such ways, Eliot's literary criticism resisted method and large claims, thriving on individual appreciations and intimacy with examples. Yet his judgments did not lack general architecture. Organisation of our aesthetic experiences is, he argues, the best critical approach, albeit the most strenuous: "the exceptional reader" is the one who "comes to classify and compare his experiences," who reaches the "second stage in our understanding of poetry, when we no longer merely select and reject, but organise" (*CP4* 582). Criticism involves "the labour of sifting, combining, constructing, expunging, correcting, testing": it is "frightful toil" (*CP2* 463). Its most basic principles of organisation, named as essential "tools of the critic" in *The Sacred Wood*, are "comparison and analysis" (*CP2* 178). To take a typical example of these in practice, Eliot elucidates the plays of Ben Jonson by this parallelism: "Whereas in Shakespeare the effect is due to the way in which the characters *act upon* one another, in Jonson it is given by the way in which the characters *fit in* with each other" (*CP2* 155). As this example suggests, however, Eliot, who is master of a negative critical grammar, falls more readily into patterns of contrast and exclusion than comparison and analysis – a point to which Christopher Ricks has given succinct expression: "Eliot was always a great one for insisting, unsentimentally and often ruefully, that to enjoy such-and-such is to be precluded from enjoying so-and-so."[27] Swinburne, Eliot writes, "was not tormented by the restless desire to penetrate to the heart and marrow of a poet, any more than he was tormented by the desire to render the finest shades of difference and resemblance between several poets" (*CP2* 118). Eliot does show flashes of this "restless desire" both to penetrate and to render. Reading, for Eliot, has fiercely visceral as well as cerebral dimensions: he experiences particular lines with a heightened responsiveness that Frank Kermode has called "a shudder."[28] Amid his organised responses, criteria and distinctions, Eliot remains open to such shudders, to the effects of erratic sensibility. A critic, he writes, if "*honest* with his own sensibility," "must now and again violate his own rules of rating" (*CP4* 662, italics added), when a line or work requires it. Such self-aware honesty remains somewhat alarming, and Eliot feigns fear of a poet such as William Blake whom he finds to possess this "peculiarly terrifying" (*CP2* 187) quality. Eliot's own form of self-awareness is of the rather more agonised kind that comes from writing in what he calls, in his introduction to Valéry's *The Art of Poetry* (1958), a "self-conscious century."[29]

In writing criticism of the words of others, Eliot creates a large-scale carapace for his self-consciousness – for his awkward awareness that he considers the most vibrant forms of insight to be those that extend or explore the poet's self. It is, after all, the "poetic practitioner" who has learned from their subject who produces the most "living criticism" (*CP2* 150) as – with the requisite indirection – Eliot remarks of Dryden on Ben Jonson. The vitality of Eliot's own critical perceptions and judgments, whether these concern the workings of Donne's conceits, Swinburne's semantic sleight of hand or Marvell's wit, also testifies to his reflective attention to the influences and legacies of these writers within his own practice as poet. This exploration of the "intimacy of the creative and the critical mind" (*CP4* 597), as Eliot terms it, represents one of his major topics and contributions to critical history. It is, of course, difficult to trace with due precision the workings of this in the practice either of his prose or his poetry. Eliot offers an over-abundance of explicit statements on the subject. In characteristic fashion, he also gives his canon of those who achieve this intimacy, or rather, he makes us acutely aware of those who do not; such intimacy, he reminds, requires much more than merely writing both forms. A "poet-critic" such as Arnold is "so little concerned with poetry from the maker's point of view" that "we can forget, in reading his criticism, that he is a poet himself" (*CP4* 657). Still better, perhaps, to forget than to offer criticism that is merely a diluted version of creative possibility: of the "several kinds of writing that pass under the name of criticism," Eliot notes, one kind, "etiolated creation," "is not worth much consideration, because it only appeals to minds so enfeebled or so lazy as to be afraid of approaching a genuine work of art face to face. Walter Pater is one example" (*CP2* 203). The only condition under which these forms of writing can profitably relate to each other is by strenuous involvement: of criticism with creation, creation with criticism.

The times at which Eliot's own criticism comes closest to this ideal are typically elusive; it is easier to say what such intimacy does not resemble. We might expect a glimpse of successful "practitioner criticism" at the points at which Eliot seems to reflect directly on creative endeavours – as, for example, in the following passage from his essay, "William Blake": "His method of composition, in his mature work, is exactly like that of other poets. He has an idea (a feeling, an image), he develops it by accretion or expansion, alters his verse often, and hesitates often over the final choice. The idea, of course, simply comes, but upon arrival it is subjected to prolonged manipulation" (*CP2* 188). Here, Eliot takes us through the stages of composition and we might hope to infer, from his description, principles for his own procedures. But, under pressure for oracular potency, such passages fall flat. Discerning what Eliot calls "the peculiar importance of the criticism of practitioners" (*CP2* 464) involves a rather more oblique approach. For Eliot, one main strength of such "practitioner critics" is that they tend to keep to technical appreciation and thus subdue the dangerous urge to interpret. His own practitioner criticism is therefore to be sought in the details of particular readings: perhaps in the minutiae of Eliot's dissection of two nymphs, Marvell's "Nymph Complaining for the Death of her Fawn" (1681), alongside William Morris's nymph singing to Hylas; or in the local acuity of his contrasts between lines from Massinger and from Shakespeare ("'Indirect crook'd' is forceful in Shakespeare; a mere pleonasm in Massinger" [*CP2* 246]); or, again, in Eliot's minimalist lines around Donne's "bracelet of bright hair." Eliot's literary criticism finds its foundations, and its ways to soar, in the workings of words on particular occasions.

"And the end of all our exploring / Will be to arrive where we started" (*CPP* 197): with Eliot's critical pseudonyms. It would seem that Eliot's performance as critic, across all its varieties, maintains a Prufrockian dimension. "No! I am not T. S. Eliot, nor was meant to be" runs the provocation or refrain behind the many voices, and occasional disguises, with which his prose experiments as it pursues a self-critical sense of what it means to be a critic; above all a poet-critic, practitioner critic or creative critic. Before Crites, Eliot wrote literary criticism under another mask, T. S. Apteryx.[30] Much like Marianne Moore, his friend and companion in reticent, impersonal forms of criticism, he found relief in emblems and masks, particularly those derived from animals or birds and he seems to have alighted on this early pseudonym after a visit to the zoo, during which, as he details in a letter of 1911, he enjoyed feeding a bun to an "aptertix" [sic] (*L1* 19). Eliot, who would open *The Sacred Wood* with a rather darker scene of feeding on songbirds – "I also like to dine on becaficas" (*CP2* 298), menaces his epigraph taken from Byron's *Beppo* – chooses here a witty disguise for his critical adventures. The apteryx, a flightless bird, has wings yet remains, undoubtedly, on its feet.

NOTES

1 T. S. Eliot, "Creative Criticism," *TLS* 1280 (August 12, 1926): 535. The phrase is not Spingarn's but a quotation from the late romantic, Barbey d'Aurevilly. Spingarn's book was first published in 1917.

2 These "Commentaries" by Crites began in April 1924, continuing until the *New Criterion* was launched in January 1926. Eliot adopts the name of Crites from John Dryden's *An Essay of Dramatick Poesie* (1668).

3 Craig Raine, "The Awful Daring of T. S. Eliot: A Centenary Essay" in *Haydn and the Valve Trumpet: Literary Essays* (London: Faber & Faber, 1990), p. 47.

4 Giovanni Cianci and Jason Harding (eds.), *T. S. Eliot and the Concept of Tradition* (Cambridge: Cambridge University Press, 2007), p. 1.

5 Arthur Quiller-Couch, *The Poet as Citizen & Other Papers* (Cambridge: Cambridge University Press, 1934), p. 46.

6 Richards wrote this annotation in his copy of *Homage to John Dryden* (1924), quoted in John Constable (ed.), *I. A. Richards and His Critics: Selected Reviews and Critical Articles* (London: Routledge, 2001), pp. xiv–xv.

7 F. R. Leavis, "T. S. Eliot as Critic" in *Anna Karenina and Other Essays* (London: Chatto & Windus, 1967), p. 179.

8 Michael Levenson, "The Role of Intellectual," in Jason Harding (ed.), *T. S. Eliot in Context* (Cambridge: Cambridge University Press, 2011), p. 66.

9 Louis Menand, *Discovering Modernism: T. S. Eliot and His Context* (New York: Oxford University Press, 1987), p.9.

10 Patricia Waugh, "Legacies: from literary criticism to literary theory," in *T. S. Eliot in Context*, p. 385.

11 William Empson, "The Style of the Master" in Richard March and Tambimuttu (eds.), *T. S. Eliot: A Symposium*, (London: Editions Poetry London, 1948), p.35.

12 Terry Eagleton, "Nudge-Winking," *London Review of Books* 24.18 (19 September 2002): 6–7.

13 Jewel Spears Brooker, "Writing the self: dialectic and impersonality in T. S. Eliot" in *T. S. Eliot and the Concept of Tradition*, p. 41.

14 Stephen Spender, *Poems* (London: Faber & Faber, 1933).

15 F. R. Leavis, "This Poetical Renascence," *Scrutiny* (June 1933), p. 70.

16 See also Chris Baldick: "it is not generally counted among T. S. Eliot's literary achievements, for example, that he was Faber's best 'blurb'-writer." *The Social Mission of English Criticism, 1848–1932* (Oxford: Oxford University Press, 1987), p. 9.

17 Figures are taken from Peter White's "Literary Journalism," in *T. S. Eliot in Context*, pp. 93–104.

18 E. M. Forster, "The Three T. S. Eliots," *The Listener*, 41 (20 January 1949), p. 111.

19 Graham Hough, "The Poet as Critic," in David Newton de Molina (ed.), *The Literary Criticism of T. S. Eliot: New Essays* (London: Athlone Press, 1977), p. 47.

20 For further details, see David Goldie, *A Critical Difference: T. S. Eliot and John Middleton Murry in English Literary Criticism, 1919–1928* (Oxford: Oxford University Press, 1998), p. 61.

21 Stefan Collini, *Absent Minds: Intellectuals in Britain* (Oxford: Oxford University Press, 2006), p. 310.

22 Hough, "The Poet as Critic," *Literary Criticism of T. S. Eliot*, p. 45.

23 Stanley Edgar Hyman *The Armed Vision: A Study in the Methods of Modern Literary Criticism* (New York: Vintage Books, 1955), p. 119.

24 Yvor Winters, "T. S. Eliot: An Illusion of Reaction," *The Kenyon Review* 3.1 (Winter 1941): 13. See also Yvor Winters, *The Anatomy of Nonsense* (1943), on Eliot as self-contradictory.

25 Frank Kermode, "Eliot and the Shudder," *LRB* 32.9 (13 May 2010), pp. 13–16. The lines are from Tennyson's "Mariana" and "In Memoriam," respectively.

26 Geoffrey Hartman, *Criticism in the Wilderness: The Study of Literature Today* (New Haven: Yale University Press, 1980), p. 175.

27 Christopher Ricks, *Decisions and Revisions in T. S. Eliot* (London: British Library, 2003), p. 9.

28 See Kermode, "Eliot and the Shudder."

29 Introduction to Paul Valéry, *The Art of Poetry* (London: Routledge & Kegan Paul, 1958), p. xi.

30 See Eliot's essays and reviews for the *Egoist* in 1918.

10

JOHN XIROS COOPER

T. S. Eliot's Social Criticism

The nineteenth century gave us the idea of "culture" as the broadest framework in which the forms of life of a society, whether a tribe or a national state, can be located. From cooking to clothing, from poetry to dance, to marriage, to religion, these and every other aspect of a society's customs, practices, and beliefs are part of something we have come to call its "culture." This is an idea that began in embryo in Giambattista Vico's *Nuova Scienza* (1725) and came fully into the light of day in Germany and France decades later in the work of Johann Gottfried Herder, Georg Hegel, Jean-Jacques Rousseau, the brothers Grimm, and others. The primacy of culture is an idea that has in the last two hundred years evolved into the social sciences as we know them today and, most brightly, in the discipline of anthropology. It found one of its strongest voices in England in the cultural criticism of Matthew Arnold in the nineteenth century. Arnold's was one of the first English voices to put the matter of "culture" on the intellectual agenda of his time.

To say that culture encompassed a whole series of pursuits such as football matches, cheese-making, and brass bands was one thing, but it was quite another when Arnold wrote that religion and the spiritual life of a people were *also* part of culture. Objections to this characterization of religion as *merely* a part of a people's culture were quick in coming. The counterclaim that culture derived ultimately from religion and that the spiritual truths of a people gave birth to any serious notion of culture was put forward in the nineteenth century by those who were seen to be defending an old idea. Progressive opinion already accommodated to the scientific cast of mind and to secularism applauded Arnold's bold claim. All the momentum of persuasion was on the side of the arguments of the secularists and the quick growth of anthropology, sociology, and political economy in the later years of the nineteenth century anchored the proposition in the academy. There were objecting voices of course – John Ruskin, Thomas Carlyle, and any number of bishops of the Church of England – but the force was with "culture," not religion, as the nineteenth century ended. For all intents and purposes, the argument was over. Game, set, and match to "culture." But the corpse of religion had not quite expired. It had one important twentieth-century champion and that was T. S. Eliot.

We sometimes overlook the fact that when studying philosophy at Harvard, Eliot was also very much aware of new developments in the new social sciences, that is, sociology, anthropology, and psychology. They had not as yet entirely broken free of their origins in philosophy. Matters of faith and belief, which he studied in 1913–14 in a seminar led by the American philosopher Josiah Royce, are themes in what we now call cultural anthropology. As the social sciences abandoned their intellectual place of birth, philosophy narrowed its range of activity. In the age of G. E. Moore, Bertrand Russell, C. S. Pierce, Franz Brentano, Henri Bergson, William James, pragmatism, logical positivism, and empiricism, there was only a very small place for religion. Eliot, the student, was never entirely comfortable with this state of affairs, and one can sense his anxieties in some of his undergraduate and graduate essays.

Eliot was trained *to think* in philosophical traditions that were primarily secular and pragmatic. He was trained *to feel*, on the other hand, in the school of Charles Baudelaire. This was not exactly a training in theology or even in religious thought, but he sensed in the French poet and many of his contemporaries, and poets such as Jules Laforgue, Charles Péguy, and Paul Valéry, the same anxieties about matters of faith and belief that Eliot felt in his youth. As his thinking matured and his convictions settled into the Christian patterns of faith that after 1927 characterized not only his thinking but his whole way of life, Eliot took as his starting point the idea that religion was the socio-historical basis of a society and its culture descended from and was shaped by the religious life of its people.

Any study of Eliot's social and cultural criticism must begin with this biographical fact and acknowledge that a good deal of his thinking and writing about society was in large part enacted as acts of resistance to the pervasive secularism of his time and especially the secularist bent in the nature and practices of the social sciences. This aspect of Eliot's thinking stands in sharp contrast to his reputation as a modernist poet, an artist who, along with others, revolutionized literature and criticism. Although modern in his creative practice, his social and cultural criticism seems intent on resisting modernity. Such an orientation positioned Eliot within a thoroughly conservative tradition, one that descended to the twentieth century through a number of British and French thinkers, including Edmund Burke and Samuel Taylor Coleridge in Britain and Joseph de Maistre, Ernest Renan, Hippolyte Taine, and, finally and most importantly, Charles

Maurras in France. These thinkers formulated different views but they did have some things in common: fear of radical social and political change and the marginalization of religion as an active spiritual and practical force in the lives of a people. This distaste for sudden social and political transformations was focused on a mutual abhorrence of the French Revolution and revolutionary ruptures in general. The displacement of religion provoked determined resistance to the advance of secularism and its accompanying materialist values.

Perhaps Eliot's resistance to modernity may explain his veneration for the "mind of Europe" (*CP2* 107) with its roots in ancient traditions and his decision after 1915 to settle in Britain rather than return to a modernity-obsessed America. These choices put him in bad odor with many American contemporaries, such as the poet William Carlos Williams who, for example, after reading *The Waste Land*, branded Eliot's Eurocentrism as little more than a species of cultural treachery. Eliot's social and cultural criticism began in America with a pronounced distaste for the popular philosophy of Ralph Waldo Emerson, an important figure in the making of nineteenth-century American culture. The Concord thinker's individualist ethic with its basis in self-reliance and his adherence to a misty and somewhat mystifying Transcendentalism did not satisfy Eliot, as it did not sit well with some nineteenth-century writers such as Nathaniel Hawthorne, in his satirical novel *The Blithedale Romance* (1852), and Edgar Allan Poe. Attempts to demonstrate Emerson's influence on Eliot, such as Lee Oser's *T. S. Eliot and American Poetry* (1998), seem a little wide of the mark, given Eliot's subsequent adherence to social and religious traditions that run dead against the Emersonian *zeitgeist*. In particular, Eliot was never convinced that the Transcendentalist faith in the essential goodness of people stood the test of experience, and neither did it square with centuries of Christian teaching about Original Sin. People are not at their best, he felt, when left to their own devices; traditional institutions, such as the apostolic churches, did not corrupt individuals but supported them. To be self-reliant and autonomous could make individuals vulnerable to narcissism, blind conceit, and demagoguery. Society, as a real community, could not be made out of self-absorbed and ultimately irresponsible social atoms. Communities are complex socio-historical organisms rooted in time and place, with living traditions, which give the individual not only a sense of belonging but a socio-cultural identity as well. Two fears – of rootlessness and of self-promoting egoism – seem to lie at the core of Eliot's sense of the social. His social criticism over the years of his mature thought was developed in a number of important prose texts, but this essentially conservative vision of society can be seen in his earliest literary criticism as well. And nowhere more prominently than in the final two essays in his first collection of literary criticism, the volume called *The Sacred Wood* (1920).

The two final essays in that book, "Blake" and "Dante," disclose in broad strokes Eliot's social and cultural leanings. The English poet, visual artist, and mystic William Blake is praised for his quite obvious genius, but the essay is very clear about Blake's limitations. They are not entirely of his making, but are the product of a society and a mind that has not inherited a viable tradition of thought and feeling that is deeply historical and collective. The mansion of Blake's thought is a jerrybuilt construction made from philosophical "odds and ends" that the poet has cobbled together into an entirely unique and original system. Where a Romantic poet or critic might praise Blake for his originality, Eliot finds only "hallucinated vision" (*CP*2 190) and isolation. Blake's genius, in order to make a great and rational contribution, needed, it seems, a living public philosophy or theology which contained the wisdom of the ages, not the siren song of an inner voice led forward by the dubious flashings of inspiration. In this respect, Blake is a flawed poet, even though he is a "poet of genius" (*CP*2 191). Eliot's ideal or classic poet is Dante, and his poetry certainly reflects Dante's own unique genius but is situated in a profound public culture that is rooted in an intellectual tradition that pervades and unifies a whole society. Dante's Catholicism, with its philosophical history and discipline, seen "as part of the ordered world" (*CP*2 232), provides just the right context for the flowering of his thought as a great collective discourse rather than thinking itself into an intellectual dead end such as we find in Blake's mythopoetics. The two essays define early in Eliot's thinking the opposed poles of Romanticism and Classicism.

Whether this literary-historical Manichaeism is an accurate and viable critical judgment or is the simplistic product of the polemics in a culture war in London during the interwar years, need not concern us here. It helped Eliot and his literary comrades-in-arms attack certain authoritative literary figures in the past that they did not like (such as Milton) and to praise others they did like (the Metaphysical poets and Dryden). The conflict between Romanticism and Classicism provided Eliot with a history and theory for the formulation of his literary criticism, even if it is mainly an imaginary history and an implausible theory that on closer inspection does not hold water. But as a starting point, in code, for making a social criticism it has some merit. What I mean is that the simplification provided by the Romantic/Classic split is actually grounded in a sociopolitical reality rather than a literary one. And this reality comes most fully into view in the responses to the revolutionary history of Europe in the late eighteenth and nineteenth centuries.

The first thing we must acknowledge is that Eliot's thinking about society and culture emerges from a French tradition of socio-historical reflection that has its origins in conservative reactions to the French Revolution of 1789 and its aftermath. The Revolution in France broke the continuity of French history by overturning the established order. In the conservative imagination of de Maistre and his successors, this was the political Original Sin of the revolutionaries. Continuity and respect for tradition were seen as paramount values. They ensured that society evolved in an orderly way with its principal parts left more or less intact over time. The underlying notion is that society is akin to a naturally growing thing and that all that a social and political elite need do is maintain its organic integrity by respecting its institutions and practices. The Revolution broke with this concept and immediately redefined society as something that is man-made, something manipulatable by human interventions. It could be changed and reshaped by the popular will, or at least by the will of a usurping elite that interpreted itself as representing the popular will. The conservative reaction to this transformation was immediate, intense, and long-lasting.

The destruction of traditional France – with its ancient hierarchies and clear lines of authority, privilege, and duty – was not only a matter of change at the level of society; it also remade the person as an individual. It had the effect of isolating and setting adrift the person from those traditional frameworks that stabilized social identities. Those contexts included the remaining constraints of feudalism, a raft of aristocratic prerogatives that very few questioned, and those clerical privileges and rights that accumulated over time in the specific institutions of the Roman Catholic Church. When the Revolution did away with these putative stabilizing forces, so the conservative argument averred, society inevitably lost its moorings and a kind of state-managed chaos ensued. The Terror after 1791 was one of its most horrific outcomes. The old regime may have had its faults but it did have a place for each individual, a social place with time-tested privileges and duties. In post-Revolutionary France, according to de Maistre, the individual was exalted in theory as the priceless subject of history, but in practice, with the guillotine in full operation, the concrete human being, when all rhetoric was stripped away, was, in fact, worthless. Some liberal thinkers and historians of the Revolution saw the Terror as an unfortunate interruption in the march of liberty, constitutionality, and progress. The conservatives, on the other hand, saw it as the inevitable result of flawed doctrines, revolutionary politics, secularism, and democracy.

The liberal program for the erection of a constitutional state and nation was not only flawed politically and philosophically but reflected a prior state that spiraled back to the origins of mankind as recounted in scripture.

Original Sin is the unavoidable stain that permeates every aspect of human life. Its presence disfigures ethics, both personal and political. All persons and the institutions they create carry the stain and it is only egotism that proceeds, at its peril, on the presumption that the doctrine of the Fall is priestly rubbish. De Maistre was very clear on this point. Divine reason was a sacred legacy vouchsafed by the scriptures, rooted in faith. Human reason was the self-willed creation of human beings answering only to their own mortal desires, desires that were, on the whole, as Kenneth Asher puts it, "uniformly perverse."[1]

De Maistre set the agenda for the conservative response to the Revolution for the rest of nineteenth century and, in the form of Charles Maurras, well into the twentieth. Ernest Renan and Hippolyte Taine, both former liberals, took up the cause in the nineteenth century. Their perspectives were shaped by two further calamities that could be laid on the shoulders of liberal and left-wing political idealists. The defeat of the French by Prussia in 1870 and the Paris Commune of 1871 were seen as the latter-day results of the revolutionary break of 1789. Renan was especially critical of individualism in liberal thinking. The Revolution had undermined traditional communal relationships; it had unwound the ties of allegiance to authority and the acceptance of one's wider social obligations. Self-interest, blatant materialism, and the pursuit of pleasure undermined the strength of the nation. What was known and accepted by all was no longer understood as a communal inheritance; the center of civil life was no longer occupied by tradition but by the individual person. Eliot would append an ancient text from the pre-Socratic philosopher Heraclitus to the first of his *Four Quartets* (*CPP* 171), which would capture, obliquely, the essence of Renan's critique: "Therefore one must follow (the universal Law, namely) that which is common (*to all*). But although the Law is universal, the majority live as if they had understanding peculiar to themselves."[2] The Heraclitean aphorism takes on a social and political dimension in addition to its philosophical implication. Renan was not alone in his criticisms; Hippolyte Taine extended the conservative argument. He shared with de Maistre a visceral dislike of the effects of the Revolution on the French language. Primarily this meant that in post-Revolutionary France the linguistic practices of old France were actively cleansed from usage, especially in the political, administrative, and cultural spheres. The language of reason and logic, the language of abstract or "enlightened" thought, crowded out the local, regional, and class-based usages of the past. French became a language of reason – abstract, precise, and colorless.

These nineteenth-century French sources were important for Eliot, but his knowledge of them was mediated by his reading of Charles Maurras

(1868–1952), a French conservative who brought the critique of revolutionary France into the twentieth century. We cannot understand Eliot's own social criticism without understanding the influence Maurras exerted on his thinking. He too condemned the effects the Revolution exercised on French society. The sweeping away of the old hierarchies – "of throne, altar, and Pre-Romantic literary decorum"[3] – gave free reign to new regimes of desire, materialism, and individualism, the principal conduits through which Original Sin enters the world. What was needed, Maurras argued, was a "*rappel à l'ordre*," a call to Order, and the restoration of traditional social forms that realized the dictates of natural law. The social composition of the nation and inherited social structures were seen as the natural expression of the life and character of a people. The integrity and purity of a nation, now defined as distinct from the apparatus of the state, became rallying points in the political expression of these general ideas. There is very little room for outsiders in this social vision. Racial or religious minorities, such as the Jews, are seen as dilutions or even threats to the national idea. Maurras labeled his restorative project "classicism" and ranged it against an implacable enemy he called "romanticism." Eliot took on board this "Manichean" model of society in the 1910s and 1920s as he read through Maurras's works and the works of Maurras's predecessors.[4] Democratic chaos, the prison house of desire, the atomized equality of mass society, egotism, and revolution were ranged against Maurras's classical virtues, namely political and religious hierarchy grounded in tradition, an organically evolving community marked by the continuity of its social, political, and cultural forms and a commitment to Order throughout the whole of social life. It needs to be said, though, that Eliot's thinking evolved beyond this rather simple dichotomy, but he never completely abandoned the lessons taught by Maurras. The fact that Maurras, in the end, took up common cause with the collaborationist, neofascist government of Vichy France during the Second World War caused Eliot some embarrassment.

Not all the influences on Eliot in the making of his views on culture and society were French. He had two important English predecessors: Samuel Taylor Coleridge and Matthew Arnold. Roger Kojecký in *T. S. Eliot's Social Criticism* (1971) demonstrates Coleridge's influence in a number of different ways. Both men became social and political conservatives; they were both raised in the Unitarian faith, but migrated spiritually to the Church of England. Both felt that national life was in need of renewal and that only reaffirmation of Christian traditions could have the required effect. But most importantly for Eliot's thinking was Coleridge's view that the conduit for revitalizing Britain by reaffirming Christian principles lay in the hands of a class of intellectual workers he called the clerisy. "Broadly speaking, the clerisy were the educated, who, having imbibed wisdom at the ancient 'halls of learning,' were able to communicate it to others throughout the country."[5] For Coleridge, the clerisy represented a social force of considerable influence in shaping the culture of English society. Eliot was drawn to this idea and adapted it for the modern world in his concept of the "Community of Christians" (*ICS* 26) in *The Idea of Christian Society*.

Matthew Arnold's influence on Eliot was more limited in scope, but important nonetheless. Active in Victorian Britain in education (as a school inspector) and in the spread of higher forms of cultural activity (as critic and social theorist), Arnold argued for a cultural activism that he had inherited from essentially liberal sources. In that respect, Arnold and Eliot were in opposed camps, but Eliot appreciated many of the ideas and strategies suggested by his predecessor in situating society on a bedrock of universal values. Arnold put great stock in the social efficacy of elites, the secular institutions of education, class, the family, and the formal pursuit of the arts. He was also a serious Christian, but not perhaps sufficiently spiritual in Eliot's estimation. Differences aside, there are many points of congruence between the two men, but none more so than in their endorsement of the need for social order. Arnold's fear of social and political breakdown was expressed most vividly in *Culture and Anarchy* (1869). In the Conclusion, he affirms without qualification the need to repress "anarchy and disorder; because without order there can be no society, and without society there can be no human perfection."[6] By "anarchy and disorder," Arnold and Eliot had the example and the excesses of the French Revolution and its possible translation to Britain principally in mind. Both viewed revolutionary violence and the overturning of the state with horror.

From these major sources, Eliot, over the course of his life, developed a coherent social criticism. Initially it took the form, primarily, of the introductory column he wrote for the periodical he edited in the 1920s and 1930s, the *Criterion*. The editorial column, running under the title "Commentary" in each number, gave Eliot the opportunity to think about society and the political and cultural events of his time. It was in those topical columns that his ideas about and vision of society began to take shape. His first attempt to give an extended exposition of these ideas came in the form of three lectures at the University of Virginia in 1933, published the following year as *After Strange Gods*. This book is not one of Eliot's more distinguished productions. It is somewhat bad-tempered and furnishes one short (and often misunderstood) example of what sounds very much like prejudice against the Jews. Those who want to demonstrate Eliot's putative anti-Semitism have usually cited it. The book presents a forceful, perhaps even extreme denunciation of liberalism in the nineteenth and twentieth centuries. He attacks not only political liberalism and its social effects but the rise of liberalism within Christianity as well. Its exasperated tone takes on a self-righteousness that may have worked as public speech to a group of like-minded Southerners in Virginia but which, when it came out in print, sounded cranky and crude. Eliot wisely never chose to reprint these lectures.

Eliot's first extended exposition of his social ideas also began life as a series of lectures, this time at Corpus Christi College, Cambridge, in March 1939, published later in the same year as *The Idea of a Christian Society*. His "point of departure," he says, "has been the suspicion that the current terms in which we discuss international affairs and political theory may only tend to conceal from us the real issues of contemporary civilization" (*ICS* 5). As in *After Strange Gods*, the problem is liberalism, but in this iteration of the old argument Eliot exerts a more certain control of the animus he feels. Liberalism, he writes, is an idea "which tends to release energy rather than accumulate it, to relax, rather than fortify" and he condemns it because

> [b]y destroying traditional social habits of the people, by dissolving their natural collective consciousness into individual constituents, by licensing the opinions of the most foolish, by substituting instruction for education, by encouraging cleverness rather than wisdom, the upstart rather than the qualified, by fostering a notion of *getting on* to which the alternative is a hopeless apathy, Liberalism can prepare the way for that which is its negation; the artificial, mechanized or brutalized control which is a desperate remedy for its chaos.
>
> (*ICS* 16)

And those "remedies" in the context of 1930s Europe are Nazi Germany and Soviet Russia. Liberalism, it seems, sows confusion and erodes traditional habits of thought, feeling, and action. This process makes individuals the likely victims of various forms of exploitation. The resulting alienation and isolation of the communal into "individual constituents" frightens people into a conformism that is the opposite of what is promised.

Liberalism's promise lies in an expanded idea of freedom. Freedom is the highest value and is entirely beneficial in its social and political effects. The faith in developing one's potential to its fullest extent and belief in equality and democracy mark the liberal mind. Eliot's argument sees these articles of liberal faith as merely liberalism's starting point. The weakness here lies in the fact that the liberal cannot foresee the end toward which liberalism is directed; he or she can only grasp the starting point because "[o]ur point of departure is more real to us than our destination." Where we end up in this process presents a "very different picture" (*ICS* 15). The dawn of a liberal era, which begins in expansive optimism, descends over time into something less idealistic, something approaching the chaos of unchecked egotism, social fragmentation, and political despair. In 1939, it was rather easy to turn to the immediate political and economic realities of approaching war, totalitarianism, economic depression, and social stagnation and ask: What more proof of this descent do you need?

When he was trying to persuade a readership he thought was hostile to his views, Eliot typically resorted to a painstaking examination of words. *The Idea of a Christian Society* begins characteristically enough with an exercise in definition. By the word "idea" he does not mean something like the word "concept" and the title "Idea of a Christian society" does not mean an examination of actual Christian societies as they currently exist. What he does mean works toward understanding the kind of values and social system necessary to produce a society worthy of the name Christian. Unlike revolutionary societies that are, in some respects, imaginary institutions, invented from abstract principles, a Christian society evolves historically and is bound to a genuine Christian tradition. So, he insists that he is not "concerned with the means for bringing a Christian society into existence; I am not even primarily concerned with making it appear desirable; but I am very much concerned with making clear its difference from the kind of society in which we are now living" (*ICS* 9). A society based on Christian values and traditions is not an ideological construct, nor is it a political party in the same sense as the term "Christian Democrat" to designate a certain political program in contemporary European politics. Neither do his lectures, he asserts, elaborate a political philosophy. A Christian society operates at a deeper level, what Eliot calls "the substratum of collective temperament, ways of behaviour and unconscious values" (*ICS* 18). Religion sustains life but not without thought and exertion. Simply to call a society Christian does not mean that certain values automatically pervade the life of the people and its institutions. Liberal societies might be nominally Christian, modern Britain for example, but one would hesitate to call them Christian societies. Values have to be put into action, and this requires adjustments in social and political activity and organization. Not revolutionary changes, but changes nonetheless that will lead to creating a proper Christian framework. Eliot's principal sociopolitical forms in the new order are the Christian State, the Christian Community, and the Community of Christians.

The foundation of a Christian State depends on a simple idea: that the rulers, those in positions of power, will act on Christian *principles*. This means a level of moral probity and religious awareness that runs against the grain of *realpolitik* as it is practiced in post-Machiavellian Europe. Eliot does not insist that the leaders should necessarily be Christian believers. Their executive, legislative, and administrative activities would be kept in check "by the temper and traditions of the people which they rule ... What the rulers believed, would be less important than the beliefs to which they would be obliged to conform" (*ICS* 27, 28). Making this paradox workable requires an education, a Christian education, which does not simply instill faith, demanding conformity even among those who doubt. Eliot's point is very clear: a Christian education schools people to think in Christian categories and as a result act within a Christian framework whether they believe or not. In this way, Eliot's assertions are not as paradoxical as they seem. Whether such a political arrangement can be achieved is another matter altogether.

The educational training of a political elite and the capacity of this elite to manage the complexities of its position in Christian society may be difficult, but it is, Eliot insists, achievable. What is not possible is the capacity of the wider Christian Community to understand or undergo the same educational program. "The great mass of humanity" can only think about faith and values in a limited way and so "their Christianity may be almost wholly realized in behaviour" (*ICS* 28, 29), both as customary practice and neighborly civility. Here Eliot's anthropological training comes into view: custom and practice strengthen a people's faith even if they do not understand its intellectual foundations. But how are these institutions and beliefs maintained? Eliot's answer requires a backward leap in time, a kind of back-to-the-future moment. He looks back to the traditional parish as the social form most capable of achieving the aims of a Christian society both at the level of the individual and at the level of the State. Only in the small local community, the parish, can there be sufficient social cohesion and coherence to counteract the atomizing tendencies of a society undergoing the liberalization process. Ordinary individuals need the close-knit support of family and parish to maintain their social and mental health. A sense of belonging and hence a substantive identity anchor the individual in a recognizable reality. The individual as social atom lives, as did William Blake, in a hallucinated state. Where Blake could turn this into great art, most of us end up suffering anxiety and despair.

Eliot is not blind to the problem this line of argument creates. He acknowledges that such a conception is seriously unhistorical as it gropes back to that turning in the road that led to modernity and then, without comment, ignores why society took, in his estimation, the wrong turn. The actual historical experience of a people is thus annulled, and we are asked to imagine a society in which a past social form, the parish in this case, had not lost its social and cultural potency. But change it did, and for real historical reasons that Eliot does not, perhaps dares not, address. Had the parish as it existed in, say, seventeenth-century England not had serious faults, the Christian Community would probably not have changed, not demanded change through political and cultural action. Without offering an explanation why the old forms of social organization were transformed or disappeared entirely, Eliot passes over, in silence, a crucial gap in his own argument.

The final pillar of Eliot's Christian Society may hold the key to these historical changes, changes that Eliot believed undermined the settledness and sanity of English culture during the Elizabethan period. Under the reign of Elizabeth I, he believed that England achieved a state of social coherence and composure that has never been reached again. This equilibrium he seems to attribute to the presence of a cultured elite. Samuel Taylor Coleridge had discussed the social importance of just such a cultured elite a century before Eliot. His term for this social formation is the "clerisy."[7] Coleridge's "clerisy" stands behind Eliot's "Community of Christians." For Coleridge, this group included dons and tutors of Oxford and Cambridge universities educated in the humanities, the clergy more generally, and schoolteachers scattered across the country, all of them socially connected to the landed gentry. Together they safeguarded a great national trust, that of preserving "civilization with freedom."[8] The clerisy, it seems, keeps the wider Christian Community in contact with the higher truths and the highest standards. This is the function as well of Eliot's Community of Christians. To Coleridge's learned men, Eliot added in addition an expanded intelligentsia that would include writers and artists, those at least with "superior intellectual and/or spiritual gifts" (*ICS* 37). This group would be the leading edge of society. It would advise the rulers and it would educate the people. It would disseminate a Christian view of the world and maintain its philosophical validity. Sharing a common background through a shared system of education, this intellectual and spiritual Community would also propagate a common culture, such that they would collectively bring to life the consciousness and conscience of the nation. Every society has had a social formation of intellectuals as one of its leading elements, and Eliot's care in delineating their composition, beliefs, and responsibilities implies their historical importance. Perhaps, it was the failure of this group to maintain its ideological unity and solidarity that led to what Eliot might characterize as the lamentable dissolution of the more integrated society of premodern Britain. Britain found its most famous and eloquent expression in Eliot's adaptation of some passages from Sir Thomas Elyot's *The Boke Named the Governour* (1531) in the first section of *East Coker*.

From these elements Eliot develops a comprehensive idea of Christian society. The relation of the State and Church provides the key to his conception. He argues that there must be a National (or Established) Church and that it must be balanced by a larger religious institution he refers to as the Universal Church. This is probably a veiled plea for Christian ecumenism centered on the Roman Catholic Church. The importance of this universality lies in the danger that a National Church might be dominated by either a particular social class or a dangerous nationalism. Such developments can only be withstood by the counterweight of a transnational Christian entity, his so-called Universal Church. Here Eliot looks back to a time when he imagines Europe, at least Western Europe, enjoyed the coherence of a universal church, a catholic church, centered on Rome. This tension of allegiances to one's homeland and to a wider transnational community of Christians is essential to Eliot's idea of society. It is also important to realize that there is no one strictly political form that ought to be considered Christian. The question of political and economic organization depends on "the character and the stage of intelligence and education of a particular people in a particular place at a particular time" (*ICS* 57). Here Eliot's anthropological imagination comes clearly into view. He believed that differences in politics and economics from one society to another depend organically on the general cultural development of a people, not on deliberate application of political theories. Revolutionary states, from the French Revolution on, have attempted to impose political abstractions on the soil of a people, with ghastly results. If a people have not matured intellectually and culturally for certain ideas to take root – the idea of democracy, for example – Church and State must guide them. If this means requiring conformity and even repression to some degree, then this is what Church and State working together must do. What the people are capable of accomplishing, not what people might think they want, is the central question at issue. For understanding *and* accepting that idea, culture is the key.

Eliot's social thought culminated almost ten years after the publication of *The Idea of a Christian Society* with a book that tackled the very question of culture head on. *Notes towards the Definition of Culture* (1948) continues his defense of Christian culture. Eliot is concerned with defining, distinguishing, and relating "the three principal uses" of that troublesome word "culture." He begins by asserting that "no culture has appeared or developed except together with a religion" (*NTDC* 15). Culture, he writes, is "essentially, the incarnation ... of the religion of a people" (*NTDC* 28). This assertion runs dead against the mainstream anthropology of his time. Instead, Eliot contends that complex cultural forms emerge from the religious beliefs, practices, and scriptures of a people. So, the draft constitution of the United Nations Educational Scientific and Cultural Organisation (UNESCO) in August 1945 is cited as a contemporary example of the contrary point of view, that is, that religion is merely a manifestation of a wider cultural reality. He criticizes Matthew Arnold's *Culture and Anarchy* from the same point of view. The fact that most social theorists in modern times have rejected Eliot's position on this fundamental issue, namely the primacy of religion, does not deter him.

Application of this social idea means that our understanding of how societies are structured needs to be rethought. Democracy and equality may be the ruling shibboleths of the modern age, but Eliot takes a different path. Of democracy he writes: "A democracy in which everybody had an equal responsibility in everything would be oppressive for the conscientious and licentious for the rest" (*NTDC* 48). In a move that runs contrary to modern egalitarianism, he defends the concept of class. He is careful to distinguish two ideas that are sometimes confused: upper classes formed through traditions of inheritance, and social elites formed by merit and measurable achievement. To sharpen his argument Eliot attacks the social theories of Karl Mannheim, an important sociologist in the mid-twentieth century. Mannheim is criticized for confusing an elite of merit with higher social classes that maintain their position through the inheritance of wealth, status, and power. Elites come into being as groups of talented individuals who are brought together by possession of particular abilities and skills. Merit binds them in intellectual, spiritual, and moral activities and as a recognizable social group. Often the members of an elite come from a dominant social class, but the two formations are not identical. However, the two groups have a clear relationship. Elites produce ideas, science, art, and other intellectual, spiritual, and moral products; traditional upper classes consume what they produce. More importantly, the higher classes transmit what they have consumed as culture to the rest of society. This then comes to constitute the way of life of a people.

Elites form and reform continuously. One cannot inherit a place in an elite; it is earned by concrete achievement. In theory, the most talented people rise to the top, but meritorious achievement is not passed on from one generation to another. Each new member of the group must continually renew legitimacy. An upper class, however, has a completely different historical presence. Class affiliations are inherited, not earned through merit. For Eliot the process of inheritance has vitally important cultural benefits; in short, an upper class transmits culture. It allows culture to suffuse a whole society. Such a class must be deeply immersed in tradition, so that the practice of inheriting wealth, status, and power ensures both the continuity of the whole society and the continuous transmission of culture: a class-divided society is more beneficial for culture than the levelling tendencies of egalitarian or democratic societies. But the divisions between classes should not be so rigid that they constitute castes with impermeable boundaries. Impermeability suffocates a living culture. Eliot writes:

> Neither a classless society, nor a society of strict and impenetrable social barriers is good; each class should have constant additions and defections; the

> classes, while remaining distinct, should be able to mix freely; and they should have a community of culture with each other which will give them something in common, more fundamental than the community which each class has with its counterpart in another society. (*NTDC* 50)

An elite, on the other hand, is an association of individuals; the talented individual constitutes the primary building block. But "differences of background will be so great" that only "common interests" will unite the group. To avoid the kind of social rootlessness among an educated elite that was one of the sources of revolutionary energy and leadership in France in 1789, it is important that "an elite must ... be attached to *some* class" (*NTDC* 42). Most probably intellectual elites will find greater affinities with the dominant class than with others. This connection between elite and class – and, hence, the subsequent vitality of the production of cultural values – ensures continuity and avoids the historical ruptures that make demagoguery, disorder, and revolution possible.

If the outstanding individual is the building block of an elite, the family serves the same role in the making of social classes. Eliot sees the family unit as the main channel in society through which culture is transmitted. We are all, he argues, products, to a not inconsiderable extent, of our early upbringing and environment. But when he speaks of the family he does not mean the nuclear family of modern times limited in extent and time-consciousness, but of an older conception.

> I have in mind a bond which embraces a longer period of time ... a piety towards the dead, however obscure, and a solicitude for the unborn, however remote. Unless this reverence for past and future is cultivated in the home, it can never be more than a verbal convention in the community. Such an interest in the past is different from the vanities and pretensions of genealogy; such a responsibility for the future is different from that of the builder of social programmes. (*NTDC* 44)

Social programs that are the product of social engineering cannot produce and sustain a culture worthy of the name. No matter how democratic and egalitarian a society may become, it cannot escape the trivialization that comes from the reduction of culture to show business and the entertainment industry.

Eliot's defense of the class structure and of the family resonates politically with the most traditionally conservative social theories of our time. And like a good conservative, he also appreciates the value and vitality of the local region. A society is not one thing; it is an amalgam of various locales and regions that allows for greater or lesser degrees of cultural diversity. But, he argues, it must be balanced by a clear unity as well. Loyalty to a particular place, like loyalty to the family, is an important aspect of culture. Even a degree of religious diversity can be a very good thing, again as long as it is balanced by an appreciation of the fundamentals of faith as the progenitors of culture and society as a whole. In the making of these delicate social and cultural equilibria, education plays a vital *social* role, as opposed to the dominant view of education as a program primarily concerned with personal self-improvement. Education, in his view, ought to preserve the integrity and legitimacy of social class, helping identify the deserving members of an elite. Eliot spends a good deal of time debunking modern educational theories as leading to the very condition of cultural breakdown that they are invoked to impede. Instead, he sees education having a more limited role, not of making people happier, or stuffing their heads with expert knowledge, or equipping them for life in the modern economy. Education should make them more receptive to culture as the expression of the traditional life of a people. And this brings us back to religion as the source of culture. A people living with the faith and experience of their ancestors are better equipped to deal with everyday life and with whatever calamities and crises history puts in their path than societies of isolated egos who are encouraged to continuously concoct shrewd curricula of self-enlargement and self-promotion. He saw no use for a religion that was simply one more tool for amplifying the self in the name of personal growth.

This social vision is deeply conservative, but not conservative in the modern neoliberal sense. Eliot was as suspicious of the deleterious effects of capitalism as he was of what is now known as liberalism and the varieties of twentieth-century collectivist ideologies. He was conservative in an older sense given its first modern expression in England by Edmund Burke at the beginning of the nineteenth century and in France by the conservative thinkers who exerted a lasting influence on Eliot's thinking about society. Respect for tradition was the key principle, but by respect Eliot meant something other than an uncritical reverence of the past. He had spent his early years as a literary critic reflecting on the relation between tradition and the individual in the field of literature. Later, after his acceptance of the Church of England, his thoughts about tradition extended over a wider field of human experience. The individual he had in mind was no longer limited to the talented artist or writer, but ordinary citizens. On that larger canvas the egotistical impulse expressed itself in the most garish colors. The only alternative, he felt, to the dominance of the cult of self-absorption was religious orthodoxy. As early as 1933, when he gave the lectures that were published in *After Strange Gods*, he saw the problem clearly. "Tradition by itself is not enough; it must be perpetually criticised and brought up to date under the supervision of what I call orthodoxy" (*ASG* 62). Baldly put, this may sound contradictory, the relation between critical thought and the "supervision" of thinking may make us uneasy and may even hide from view an authoritarian tendency. But although Eliot never veered from this basic position, his subsequent extended meditations on society grew more sophisticated and he developed a serious body of social criticism that in its day was much discussed but, as the world was headed in a different direction, was largely ignored by those who shaped Western societies after the cataclysm of the Second World War.

NOTES

1 Kenneth Asher, *T. S. Eliot and Ideology* (Cambridge: Cambridge University Press, 1996), p. 13.
2 Kathleen Freeman (trans.), *Ancilla to the Pre-Socratic Philosophers: a Complete Translation of the Fragments in Diels, Fragmente der Vorsokratiker* (Oxford: Blackwell, 1948), pp. 24–5.
3 Asher, *T. S. Eliot and Ideology*, p. 161.
4 Asher, *T. S. Eliot and Ideology*, p. 23.
5 Roger Kojecký, *T. S. Eliot's Social Criticism*, (London: Faber, 1971), p. 23.
6 Matthew Arnold, *Culture and Anarchy*, in *Culture and Anarchy and Other Writings*, Stefan Collini (ed.) (Cambridge: Cambridge University Press, 1991), p. 168.
7 Samuel Taylor Coleridge, *On the Constitution of Church and State* (London: Hurst, Chance, 1830), p. 47.
8 Coleridge, *On the Constitution of Church and State*, p. 57.

11

GAIL MCDONALD

Gender and Sexuality

The previous *Cambridge Companion to T. S. Eliot*, first published in 1994, contained no essay on the subject of Eliot and gender, and had only one page reference to gender in its index: "gender, rendering of." There were eleven references to sexuality, three of which appeared under the subheading "insecurity of." Ten years ago, a substantial volume written by distinguished scholars did not dwell upon the significance of gender and sexuality to Eliot's work. An earlier publication, Mildred Martin's *A Half-Century of Eliot Criticism* (1972), a thorough annotated bibliography of English-language books and articles for the 1916–65 period (2,692 items), makes it clear that the controversies in Eliot studies in the first half of the twentieth century were far more likely to center on the poet's putative obscurity, his religious conversion, and his conservative politics than on his attitudes toward women or sexuality. "Politics," at that point, had barely begun to be associated with feminist theory: the politics of gender and identity were still in the making. My first task, then, is to justify the inclusion of an essay on this topic now.

Although the configurations, definitions, and theories of gender and sexuality are unsettled and the contours of the fields variable, it is now nearly impossible to imagine studies of modernism and its major writers without these categories of investigation. To neglect them is to ignore several decades of significant developments in literary criticism generally and modernist studies particularly: influential work recovering and revaluing modernist women writers, critical examination of gender representation in literary works, analyses of style through the lens of sexuality, and investigations of gender and sexuality in the cultures of modernity and modernism. Surveying the development of criticism over the last half-century, one need not be a fashion-monger to recognize that poststructuralism, feminist studies, cultural studies, and gender and queer studies have had a transformative effect on the way we now read. New Modernist Studies, announced in the *Chronicle of Higher Education* in 1999 and institutionalized in the now well-established Modernist Studies Association, would have been unthinkable without the significant shifts in critical perspective brought about by these new modes of analysis.

To the extent that these approaches came about in an atmosphere that had grown impatient with the limitations and repetitive formulae of New Critical reading (strongly, if sometimes erroneously, associated with T. S. Eliot), and to the extent that revised modes of reading were driven in many cases by a desire to rewrite certain narratives of what modernism was, a figure like Eliot, indisputably an icon of male modernism, presented an irresistible target for revisionism. It is unsurprising that the Anglo-American academy, having embraced Eliot so firmly between 1920 and 1960, would come to view its near-adulation of Eliot with considerable suspicion, if not revulsion. In "T. S. Eliot at 101," a *New Yorker* essay of 1989, Cynthia Ozick announced, "It is now our unsparing obligation to disclaim the reactionary Eliot."[1] It could be argued that this call to reject Eliot blinds potential readers to the accomplishments of his poetry, drama, and criticism. Along with charges of anti-Semitism, accusations of misogyny have been among the most powerful forces employed in the project of repudiation. Rachel Blau DuPlessis, however, offers an alternative view of the effects of rethinking Eliot: "Some critics have resisted recent sex-gender interpretations and biographical readings with enraged dismissal, seeing these investigations as an unseemly, even prurient revolt against this iconic, canonical writer. But in truth explorations of modernism and sex-gender materials have been critically productive in discussions of Eliot's work."[2] With DuPlessis, I believe that these historical and theoretical frameworks enrich rather than diminish our understanding of Eliot.

Before surveying the critical landscape, however, it is crucial to raise the question of *evidence*. To what extent can biography (even that shored up by letters, memoirs, and "hard" facts) be taken as evidence of a figure's gender affiliations or sexual proclivities? More problematic still, to what extent can a writer's poetry or plays be taken as evidence of his attitudes and beliefs? In "Facts and Theories about Shakespeare's Sonnets," Stephen Booth waves a warning flag at those who would seek to discover Shakespeare's sexuality in his verse: "William Shakespeare was almost certainly homosexual, bisexual, or heterosexual. The sonnets provide no evidence on the matter."[3] Booth's witty dismissal of the sexual guessing game is only partly a joke. Neither Shakespeare's life, so far as it is known, nor his poetry furnish adequate "evidence." Similar limitations apply to Eliot. My suspicion is that the outrage and accusations of "prurience" to which DuPlessis refers derive not only from a misplaced desire to protect an icon but also from an intellectually defensible position that it is unethical to draw conclusions from scant evidence.

Eliot's biographers and the editors of his letters have provided abundant material for study of his life and work, but scholarship is unlikely to turn up incontrovertible evidence of sexuality that contradicts the public record. The events of his public life point to heterosexuality. He was twice married, first to Vivien Haigh-Wood and then to Valerie Fletcher. It is a truth universally acknowledged that the first marriage was miserable for both parties. Virginia Woolf's memorable image of Vivien as a "bag of ferrets" around Eliot's neck comes to mind.[4] The first volume of letters is replete with accounts of the couple's illnesses and domestic difficulties. The narrative of Eliot's efforts to separate himself from Vivien has been retold in biography, drama, and film with varying degrees of accuracy and special pleading.[5] The second marriage, a surprise even to Eliot's closest associates, appears to have been blissful. In between the two marriages, Eliot was romantically involved with Emily Hale. Over a thousand letters from Eliot to Hale are famously sequestered at Princeton until 2020; Hale's letters to Eliot were destroyed. He also had a long-term but apparently platonic relationship with Mary Trevelyan. These associations have been examined in detail by Lyndall Gordon. A youthful friendship with Jean Verdenal during Eliot's sojourn in Paris in 1910–11 was memorialized in the dedication to *Prufrock and Other Observations* ("For Jean Verdenal, 1889–1915, mort aux Dardanelles" [*CPP* 11]). This brief but intense attachment has been the focus of arguments positing Eliot's homosexual attraction to Verdenal, a possibility sometimes milked to strengthen an argument that Eliot was "really" a homosexual. At various points in his life after Eliot left Vivien, he shared housing with three homosexual men, one priest, and, at greatest length (some eleven years), with John Hayward, who declared himself "the most un-homosexual man in London."[6] These flat-shares occurred in a period in which Eliot claimed to be celibate, having taken a vow of chastity in 1928. No reliable evidence has arisen to suggest he broke this vow.

In the one instance during Eliot's life in which a critic, John Peter, argued that *The Waste Land* was an elegy for a homosexual lover, the poet acted swiftly through his legal representatives to suppress the article. What does this action prove? That he wished to hide his "real" sexuality? That he resented a critic reading his life on the grounds of his poetry? That he considered the article an invasion of privacy? The letter to Peter from Eliot's legal representatives declared that Eliot found the essay disgusting and "completely erroneous."[7] Without significant new evidence, how can we be certain of Eliot's motives? And why is it important to know one way or the other? This last is a serious question. For perhaps the first time in Western culture, there is greater readiness to take sexual preferences in stride: the younger generation in particular are comfortable with the idea of gender as performed and malleable and regard a lengthy menu of sexual practices without concern. Social mores have become less punitive and judgmental. Nevertheless, there are several reasons investigations of gender and sexuality still matter to Eliot studies.

First, one cannot read the poetry without a sense that sexual relations, especially those between men and women, are uneasy, unfulfilling, or painful. Readers of Eliot's early poetry, of whatever critical bent, generally agree in observing an air of sexual discomfort in the poems prior to Eliot's public announcement of his religious commitment in 1927. Tensions between mind and body, or body and soul, are, in the later poetry, less frequently made manifest in desolating sexual failures and miscommunications, but even essentially meditative poetry like *Four Quartets* continues to allude to human love. Taking the long view, both of the poetic career and of twentieth-century literary criticism, these basic observations have wide acceptance. Second, critical theory during much of the second half of the twentieth century was dedicated to understanding the power relationships and institutions that are shaped by sex and gender. Eliot lived, it should be remembered, within a social regime that policed sexual practices. Peter's article appeared in 1952. Homosexual acts between two men were not legalized in England until 1967. Third, Eliot (like a number of his peers) wrote about women with apparent misogyny, implying a fear of or disdain for the strengthening position of women in modern life. Evidence of resentment among the male modernists has implications for the recovery of forgotten writers, for publishing, for canon formation, and for understanding the social and historical contexts of modernist literature. Fourth, questions of sexuality and gender are fundamental to the humanities and should not be ignored.

Biographical study is, of course, too useful to be dismissed. The trouble with the facts of a biography, however, is that they require interpretation, and interpretation is susceptible to error. Eliot was not called "Possum" because of his relish for self-revelation. One might consider, for example, the first volume of his letters. These teem with information, but even to a reader not previously aware of the many voices Eliot employs in his correspondence, it soon becomes clear that Eliot does not write to everyone in the same way: he adopts one stance with Ottoline Morrell, quite another with Eleanor Hinkley, and still another with his mother Charlotte. We all write different letters to different recipients – no accusation of insincerity need be leveled. But when letters are used as proof, then matters of tone, of intended recipient, of degrees of intimacy must all be considered. Eliot could joke about a "Big Black Kween" (*L1* 93) to Ezra Pound or Conrad Aiken because that was the rather juvenile mode in which they had been corresponding. Is the language racist and misogynist? Yes. Does context make it less deplorable? No. And yet the context of ribald "guy-talk" affects our understanding of what has been written. Eliot razored out the bawdy poems of the notebook labeled *Inventions of the March Hare* and sent them to Pound: it was only with Christopher Ricks's 1996 edition that the poems were restored to the context in which they had first appeared. Eliot's excision of the coarse poems is typical of his self-awareness and selectivity in what he says to whom. His sense of himself as a public figure with a reputation to protect came to him early and persisted throughout his life.

If the facts of a life are slippery, surely the evidence of the poetry is even more so. During the period of New Criticism's ascendancy, budding critics were cautioned against seeking meaning in the world outside the poem. Having moved away from such strictures, and with historical contexts now seen as crucial to readings of texts, we nevertheless move cautiously in identifying a specific referent for a specific poem. Even the confessional lyric – which seems to invite one to say, "Sylvia Plath cut her finger while slicing an onion on such and such a day: the consequence is 'Cut'" – is usually not well served by such naïve connections. A reductive reading of a poem heavily dependent on referentiality is likely to foreclose rich analysis of the artistry and relevant contexts that produced it. Employing poems as "evidence" in so direct a way is therefore normally avoided in persuasive critical readings. On the other hand, as the controversy over the 1949 awarding of the Bollingen Prize to Ezra Pound's *Pisan Cantos* illustrated, willful refusal to acknowledge evidence of obnoxious views expressed in poetry can also be irresponsible. Criticism surveys a poet's oeuvre to observe the patterns of the writer's opinions, engagement with historical events, deployment of imagery, diction, symbols, allusion, and other figures – these materials, in the aggregate, are the contours of the poet's imaginative world. Interpretation, whether of biographical, psychological, literary historical, or other matters, also (and inevitably) suggests the critic's imaginative world. Readers of literary criticism, recognizing the subjectivity and historicity of critical views, rightly expect evidence to be persuasive rather than conclusive.

Such attention to what he perceived as the preponderance of the evidence underpinned Peter's 1952 reading of *The Waste Land*. Peter's was the first scholarly article to suggest a homoerotic backstory to the poem and is today known largely because of Eliot's efforts to suppress all copies of the journal *Essays in Criticism* in which it appeared. In his 1969 postscript to the article, four years after Eliot's death, Peter describes his evidence as "like straws, attaining some weight through accumulation."[8] Peter did not name Verdenal as the probable subject of the poem until this postscript. The 1952 article has an air of polite humility: there is none of the accusatory rhetoric sometimes seen in the "outing" of a closeted homosexual. He offers the notion of the Phlebas figure as a "useful entry into the poem" and, in fact, makes no outright claim regarding Eliot's own sexuality. He understands the speaker to be both grieving and guilt-ridden and he moves in the direction of reading *The Waste Land* not as a commentary on the postwar world, but as a "personal tragedy." The word "personal" is used carefully to avoid any suggestion that the speaker is in fact Eliot. Peter's focus is not on biography but on references to Augustine's *Confessions*, Dante's Arnaut Daniel, Mr. Eugenides, and the hermaphroditism of Tiresias. His most controversial contention is that students of the poem would be well served by an introduction before the "monologue" begins. Here is what he refers to as "his rather clumsy stage direction":

> At some previous time the speaker has fallen completely – perhaps the right word is "irretrievably" – in love. The object of this love was a young man who soon afterwards met his death, it would seem by drowning. Enough time has now elapsed since his death for the speaker to have realized that the focus for affection that he once provided is irreplaceable. The monologue which, in effect, the poem presents is a meditation upon this deprivation, upon the speaker's stunned and horrified reactions to it, and on the picture which, as seen through its all but insupportable bleakness, the world presents.[9]

For a reader today, one schooled in the polyphonies of modernism, the most incredible claim being made here is that there is an identifiable single speaker in *The Waste Land*, not that this speaker has felt love for a young man.

Peter's essay and his postscript are of interest not only for the claims he makes, nor even for Eliot's reaction, but for the insights they provide into what might be called the changing "etiquette" of literary criticism. Peter's is very much a New Critical reading, informed by attention to literary allusions, but still maintaining the distinction between speaker and poet. It is not given to ad hominem attacks – nor even impolite. The documents of Eliot criticism have not always been so mannerly. Tim Dean quotes one of the more egregious examples of recent years as an epigraph to his essay, "T. S. Eliot, famous clairvoyante": "Anyone who announces, as Eliot did, that poetry is an escape from personality can expect, now more than ever, to have his personality ripped open like a fox."[10] Those familiar with the debate about Eliot's anti-Semitism will no doubt recognize the author as Anthony Julius. Why the angry, even vindictive attitude? Why "now more than ever"? Without question, all literary criticism is driven by ideology of some kind, polite New Critical readings decidedly included. Still, it seems fair to ask, what happened between 1952 and 1995, the date of Julius's *T. S. Eliot, anti-Semitism and Literary Form*, that could explain this change of tone?

Analyses focused on gender and sexuality will inevitably be shaped by the kinds of questions being asked; those questions will stem not only from the texts under consideration but also from current critical practices. Two examples will suggest the interpretative differences that arise from different premises. Tony Pinkney's *Women in the Poetry of T. S. Eliot: A Psychoanalytic Approach* (1984) frames his study of Eliot according to the psychoanalytic theories of D. W. Winnicott and Melanie Klein, and finds that violence toward women is constitutive of Eliot's poetics: "any Eliotic text has to, needs to, wants to in one way or another, do a girl in; and if it fails to achieve that goal, it is itself murderously threatened by the girl."[11] Pinkney's argument may or may not convince a given reader, but its effectiveness depends on accepting certain premises of psychoanalysis. Carol Christ reads the same poems as Pinkney and reaches a quite different conclusion:

> If one were seeking to articulate a motivating psychology for Eliot's poetry, one might argue that difficulty in separating himself from woman leads, among other things, to various attempts to do her in. But such a misogynistic reading would be at the cost of simplifying both the violence of his poetry and the ambiguity in its representation of gender.[12]

Christ focuses instead on the ways in which the corporeal fragmentation of women's bodies is a function of Eliot's efforts to create a strong poetic voice. "He locates his strongest voice not only by fragmenting the body but by making ambiguous its identification with both character and gender." Eliot, she concludes, comes to avoid "attaching gender to bodies." In Eliot studies, controversies, accusations, attacks, and defenses have arisen less from the evidence of sexual discomfort in the poetry, upon which there is general agreement, than from speculation (in biographical and psychological studies) about the causes and motivations behind the discomfort or (in historical and contextual studies) about the larger cultural meanings of misogyny or sexual disgust. What is striking about "fox-ripping" readings of Eliot's work is the sense of glee at having uncovered a well-guarded secret. Like Henry James's unnamed biographer in *The Aspern Papers* (1888) or Vladimir Nabokov's Charles Kinbote in *Pale Fire* (1962), the critic acts as detective, seeking the clues that will reveal the Real Truth in an artist's creation. The governing assumption is that the real thing is always the hidden thing, and of course the personal and intimate aspects of sex and gender affiliation are perfectly suited to vocabularies of the secret. By this logic, a poet who has publically aligned himself with the word "impersonality" is invariably a poet who has something to hide.

Even casual readers of Eliot's poetry will find numerous unflattering portraits of women: the dismissive woman who tells Prufrock "That is not what I meant at all" (*CPP* 16); the woman in "Preludes" whose feet have "yellow soles" (*CPP* 23); the "female smells in shuttered rooms" (*CPP* 25) of "Rhapsody on a Windy Night"; the "damp souls of housemaids" (*CPP* 27) in "Morning at the Window"; Cousin Harriet, the dull reader of "the *Boston Evening Transcript*" (*CPP* 28); Helen Slingsby, the dead maiden aunt unmourned by her dallying footman and second housemaid; the *vagina dentata* of "Hysteria"; nicely "pneumatic" Grishkin (*CPP* 52) in "Whispers of Immortality"; "blue-nailed" Princess Volupine (*CPP* 41); toothless Lil in *The Waste Land*. Women haunting doorways, women twisting paper roses or stalks of lilac, women combing their hair into fiery points or fiddle strings. We may call these images decadent or morbid or even derivative (of French Symbolism, of Swinburne, or of any number of anti-Petrarchan or misogynist literary traditions dating back to the medieval period). Such catalogs of ugliness are not difficult to assemble. It might be noted that the list of attractive male figures in Eliot's poetry is as short as the list of unattractive female ones is long. By a stretch, one might see the highly sensitive and observant Laforguean personae of Eliot's early poems as appealing. Coriolanus (who makes several appearances in Eliot's oeuvre) is hardly a portrait of unalloyed heroism. Other male figures are either vulgar (the young man carbuncular and Mr. Eugenides of *The Waste Land*, ape-necked Sweeney), elderly and defeated (Gerontion; the speaker of "Journey of the Magi"), crippled by feelings of impotence, fear of rejection, and sexual uncertainty (Prufrock; the speaker of "Conversation Galante"), or haunted by guilt (a repeated topic of the plays). To what extent, then, is Eliot's representation of gender and sexuality misogynistic? To what extent might it, with equal correctness, be labeled misanthropic? In the 1980s and early 1990s the emphasis fell more heavily on the former than the latter; this emphasis may be accounted for by the emerging strength of feminist criticism and its powerful attention to the representation of women in literary texts. More recently, as the performativity of gender and the recognition of fluidity in sexual desire have been more thoroughly explored, the emphasis has fallen more heavily on the meanings of sexuality more broadly defined – and this shift in focus has raised other sorts of questions, about transgressive desires, queer perspectives, and the cultural constructedness of gender and sexuality.

The "Eliot" we have is the "Eliot" we make. There will be many more prose pieces to study once the new Eliot editorial project is complete and its findings are online for new readers to discover. With more than a hundred previously unpublished pieces found to date, the editorial project will provide material of great interest. I am nevertheless willing to hazard the guess that new prose materials, with the possible exception of the sequestered Hale letters, are not likely to reshape the fundamental understanding of Eliot's relationship to matters of sex and gender. Further, although we may expect superb editorial work on the poems from Christopher Ricks and Jim McCue, the poetic record will not be substantially altered. The change that has counted most in Eliot criticism is not the printed record but readers' views of that record. We must therefore look to the evolution of literary criticism for an understanding of Eliot's fall from guardian of tradition to violent misogynist, secret homosexual, or indeed to any other refiguring of the poet still to come. In the last half-century, the idea of a canon, the aesthetic standards by which male and female modernists are judged, the meanings of linguistic strategies, the questioning of modernism's status as experimental or avant-garde – all these changes have altered our understanding of T. S. Eliot.

A decade ago, the feminist scholar Lisa Rado introduced her collection, *Rereading Modernism: New Directions in Feminist Criticism*, by offering a survey of the ways in which that criticism had addressed the "massive cultural 'forgetting'" that had undervalued, if not erased, the contributions of central female modernist writers like H. D., Marianne Moore, Djuna Barnes, Gertrude Stein, Rebecca West, and others.[13] Recovery work of this kind was the first accomplishment of feminist literary criticism. Other stages of the project included revising the literary histories that had promoted labels like "The Pound Era" and "The Men of 1914"; establishing a "matrilineal" literary tradition parallel to that of the male writers; reexamining the effects of friendship, mentorship, financial support, and collegial relationships among male and female writers of the modernist era; and attending to the portrayal of female characters and the deployment of tropes such as the femme fatale, the angel of the hearth, and the muses. Key texts of this critical moment include Elaine Showalter's *A Literature of Their Own* (1977), Rachel Blau DuPlessis's *Writing Beyond the Ending* (1985), Toril Moi's *Sexual/Textual Politics* (1985), Shari Benstock's *Women of the Left Bank* (1986), Sandra Gilbert and Susan Gubar's *No Man's Land* (1988), and Bonnie Kime Scott's *The Gender of Modernism* (1990).[14] Moi's work was especially useful in delineating the differences between Anglo-American feminism, largely devoted to the content of texts, and French feminism, more focused on the linguistic strategies of texts. From the latter (notably in the work of Hélène Cixous) came the notion of *l'écriture féminine*, the *jouissance* of which seemed to grant a kind of feminist stamp of approval to the experiments of modernist writers like Joyce. "As a result of these dichotomies," Rado writes, "two very different portraits of the modernist period have emerged: one as conservative, patriarchal, and repressive, the other as radical, feminist, and subversive."[15] While some of these texts were polemical (Gilbert and Gubar's hyperbolic description of modernism as a war between the sexes) and others more measured (Kime Scott's anthology included essays on both male and female modernists from a range of critical viewpoints), in general the view of Eliot placed him firmly in the conservative-patriarchal-repressive camp. In a period in which the words "subversive," "radical," and "transgressive" were like shiny medals handed out to worthy recipients, Eliot was, predictably, not among the favored.

By 1994, when Rado was evaluating the state of feminist criticism, significant changes were already afoot that would lead to more historically informed work and, in my view, to more nuanced portraits of modernist writers, including Eliot. As Rado herself worried, "How useful is it to prove over and over again that Hemingway, Faulkner, or Joyce [or, I would add, Eliot] was or was not a misogynist?"[16] Rado predicted that "images of women" – criticism and reiterations of blame aimed at an essentialist or nebulous conception of the patriarchy – would decline as critics moved in the direction of historical and interdisciplinary approaches. And this in fact occurred. Judith Butler's *Gender Trouble* (1990) reframed the question of gender so thoroughly that the usual binaries underpinning sex and gender criticism came to seem inadequate. Kime Scott's famous "web" of influence provided a visual metaphor more capacious than oppositional binaries. Critics like Rita Felski questioned the blanket approval of Joycean experimentation: "The assumption that the political value of a text can be read off from its aesthetic value as defined by a modernist paradigm, and that a text which employs experimental techniques is therefore more radical in its effects than one which relies on established structures and conventional language is too simple." Felski argued for attention to "contingent functions of textual forms in relation to socially differentiated publics at particular historical moments."[17] Recognition of contingent functions of form, socially differentiated publics, and particular historical moments has increasingly marked the work undertaken by scholars of modernism in the last quarter-century. Even the titles of recent influential studies suggest the move toward complicating the understanding of what modernism was: we might note as evidence the plural nouns in Peter Nicholls's *Modernisms* (1995) and Lawrence Rainey's *Institutions of Modernism* (1998) or the detailed concentration on a single year, as in Michael North's *1922* (1999) or Jean-Michel Rabaté's *1913* (2007).

In 2004, a decade on from Rado's survey, Cassandra Laity noted that:

> Eliot's unusually prolonged association with a monolithically elitist, masculinist, and reactionary conception of early modernist culture may be among the chief obstacles to his resituation in the sex/gender/erotic contradictions of his own milieu. However, increasing critical attention to a refocused "modernity" which enters early modernism alternatively from the perspective of its complex gender dynamics as well as its negotiations between high and low culture brings to view ... Eliot's largely unexplored engagement with various public and private worlds of women, eroticism, and the feminine.[18]

What Laity proposes – and what the essays collected in the volume illustrate – is that a revised conception of modernism opens the possibility of a revised conception of Eliot. This is not to say that we will suddenly discover an Eliot who was not in the main classicist, royalist, and Anglo-Catholic. But attention to detail may at minimum complicate our understanding of the poet's opinions, beliefs, and reception, and of his positioning of himself as a gendered subject. My own article in the Laity and Gish volume argues that academic women such as Muriel Bradbrook found *The Waste Land* exhilarating rather than oppressive, that young women who heard Eliot's lectures at Cambridge took quite a different view of Eliot than did, for example, Gilbert and Gubar. Tim Dean's essay in the same volume revisits the meanings of Eliotic "impersonality" – which has often been the basis for accusations that Eliot's aesthetic principle is actually a strategy for evading or concealing genuine intentions. What Dean calls the "logic of demystification" employed by critics aiming to reveal the true motives of impersonality has, he argues, made Eliot's imaginative impersonations in his poetry seem nothing more than a ruse. Dean reads the evidence differently: "More than a camouflage, impersonation may represent a way to inhabit other existences – a way to transform oneself by becoming possessed by others. This distinction furnishes us with a rationale for approaching modernist impersonality as a strategy not of dissimulation but of access to regions of voice beyond the self."[19]

Dean's argument is convincing not least because it points toward another aspect of Eliot that can and should be a context for the study of gender and sexuality in his work: his religious life. Religion and sex have long been a potent combination, sometimes fierce opponents and sometimes uncanny twins. Eliot's poetry partakes of both. His recurrent attention to the penetrated body (as in the oft-studied "The Love Song of St. Sebastian") may be read as homoerotic, but it may also, and simultaneously, be read as a fascination with ecstatic transcendence of the body. His life-long dedication to the study of Dante has many explanations, but one of them must be the argument of *La Vita Nuova*, that is, that human love may be a route to divine love: "that beatitude which is the goal of desire" (Section XVIII).[20] Eliot's sexual desires (of whatever kind) and his equally strong desire to be "a dancer before God" (*CPP* 605) mean that his poetry at times displays an ascetic's horror of flesh and at other times a yearning for the joys of human love. Colleen Lamos in *Deviant Modernism* refers to Eliot's "errant female sexual energies."[21] "Errancy" seems to me a rich metaphor for gender and sexuality, if we can think of the word not with the emphasis on "error" but on a notion of creative wandering, the alternating energies of strict control and letting go, of following a path or deviating from it. A struggle between discipline and release is not a one-time event, but a process, the messiness and unendingness of which is precisely in keeping with Eliot's temperament, an agon at least hinted at in a line from *The Waste Land*: "The awful daring of a moment's surrender" (*CPP* 74).

NOTES

1 Cynthia Ozick, "T. S. Eliot at 101," *New Yorker* (20 November 1989), p. 119.
2 Rachel Blau DuPlessis, "Gender" in *T. S. Eliot in Context*, Jason Harding (ed.) (Cambridge: Cambridge University Press, 2011), p. 296.
3 Stephen Booth, "Facts and Theories about Shakespeare's Sonnets," in *Shakespeare's Sonnets* (New Haven: Yale University Press, 1977), p. 548.
4 Diary entry for 8 November 1930 in *The Diary of Virginia Woolf. Vol. 3, 1925–30*, edited by Anne Olivier Bell (Harmondsworth: Penguin, 1980), p. 331.
5 Examples include Carole Seymour-Jones's *Painted Shadow: A Life of Vivienne Eliot* (London: Constable, 2001) and a 1984 play *Tom and Viv* by Michael Hastings, which was made into a film in 1994, directed by Brian Gilbert.
6 For a detailed examination of Eliot's friendship with Hayward, see John Smart, *Tarantula's Web: John Hayward, T. S. Eliot and Their Circle* (London: Michael Russell, 2013).
7 John Peter, "A New Interpretation of *The Waste Land* (1952)," *Essays in Criticism* 1969 XIX (2): 173.
8 "A New Interpretation of *The Waste Land* (1952)," *Essays in Criticism*, p. 172.
9 "A New Interpretation of *The Waste Land* (1952)," p. 143.
10 Tim Dean, "T. S. Eliot, famous clairvoyante" in *Gender, Desire, and Sexuality in T. S. Eliot*, eds. Cassandra Laity, Nancy K. Gish (Cambridge: Cambridge University Press, 2004), p. 43.
11 Tony Pinkney, *Women in the Poetry of T. S. Eliot: A Psychoanalytic Approach* (London: Macmillan, 1984), p. 18.
12 Carol Christ, "Gender, Voice, and Figuration in Eliot's Early Poetry" in *T. S. Eliot: The Modernist in History*, ed. Ronald Bush (New York: Oxford University Press, 1991), p. 29.
13 Lisa Rado, "Introduction," *Rereading Modernism: New Directions in Feminist Criticism* (London: Routledge, 1994), p. 4.

14 Jane Gallop's *Around 1981* offers a useful summary of feminist criticism in the academy.
15 Rado, *Rereading Modernism: New Directions in Feminist Criticism*, p. 8.
16 Rado, *Rereading Modernism: New Directions in Feminist Criticism*, p. 6.
17 Rita Felski, *Beyond Feminist Aesthetics* (Cambridge, MA: Harvard University Press, 1989), p. 161.
18 Laity, "Introduction," *Gender, Desire, and Sexuality in T. S. Eliot*, p. 2.
19 Dean, *Gender, Desire, and Sexuality in T. S. Eliot*, p. 54.
20 *La Vita Nuova*, translated by Dante Gabriel Rossetti in *The Early Italian Poets*, p. 195. Eliot used this translation in his Clark lectures (*CP*2 661).
21 Colleen Lamos, *Deviant Modernism: Sexual and Textual Errancy in T. S. Eliot, James Joyce, and Marcel Proust* (Cambridge: Cambridge University Press, 2004), p. 103.

12

JEWEL SPEARS BROOKER

Eliot's Philosophical Studies: Bergson, Frazer, Bradley

In July 1922, as part of an attempt to assemble a list of distinguished writers for the *Criterion*, Eliot contacted E. R. Curtius, professor at the University of Marburg, to express admiration for his recent book, *Die literarischen Wegbereiter des neuen Frankreich* (1919) [Literary Precursors of the New France] (*L1* 694). When Curtius responded positively, Eliot expressed "the hope that we may some day see a work from you on English literature comparable to your book on contemporary France" (*L1* 721). In August 1923, Eliot repeated his suggestion: "I wish you wd do a series of *English Wegbereiter*," adding that "*my* choice" would include Henry James, Joseph Conrad, and Rudyard Kipling, and "I shd be tempted to add *Frazer* and *Bradley*" (*L2* 186). Curtius did not write such a book, but two months later, in October 1923, Eliot finished an essay for *Vanity Fair* making his own case for James, Frazer, and Bradley as precursors: "A Prediction in Regard to Three English Authors: Writers Who, Though Masters of Thought, are Likewise Masters of Art." He claimed that these writers had shaped the sensibility of a generation and predicted that they would endure because their work, compared to that of their contemporaries, "throbb[ed] at a higher rate of vibration with the agony of spiritual life" (*CP2* 517). Of the three "masters," only James, strictly speaking, is a "literary" precursor; Frazer is a social scientist and Bradley a philosopher. The author of *The Golden Bough* undoubtedly influenced the sensibility of a generation, but the author of *Principles of Logic* and *Appearance and Reality* was relatively obscure, known primarily to students and fellow philosophers. Frazer and Bradley made Eliot's list in large part because they were his own precursors, touchstones in his intellectual biography. With James, they represent the three core areas of his university education: literature, social science, and philosophy.

Eliot was educated, chiefly at Harvard, between 1906 and 1916. In June 1910, he received his B.A, and in October, he crossed the Atlantic to attend the lectures of Henri Bergson. At the end of his year in Paris, he returned to Harvard to work on a Ph.D. in philosophy, in the course of which Frazer and

Bradley joined Bergson as major influences. In the fall of 1914, he began a year's study of Aristotle and modern philosophy at Merton College, Oxford, during which he completed a draft of a Ph.D. thesis on Bradley's epistemology. These years include two watershed moments in Eliot's intellectual and spiritual life: the first, associated with Bergson, was the decision to pursue a career in philosophy; the second, associated with Bradley, was the decision to abandon it.

The essential context informing Eliot's philosophical studies is the temporalization of the chain of being that occurred at the end of the eighteenth century and prepared the way for developments in the natural and social sciences. The shift from a view of reality consisting of more or less static entities linked in space to a view consisting of fluid entities moving through time is at the heart of nineteenth-century intellectual life. It was a shift of emphasis from mechanism to organicism, from Being to Becoming. This interest in history and in change over time – a major element in Romanticism – stimulated an interest in old languages and folk tales that led linguists such as Rasmus Rask and folklorists such as Max Müller to trace the origins of language and myths. The emphasis on change over time was liberating for scientists, including Charles Lyell, author of *Principles of Geology* (1830–3) and Charles Darwin, author of *On the Origin of Species* (1859), who argued that the earth and its inhabitants are immeasurably old and still changing. In subsequent generations, the quest for origins begun in geology and biology led to an explosion of activity in the social sciences, including anthropology, sociology, psychology, and religion.

The special focus on time in the sciences had an enormous influence on philosophy, which to remain relevant had to deal with the implications of evolutionary models and the dissolution of boundaries between categories. In a landmark study, *The Revolt Against Dualism* (1929), A. O. Lovejoy assessed the situation in philosophy in the early twentieth century. Descartes, Locke, and Newton, he argued, had dominated Western thought for three centuries, their bedrock assumption being that the precondition for understanding the world was the strict separation of subject and object. In the post-Hegelian, post-Darwinian reconsideration of the subject-object question, major philosophers rejected the division of the world into irreconcilable parts. Their attempts to overcome dualism typically involved privileging one extreme or the other: the subject absorbing the object (mysticism, neo-idealism) or the object subsuming the subject (materialism, neo-realism). Some thinkers, of course, claimed to be neither idealist nor realist, but they inevitably slipped into a weak version of one or the other. The philosophers to whom Eliot was most indebted included distinguished representatives of the various camps – the idealists Josiah Royce and Bradley, the realists Bertrand Russell and

Ralph Barton Perry, and, fence-straddlers, the Pragmatist William James and the "vitalist" Bergson. Eliot's retrospective understanding of his work in the social sciences is suggested in the *Vanity Fair* essay. Frazer, he maintains, is the most eminent of the scholars who have contributed to an understanding of the past, in large part because he gradually withdrew from the attempt to impose an interpretation on the vast data regarding human consciousness that he had assembled. His material, collected in *The Golden Bough*, "extended the consciousness of the human mind into as dark a backward and abysm of time as has yet been explored" (*CP2* 515).

Eliot's discussion of philosophy in the *Vanity Fair* essay is also illuminating. Bradley's methodology, Eliot suggests, is more important than his conclusions. He contrasts Bradley's approach to that of Bergson and Russell, the first of which is "pure" and the second "impure." The first brings no commitments and has no agenda; it simply follows the argument to its end; the second, on the other hand, knows where it is going and builds that knowledge into its argument. Impure philosophy begs the question by beginning with premises that guarantee a desired end (*CP2* 515–16). Bergson brought to philosophy a commitment to biology and psychology, and Russell brought a commitment to mathematics; Bradley, on the other hand, brought no commitments whatsoever. Like Aristotle, "he looked solely and steadfastly at the object" (*CP2* 267). Bergson's premises led him to affirm the immortality of the soul; Russell's foreordained him to deny it. In a 1927 review of Russell's *Why I Am Not a Christian*, Eliot remarked that one should be "prepared to find that [Russell's] reasons will be such as the author thought of afterwards, in order to fortify his faith" (*CP3* 160) in scientific materialism. Pure philosophy is "infinitely more disillusioned" and much "harder" (*CP2* 517). In accepting the data and following the argument without prejudice, one risks ending in "resignation or despair – the bewildered despair of wondering why you ever wanted anything, and what it was that you wanted, since this philosophy seems to give you everything that you ask and yet to render it not worth wanting." But although more dangerous, philosophy without prejudice is more vital, more in touch with the "agony of spiritual life" (*CP2* 516, 517).

Eliot's decision to pursue graduate work in philosophy occurred in 1911 when, as a student at the Sorbonne, he experienced what he later called a "temporary conversion to Bergsonism."[1] As suggested by the term "conversion," his initial attraction was both personal and doctrinal. The personal element, repeatedly dramatized in the early poems, was the pain associated with a conflict between mind and body, a gap between intellect and feeling. The doctrinal was Bergson's claim to have resolved these antinomies, a claim that Eliot tested in Paris and rejected as inadequate. His disappointment is evident in several poems, including "Rhapsody on a Windy Night" and "He said: this universe is very clever," both written in March 1911.[2] His reasoned dissent will appear two years later in a lecture for the Harvard Philosophical Club titled "Inconsistencies in Bergson's Idealism."

In 1910, in anticipation of attending Bergson's lectures, Eliot read *Time and Free Will* (1889) and *Matter and Memory* (1896).[3] Both are informed by the post-Darwinian focus on time, and both are framed by Bergson himself as critiques of dualism. In the first, he attacks Kant's separation of perception and reality (subject and object); in the second, Descartes's separation of mind and body; and in both, he claims to have bridged the gap. The subject of *Time and Free Will* is the debate between free will and determinism, and the argument is that an understanding of the debate is contingent upon an understanding of time, and an understanding of time contingent upon an understanding of consciousness. Bergson dwells on Kant's distinction between *phenomena* and *noumena*, that is, between things as perceived and things as they are in themselves.[4] The first is knowable, the second unknowable; the first is associated with cause and effect (and thus determinism), and the second with freedom. Bergson argues that Kant's error was a failure to distinguish between two different aspects of time. The first, associated with clocks, assumes identical and thus repeatable units – minutes, hours, years. The second (*durée réelle*), associated with consciousness, assumes an undivided continuum of heterogeneous and thus unrepeatable elements. The first treats time, which is a process, as if it were space with parts that could be separated, counted, and placed side by side. The second treats time as an indivisible part of consciousness. Bergson discredits determinism by associating it with a lock-step notion of time and validates freedom by associating it with the unpredictable play of consciousness. In a related move, he maintains that Kant overlooked the distinction between two modes of knowing – intellect and intuition, the first based on logical analysis and the second on intellectual sympathy.[5] Bergson's basic methodology, also revealed in *Time and Free Will*, has three interconnected steps: (1) focusing on well-known binaries, such as perception and reality; (2) generating smaller, more subtle binaries, such as clock time and *durée réelle*, that can be used to dismantle the larger ones; and (3) folding the quantitative, associated with logic, into the qualitative, associated with consciousness.

Bergson's claim to have overcome dualism is even more emphatic in *Matter and Memory*. His stated goal is to show how mind and body are related. He admits that his view is "frankly dualistic" in that it affirms the reality of both matter and spirit, but he promises to deal "with body and mind in such a way as to lessen greatly, if not to overcome, the theoretical difficulties which have always beset dualism."[6] His argument turns on an analysis of memory, which he divides into motor memory (habit), ingrained in the body, and "pure memory," part of consciousness. The first is associated with the mechanical, the second with the *durée réelle*. Bergson's solution to mind-matter dualism involves redefining matter as "an aggregate of 'images' ... more than that which the idealist calls a *representation*, but less than that which the realist calls a *thing*," and redefining memory as the halfway house in which matter, as redefined, interacts with spirit.[7]

After Eliot returned to Harvard and entered the Ph.D. program in philosophy, he began to consider Bergson in the context of the contemporary philosophical debate between idealism and realism. In a 1913 address to the Philosophical Club, he argued that Bergson's claim to have mediated between idealism and realism, in the process overcoming dualism, is too weak to warrant assent. En route to this conclusion, he considered three interrelated steps in Bergson's methodology: (1) the focus on received antinomies, such as idealism and realism; (2) the use of a distinction between quantity and quality to generate his own more nuanced binaries, such as the two aspects of time; and (3) the use of his pairings to overcome the larger ones with which he had begun.

Eliot begins by scrutinizing the sine qua non of Bergson's philosophy: the assumption of a clear distinction between quantity and quality. The quantitative assumes that reality is composed of parts that can be separated and counted, the qualitative that it consists of indivisible interpenetrating states of consciousness. One is associated with exterior objects immobilized in space, the other with interior states fluctuating in time. Eliot examines the examples that Bergson presents in support of this distinction and finds that most actually subvert his argument. He points to Bergson's claim that there are two ways of knowing that a bell has tolled four times. One is by counting the strokes; the other is "not by counting, but because *four* strokes is a quality, different from three, five, and the rest" (*CP1* 69). The notion that a specific number of strokes can be perceived as a quality, Eliot says, is inherently contradictory (*CP1* 70). He shows that, even for Bergson, qualitative perception is never pure, that it inevitably includes an element of number and thus of spatiality. Number exists in both "the physical world ... and the world of introspection," in the extrinsic world where the bell tolls and intrinsic one in which it is heard. There is "no essential difference" (*CP1* 70). In undermining the antithesis between quantity and quality, Eliot discredits the most famous part of Bergson's thought – his signature binaries – concluding: "We cannot rest at the *durée réelle*. It is simply not final" (*CP1* 79).

Eliot is especially critical of Bergson's attempt to overcome dualism by redefining reality as an image that exists *between* the subject and the object. He quotes Bergson's insistence that "What is given, what is *real, is something intermediate between divided extension* [space] *and pure inextension* [time]" (*CP1* 71, 74, Eliot's emphasis).[8] Eliot suggests that this passage reveals the soft spot in Bergson's metaphysics. "The crux of the *affaire Bergson* ... is his attempt to invest with the title of reality this middle territory ... this territory cannot be regarded as *selbstständig* [self-sufficient]."[9] The discrediting of Bergson's intermediate or bridge reality leads Eliot back to his opening point – Bergson's claim to be neither a realist nor an idealist. Based on the fact that he consistently explains the quantitative as an aspect of the qualitative, Eliot argues that he is an idealist, albeit a very weak one. Because most or all of Bergson's attempts to reconcile oppositions entail this slide into subjectivism, Eliot in later contexts would associate him with romanticism.

When Eliot entered the Harvard Philosophy Department in 1911, it was also dealing with the need to reconcile the polarity between idealism and realism. In the first decade of the century, the department was at the pinnacle of its prestige, largely due to the eminence of two philosophers, William James and Josiah Royce, and to the distinction of visitors such as Bertrand Russell. James, like Bergson, positioned himself as a bridge builder. As Eliot noted in 1917, both "the oppression of idealistic philosophy and the oppression of scientific materialism were very real to him" (*CP1* 582). His attempt to mediate between idealism and materialism by focusing on results is evident in his definition of Pragmatism "as the *attitude of looking away from first things, principles, 'categories,' supposed necessities; and of looking towards last things, fruits, consequences*."[10] Russell, who taught a course in symbolic logic at Harvard in 1914, had important disciples in the department – the Neo-Realists, described by Eliot as "animated by a missionary zeal against the Hegelian Idealism which was the orthodox doctrine of the philosophical departments ... [They] were on the whole anti-religious and professed considerable respect for Mr. Bertrand Russell" (*L1* 156). Royce was a neo-idealist and, after the death of James in 1910, the department's most influential thinker. In *The World and the Individual* (1901), he addressed the issue that was always at the core of his thought: the attempt to connect the finite and the infinite, the individual and the Absolute. "The essence of this doctrine of Evolution," he claimed, "lies in the fact that it recognizes the continuity of man's life with that of an extra-human realm whose existence is hinted to us by our experience of nature."[11] The department as a whole tended toward idealism, and the critical idealism of Kant and the absolute idealism of Hegel and F. H. Bradley were central in the curriculum.[12]

Eliot worked with figures across the department, but in retrospect, it is evident that he was most influenced by the idealists. In 1913, he took a seminar on the philosophy of Kant, whose work had been the chief target of Bergson's critique of modern philosophy. In the second of three papers surviving from this course, he praises the German thinker for understanding that dualism is inherent in the human condition. In 1913, he took a seminar with Royce that, according to Bruce Kuklick, was "the core of the graduate curriculum."[13] The topic for the year, Royce remarked, was not idealism per se ("no theory of my own"), but the usefulness of Darwinian methods for addressing issues in the human sciences.[14] Each student was required to contribute one long paper and four short ones. Eliot's long paper, presented on 9 December 1913, and his short pieces, given at intervals during the spring term, deal with the validity of applying post-Darwinian scientific methods to a study of primitive religion.

Eliot's long paper for Royce, "The Interpretation of Primitive Ritual," is arguably the most significant of his surviving graduate essays. His topic is one that the department had been preoccupied with for decades – the conflict between science and religion. By focusing on the role played by interpretation in the social sciences, Eliot carves out a position of his own. He begins by stating his questions: "On what terms is a science of religion possible? Can it be treated wholly according to the methods of sociology? And are these methods ever wholly scientific?" (*CP1* 106). As Royce's class secretary accurately reports, Eliot's paper concerned "theories about comparative religion and in how far they were description and in how far interpretation."[15] In attempting to explain the difference between description and interpretation, Eliot refers to the most distinguished figures in the field, including Frazer, but his main reference points are Émile Durkheim, author of *Les Règles de la méthode sociologique* (1895), and Lucien Lévy-Bruhl, author of *Les Fonctions mentales dans les sociétés inférieures* (1910). Eliot tries to show that sociologists and anthropologists often conflate description and interpretation, and argues convincingly that what is usually called science in these fields is really interpretation. "What seemed to one generation fact is from the point of view of the next a rejected interpretation." Eliot protests against the use of the phrase "evolution of religion," saying that "evolution" is a term that describes a value-free relation between organic tendency and environment. In social and religious progress, there can be no value-free descriptions. His conclusion is that neither Durkheim's group consciousness nor Lévy-Bruhl's pre-logical mentality enables us to understand the primitive mind. Their theories are a negative example, reminding us "that primitive reality ... cannot be put together out of the abstractions of social psychology which are torn from our sophisticated and conscious life" (*CP1* 115) A decade later, in the introduction to his mother's *Savonarola: A Dramatic Poem* (1926), he summarized his paper from memory:

> Some years ago, in a paper on *The Interpretation of Primitive Ritual*, I made an humble attempt to show that in many cases no interpretation of a rite could explain its origin. For the meaning of the series of acts is to the performers themselves an interpretation; the same ritual remaining practically unchanged may assume different meanings for different generations of performers; and the rite may even have originated before "meaning" meant anything at all. (*CP2* 771–2)

The methodology studied in the Royce seminar had enduring effects on Eliot's mind and art. It informs most of his literary criticism of the 1920s and his social criticism of the 1930s, and it can be seen in his structural experiments in poetry, notably in the "mythical method" (*CP2* 479) of *The Waste Land*. The meditation on language and interpretation commenced in this paper, moreover, was to remain at the heart of Eliot's work, culminating in *Four Quartets*.

Eliot's first in-depth engagement with F. H. Bradley, the idealist on whose work he was to write his thesis, occurred in the Kant seminar. In contrast to Bergson, who defined reality as something that exists between the subject and object, Bradley defined it as something that comprehends both in a dialectical process of transcendence that is continuously moving forward and looping back. Bradley's metaphysics (what reality is or isn't) and his epistemology (how one can know) should be seen in the context of the long conversation on dualism initiated by Descartes. The emphasis on reason by the French rationalists, for example Descartes, had been answered by the emphasis on experience by the British empiricists Locke and Hume, and the two had been brought together by the German idealists, notably Kant and Hegel. Far from overcoming dualism, however, Kant's synthesis confirmed it by arguing that there is an unbridgeable gap between perception, which by definition is limited (a point of view), and reality. Hegel responded by moving to an absolutist position, arguing that the real and the rational are one and the same. Bradley demurred, pointing out that Hegel's solution overcomes dualism by tossing out the material world. He tried to reintegrate the world of human experience into his own version of the Absolute, thus creating a model that includes both the world of nature and the world of ideas. As evidence of Bradley's resistance to Hegel, Eliot quotes a passage from *Principles of Logic*:

> [T]he notion that existence could be the same as understanding strikes as cold and ghost-like as the dreariest materialism. That the glory of this world in the

> end is appearance leaves the world more glorious, if we feel it is a show of some fuller splendour; but the sensuous curtain is a deception and a cheat, if it hides some colourless movement of Atoms, some spectral woof of impalpable abstractions, or unearthly ballet of bloodless categories ... Our principles may be true, but they are not reality.[16]

"There is but one Reality," Bradley argues, "and its being consists in Experience. In this one whole all appearances come together."[17]

Bradley's epistemology, the focus of Eliot's thesis, descends from his metaphysics. If reality is an all-inclusive "Experience," then subjects and objects in themselves are not ultimates, but rather parts of something larger than either one. One can never discover truth through analysing subjects and objects, because analysis by its very nature divides reality into this and that, temporal and spatial, mind and matter. Knowledge, Bradley maintains, does not begin with thought, but with feeling. He posits an epistemological triad: "immediate experience," "intellectual experience," and "transcendent experience," with the first and third phases made up of feeling, and the intermediate term made up of thought.

> We in short have experience in which there is no distinction between my awareness and that of which it is aware. There is an immediate feeling, a knowing and being in one, with which knowledge begins; and, though this ... is transcended, it nevertheless remains throughout as the present foundation of my known world.[18]

It is the nature of immediate experience to fall apart, to make way for perception in terms of self and not-self. This is the level of analytical (intellectual) experience, the dualistic level of knower and known, subject and object. Although most people never get beyond this level, a few transcend it, achieving a sort of non-analytical comprehensive wisdom. This empirical wisdom, in Bradley's view, involves a return to the wholeness and unity of immediate experience, but not to its innocence. Whereas immediate experience is characterized by a *knowing and feeling* that comes before thinking, transcendent experience is characterized by a *thinking and feeling* that comes after and is achieved through thought. This is the level that Eliot refers to as "a direct sensuous apprehension of thought, or a recreation of thought into feeling" (*CP2* 379). In his Ph.D. thesis, Eliot accepts the idea that intellectual experience is enclosed in an envelope of pure feeling: "We are led to the conception of an all-inclusive experience outside of which nothing shall fall." He admits that the first and last terms in this triad can only be known hypothetically, but maintains that they are "necessary postulates because thinking occurs only in time" (*CP1* 256).

Eliot began his work on Bradley at Harvard, but he completed it at Merton College, Oxford, in the fall of 1914. Bradley was by this time in ill health and a recluse, but Harold H. Joachim, a specialist in both modern idealism and in Aristotle, was also at Merton and was available. Eliot spent the year studying both Bradley and Aristotle under his supervision. During Michaelmas 1914, they worked primarily on modern philosophy and in Hilary and Trinity terms 1915 chiefly on Plato and Aristotle. Eliot's weekly essays during Michaelmas all dealt in one way or another with "the questions considered in the thesis which I hope to present for the degree of Ph.D." (*L1* 92). In dealing with the issues raised by Bradley, Eliot also considered the counterarguments of Russell and other thinkers. In the last of six surviving Michaelmas essays, "The validity of artificial distinctions," he accepts the dialectic implied in Bradley's thought, the idea that moving forward always involves moving back. "The token that a philosophy is true is ... the fact that it brings us to the exact point from which we started" (*CP1* 191). He claims to accept Bradley's conclusions in *Appearance and Reality* "with certain reservations"; at the same time, he scribbles in the margin: "I cannot see my way to the admission that 'Reality is spiritual' " (*CP1* 192n7). This is more than a "certain reservation"; it is a rejection of Bradley's core principle, as stated in the closing lines of *Appearance and Reality*: "We may fairly close this work then by insisting that Reality is spiritual ... Outside of spirit there is not, and there cannot be, any reality."[19]

A month after finishing his draft, Eliot confessed in a letter to fellow student Norbert Wiener that, on both personal and professional levels, his philosophic quest had brought him to a dead end. "[A]ll philosophizing is a perversion of reality: for ... no philosophic theory makes any difference to practice ... It invariably involves cramming both feet into one shoe" (*L1* 80). Unable to accept either idealism or realism, he identified himself as a relativist. "[O]ne has got to neglect some aspects of the situation, and what relativism does ... is to neglect *consciously* where realism protests that there is nothing to neglect, and idealism that it has neglected nothing." The "lesson of relativism," he claimed, is "not to pursue any theory to a conclusion, and to avoid complete consistency." In regard to his dissertation, Eliot added: "my relativism made me see so many sides to questions that I became hopelessly involved, and wrote a thesis perfectly unintelligible to anyone but myself" (*L1* 80–81).

At the time of his correspondence with Wiener on relativism, Eliot was working on a talk to be given a few weeks later in Bertrand Russell's rooms at Cambridge. In "The Relativity of the Moral Judgment," presented on 12 March 1915, he again describes himself as a relativist and argues that neither realism nor idealism is any help in ethics, for "to reduce the world to a set of formulae is to let it slip through our fingers in a fine dust; but to fly into an emotional orgy or retire into a sunlit stupor is to let the world slip through our fingers in a thin smoke" (*CP1* 198). His recommendation is that one should avoid committing oneself to any theory, but rather view philosophical extremes as two points in a conversation, "upon which intelligence feeds" (*CP1* 198).

Eliot concluded his formal studies in 1915 with a weekly tutorial on Aristotle's metaphysics and ethics. In 1916, when he began his career as a man of letters in London, he kept Aristotle in mind as a model of intelligence, generosity, and objectivity, and tried to cultivate these virtues in his own criticism. In "The Perfect Critic," he praises Aristotle as remarkably brilliant, a man of "universal intelligence, and universal intelligence means he could apply his intelligence to anything." Aristotle was a perfect critic because he had no "impure desires to satisfy; in whatever sphere of interest, he looked solely and steadfastly at the object" (*CP2* 267). In the *Vanity Fair* essay quoted earlier in this essay, Eliot uses similar language in his praise of Bradley. Like Aristotle, he practiced philosophy without prejudice.

By the time Eliot finished his work at Oxford, he was thoroughly disillusioned with philosophy, but in deference to his parents, he revised the dissertation and submitted it to Harvard in the spring of 1916. Professor Woods informed him that Professor Royce considered it "the work of an expert" and that it had been accepted "without the least hesitation" (*L1* 156). Eliot responded gracefully, saying, "I shall try to justify its acceptance by passing a good examination when I come. I don't know at all when that can be" (*L1* 167). In fact, it would never be. In 1915, he married an English woman who needed financial and emotional support, and they decided to live in England, then mired in what seemed to be a never-ending war. In 1929, in a letter to his mother, Eliot reflected on this turning point in his life: "I am sure that I should have made a very poor professor of Philosophy, because, after my first enthusiasm, I found modern philosophy to be nothing more than a logomachy." He assured her that her unstinting support during his years of study had not been in vain, and indeed, that his philosophical studies had turned out to be "a great advantage" (*L4* 411–12) for his future work. The truth of this reflection is amply borne out by both the substance of his criticism and the expressions of gratitude to his precursors, including Frazer and Bradley, "who, though masters of thought, are likewise masters of art" (*CP2* 513).

NOTES

1 Eliot, *A Sermon preached in Magdalene College Chapel* (Cambridge: Cambridge University Press, 1948), p. 5.

2 "He said: this universe is very clever" is an unpublished sonnet dated March 1911 in Eliot's notebook drafts (see *IMH* 71).

3 The following analysis of Eliot and Bergson draws upon Jewel Spears Brooker, "Eliot and Bergson: 'Rhapsody on a Windy Night' and the Intractability of Dualism," *Partial Answers* 13:1 (January 2015), pp. 1–30.

4 Henri Bergson. *Time and Free Will: An Essay on the Immediate Data of Consciousness* (1889), trans. F. L. Pogson (London: George Allen, 1912), p. 235.

5 Henri Bergson. *An Introduction to Metaphysics* (1903), trans. T. E. Hulme (London: G. P. Putnam's Sons, 1912), pp. 84–5.

6 Henri Bergson. *Matter and Memory* (1896), trans. N. M. Paul and W. S. Palmer (London: George Allen and Unwin, 1911), p. vii.

7 *Matter and Memory*, p. vii.

8 Eliot's quotation of Bergson is from *Matter and Memory*, p. 326.

9 *Matter and Memory*, p. 78.

10 William James, *Pragmatism* (New York: Longmans, Green, 1907), pp. 76–7. James's italics.

11 Josiah Royce, *The World and the Individual* (New York: Macmillan, 1901), p. 242.

12 Bruce Kuklick, *The Rise of American Philosophy: Cambridge, Massachusetts, 1860–1930* (New Haven: Yale University Press, 1977), p. xxi.

13 Kuklick, pp. 249–50.

14 John Clendenning, *The Life and Thought of Josiah Royce* (Madison: University of Wisconsin Press, 1985), p. 378.

15 *Josiah Royce's Seminar, 1913–1914 as Recorded in the Notebooks of Harry T. Costello*, ed. Grover Smith (New Brunswick: Rutgers University Press, 1963), p. 77.

16 F. H. Bradley, *Principles of Logic* (New York: G. E. Stechert, 1912), p. 533. Quoted by Eliot in "Francis Herbert Bradley" (1927) (*CP3* 306).

17 F. H. Bradley, *Appearance and Reality: A Metaphysical Essay* (1893), 2nd ed. (Oxford: Clarendon, 1897), pp. 405, 403.

18 F. H. Bradley, "On Our Knowledge of Immediate Experience," in *Essays on Truth and Reality* (Oxford: Clarendon, 1914), pp. 159–60.

19 Bradley, *Appearance and Reality*, p. 552.

13

BARRY SPURR

"Anglo-Catholic in Religion": T. S. Eliot and Christianity

Of the significant influences on T. S. Eliot's life and work, religion is the most often misunderstood and misrepresented. The essential reason for this is the failure to take the poet at his word in several important statements that he made about his Christianity, at different points in his life. We also need to give careful attention to the ways in which he wrote about the experience of faith in his poems, and in his correspondence, too, now that several volumes of his letters have been published.

Eliot announced, in 1928, that the position that he had adopted (with regard to religion) was that of an "anglo-catholic" (*CP3* 513). It is necessary to be clear about what that statement means and what it does not mean. Characteristically, Eliot presents us with a precise formula. And his declaration, especially in that twentieth-century inter-war period of burgeoning conviction and confidence in the Anglo-Catholic movement in the Church of England, amounted to an unequivocal public expression of allegiance to an increasingly conspicuous variety of faith and practice. Eliot was to remain faithful to this for the rest of his life. He was not merely a "High Church" Anglican; he had not, by embracing Anglo-Catholicism, joined the "establishment" (quite the contrary, in fact), and he had not become, as some confused commentators seem to believe, a "Catholic," apparently meaning to designate, by that term, a Roman Catholic. "Mon point de vue est Anglo-Catholique et pas Catholique de Rome," ["My point of view is Anglo-Catholic and not Roman Catholic"] Eliot wrote to Jacques Maritain in 1927 (*L3* 620). Others refer to "the Anglo-Catholic Church" and Eliot joining it. There was and is no such body. Eliot pointed out emphatically in some notes on Northrop Frye's book about him: "One does not *join* an Anglo-Catholic wing!" (*L3* 573n1). And, usually, people speak of Eliot's "conversion" to Christianity. Not only did Eliot not undergo a conversion experience, but he firmly deprecated the idea, both with regard to his own religious experience and to any influence that his faith or his references to it in his work might have on others.

This stubbornly persistent conversion theory leads commentators into misreadings not only of Eliot's thought but of his poetry, propagating (for example) ideas that Eliot "refashions himself from the poet of *The Waste Land* into the Christian poet" with "an entirely new manner and vision" (*L3* xiii). In what sense did Eliot ever become a "Christian poet," in the sense that that term is usually understood? The continuities in his oeuvre, thematically and technically, are more remarkable than any striking change of manner and vision as the result of a mid-career renunciation of his former life and a new beginning. Reflecting on the concept of his conversion in a letter to Paul Elmer More in 1936, Eliot wrote: "[W]hat appears to another person to be a change of attitude or even a recantation of former views often appears to the author himself rather as part of a continuous and more or less consistent development."[1]

The pre-conversion *Waste Land*, with its dependence on the myth of the Holy Grail and the Passion story, is at least as much a "Christian" poem as *Four Quartets*, which is an extended philosophical meditation on time and timelessness only intermittently specifically Christian in reference. And in that later work, the sense of the wasteland experience of most human beings (such as the "Eructation of unhealthy souls / Into the faded air") pointedly persists, even if it is now punctuated with the possibility of tentatively realised "hints and guesses" (*CPP* 174, 190) of an alternatively redemptive and transcendental experience and domain. The "gloomy hills of London" in *Burnt Norton*, the first Quartet, belong to the same mindset of the poet who lamented the spiritual death of the "crowd" that "flowed over London Bridge" in *The Waste Land* (*CPP* 62). And the qualities of the prosody – such as the haunting use of incantation – are sustained from Eliot's earliest work to the last. Of his first Christian poems, "Journey of the Magi" (1927) and "A Song for Simeon" (1928), Eliot opined that both works posed a question (rather than supplying an answer): "how fully was the Truth revealed to those who were inspired to recognise Our Lord so soon after the Nativity?" (*L3* 641n1). And Eliot's flippant account of the circumstances of writing the former of these works is a warning, too, against an over-solemn reading of such expressions of reputedly assured faith: "I have no illusions about it: I wrote it in three quarters of an hour after church time and before lunch one Sunday morning, with the assistance of half a bottle of Booth's gin" (*L3* 700). The final reflection of the solitary magus, "I should be glad of another death" (*CPP* 104), ends the poem not with closure but in an open-ended reflection on a longed-for but uncertain future state of belief.

The poet's slowly developing apprehension of the intimations of religious truth cannot be reduced to a simplistic chronological narrative of pre- and post-conversion, especially with the implications of arrival at assurance that such crude terminology invites. In a typical statement, Eliot wrote to his brother Henry (with whom he corresponded "more frankly" than with "anyone else in the world" [*L3* 230]) that "One realises that one never arrives at anything, but must just go on fighting every day as long as the strength lasts" (*L3* 229).

The necessity for conscientious journeying in the quest for ultimate wisdom remains a potent idea from the beginning to the end and climax of Eliot's poetic career; from Prufrock's determination to set out on a night-time's peregrination for illumination regarding overwhelming questions of existence, and the querent's pursuit of the Grail in *The Waste Land*, to *Four Quartets*. There, initially in *Burnt Norton*, we follow a journey-in-miniature in the form of an excursion into the rose garden that proposes nothing less than a recovery of "our first world" of Edenic innocence. It is a fleeting experience, for "human kind / Cannot bear very much reality" (*CPP* 172). Earlier, in *Ash-Wednesday*, the arduousness of pilgrimage is configured in terms of oscillating ascent and descent. A painful exercise of stair-climbing in its third section dramatizes a persona who would attain spiritual perfection, renouncing worldliness, but is constantly and literally bedevilled in his quest, as he is also represented, repeatedly, posing a series of queries, with incantatory insistence, about both a life lived in accord with the Word and the means of giving voice to a compelling, contemporary poetic language in which to express it. With regard to Eliot's later poems, Kenneth Graham puts the matter succinctly when he writes that they "ask more questions than they answer."[2]

None of this is to say that there was any tincture of insincerity or a fatally disabling doubt in Eliot's faith, but, equally, such reflections indicate how completely ideas of a radical refashioning of thought and artistry as the result of a "conversion" experience miss the mark. For him, religious belief was in constant tension with scepticism: "it takes application, and a kind of genius, to believe anything, and to believe *anything* ... will probably become more and more difficult as time goes on ... There is always *doubt*" (*CP3* 20). Eliot published these reflections, with those emphases, in the very year of his Baptism and Confirmation. For him, what he called "the truths of religion" were not "a question of something absolutely true (or false) in so many words; but they are more nearly true than is the contradiction of them" (*L3* 648).

By embracing Anglo-Catholicism, the poet was formally committing himself to a range of beliefs, spiritual disciplines and liturgical practices, deriving from the Catholic tradition of Anglican theology and worship, which had been given particular prominence by the nineteenth-century Oxford Movement and which were the antithesis of what he had known of Christianity in the untheological, terrestrially focused moralism of the Unitarianism of his upbringing. He had repudiated this by the time he was a university student.[3] Anglo-Catholicism was a school of ecclesiastical thought and practice that was insistently mindful of belonging to Western Christendom at large.

Indeed, in the 1920s, Anglo-Catholicism was actively aspiring to full reunion with Rome, notably in the Malines Conversations from 1921 to 1926 between Viscount Halifax, lay leader of Anglo-Catholics in Britain, and Cardinal Désiré-Joseph Mercier. This unity had been ruptured by the sixteenth-century Protestant Reformation, which Eliot, typically of an Anglo-Catholic, regarded as an unmitigated disaster. Writing to a Jesuit priest about the founding of the Society of Jesus, Eliot commented: "What I really regret ... is the intellectual break up of Europe and the rise of Protestantism" (*L3* 131). He believed that it was "almost inevitable that Canterbury should eventually be superseded by Rome" (*L3* 254). But he eschewed contemporary English Roman Catholicism, which, in its literary and intellectual guise, he personified as "Bellochesterton" (reflecting the collaboration of the Anglo-Frenchman Hilaire Belloc and G. K. Chesterton). He wrote that, in contrast, "I cling to some alternative ... I cling to my martyr'd archbishop, Wm. Laud" (*L3* 520), indicating there an inspiration of Anglo-Catholicism much earlier than the Oxford Movement, in the Catholicity of the Caroline divines of the early seventeenth century who, in turn, looked back to the early Church for the inspiration of a primitive Catholicism uncorrupted by later papal medievalism. "I am associated with what is called the Catholic movement," Eliot wrote in 1932, "as represented by Viscount Halifax and the English Church Union. I accordingly believe in the Creeds, the invocation of the Blessed Virgin and the Saints, the Sacrament of Penance etc." (*L3* 572–3n1).

What was most appealing to Eliot in Anglo-Catholicism was the movement's bringing into lively relationship two elements which, by the 1920s, he had come to value very highly, intellectually and personally. These were the historical and cultural heritage at the centre of the life of a society (in his case, England – where he had been in permanent residence from 1915 and where he acquired citizenship in November 1927 – with the English Church at the heart of that society, as it still was, if increasingly precariously, in those days) and the theology, spirituality and ritual of the Western Catholic Church at large, as he had encountered it during several visits to Europe, especially in France and Italy. This, through the centuries, had given Western civilisation its meaning and purpose, as well as its great artistry (in the works of poets such as Dante, whom Eliot came to value above all others), however dimly that heritage was understood and appreciated by the time of the twentieth century. For him, in England, the Church of England (for all its shortcomings and, in its Protestant elements, its compromising of Catholic doctrine and practice) was the Catholic Church in the land; the Roman Catholic Church there being merely a sect because of its long separation from the mainstream of the nation's cultural life and heritage. And where that Catholicity of Anglicanism was most evident was in Anglo-Catholicism, especially in parishes which were strongly committed to the movement's theological and liturgical principles, such as St Stephen's, Gloucester Road, in London, Eliot's parish church throughout his Christian life.

Indeed, it was the Anglo-Catholic tradition that made it possible for Eliot to join the Church of England in the first place, as he noted in "Thoughts after Lambeth" (1931):

> [I]f Anglo-Catholicism has assisted a few persons to leave the Church of England who could never have rested in that uneasy bed anyway, on the other hand it has helped many more, I believe – one cannot quote statistics in the negative – to remain within the Anglican Church. Why, for instance, has Lord Halifax not saved himself a deal of trouble, of generous toil and disappointment, by becoming a convert out of hand? (*CP4* 239)

Halifax – "the greatest living figure of the Catholic movement"[4] – received Eliot at Hickleton Hall in Yorkshire in October 1927, a few months after his Baptism and Confirmation (on 29 and 30 June), and Eliot

> accompanied his host each day to Hickleton Church ... where they worshipped in a form which only an expert could have detected was other than the Roman Catholic mass, and where the building was exactly arranged with lights, lamps, pictures, images and the redolence of incense so as to have what one could only call a Catholic atmosphere.[5]

Eliot described Halifax to his mother as "a very saintly man" (*L3* 734) and, after the visit, they engaged in a warm correspondence, focused on Halifax's ecumenical preoccupation about which Eliot expressed his reservations in a lengthy letter on the subject to his host, including this reflection: "I believe that the immediate difficulties in the way of Anglo-Roman reconciliation are great. I fear Rome at present, because I fear that it would welcome any movement towards the abolition of the Kingship in Britain" (*L3* 756–7). The "anglo-catholic in religion" was, we remember, also a "royalist in politics" (*CP3* 513).

The appurtenances and environment of worship that Eliot shared with Halifax at Hickleton are usually seen by those unsympathetic to Anglo-Catholicism as evidence of its disreputable preoccupation with the aesthetic externals of Christianity, "bells and smells." But for Eliot, as for Halifax and all devout Anglo-Catholics, the outward and visible signs of liturgy and church adornment are not only beautiful in themselves, and, thereby conducive to stirring the sense of "the numinous" appropriate to prayer and worship, but – more importantly – they testify, in their created beauty, to the central truth of Catholic theology at large (and which was at the heart of Eliot's Christianity): the doctrine of the Incarnation.

This and the belief in Original Sin were the key tenets of Eliot's religion, combining his emerging Catholicism with the Puritan heritage of his ancestors with its relentless stress on man's fallen nature. Eliot reflected late in his life that he possessed "a Catholic cast of mind, a Calvinistic heritage, and a Puritanical temperament" (*OPP* 209).

The poet's conviction of the implication of all humanity in what Newman called the "aboriginal calamity" of original sinfulness (implicit everywhere in the wasteland world of Eliot's earlier poetry) came to be balanced by a deep appreciation of the redemptive "gift" – "half guessed" and "half understood" – of the "Incarnation" (*CPP* 190), as he puts it, with the telling capitalisation.

The participation of the Word made flesh in the created order indicated the potential for the hallowing of this fallen world, "spitting from the mouth the withered apple-seed" (*CPP* 97). Because this is rarely experienced in its fullness of meaning and is configured by the poet in terms of the brief, timeless moment in time, "the still point of the turning world" (*CPP* 173), Eliot is always stressing the need for constant journeying in understanding and striving for such epiphanies: even the "old men" of *Four Quartets* must be "explorers" (*CPP* 182).

Anglo-Catholicism provided encouragement in what Eliot more than once referred to as "the struggle for existence" (*CP2* 95, 503), by teaching that the graces of the Church's sacramental life, in particular, were an extension of the Incarnation. His devout participation in the sacraments, especially of the Mass and – notably, for one so conscious of sin, both universal and personal – in Penance (or Confession) was a conspicuous expression of his Incarnational Christianity. It is noteworthy, in the summary of his beliefs as an Anglo-Catholic which Eliot gave to Sister Power (to which we referred earlier), that it is "the Sacrament of Penance" which is singled out amongst the seven sacraments for listing as one of the elements of his faith.

Eliot commented that "ritual and habit" were "essential to religion" (*CP3* 457), and even by Anglo-Catholic standards he brought a rigorous commitment to the observance of the Church's disciplines in the course of each liturgical year. He participated, for example, in the annual Holy Week "watch" before the tabernacle at St Stephen's Church, an ancient liturgical custom drawing attention both to Christ's Real Presence in the Eucharist and to his Passion ("Could ye not watch with me one hour?" Matt. 26:40), taking place between the Maundy Thursday liturgy and the Good Friday liturgy of the Passion. His fellow parishioner, Mary Trevelyan, records in her diary for 1950 that Eliot insisted on taking the 1 a.m. to 2 a.m. watch before the Sacrament that Easter, and the next day looked particularly exhausted.[6]

In addition to High Mass on Sundays, he observed all the holy days of obligation (usually falling on weekdays), by Mass attendance, involving early rising and, of course, fasting. Eliot's rigorous observance of the Eucharistic fast (in those days, from midnight to the reception of communion the following morning) is an example of the importance to him not only of ritual and habit, and of obedience to authority and order (resonating, too, with the principles of classicism that he so often commended), but of mortification of the flesh. It included the Friday rule of avoiding meat. The poet, Anne Ridler, told me that Eliot would warn prospective Friday hostesses of the necessity (in his case) for fish. This would have been an exceptional request from an "ordinary" Anglican, even a High Churchman. But Eliot was adamant that others should be aware of his position and the implications of his commitment. Herbert Read noted of his friend: "[A] statement of differences he could respect; what he could not tolerate was any false interpretation of the position he himself held."[7] From the beginning of his Anglo-Catholic life, Eliot was a devoted Mass-goer. He told William Force Stead that he found the sacrament "indispensable" and within months of his Baptism had established the habit of attending Mass on weekdays as well as the obligatory Sunday, writing: "(strictly private) I communicate three times a week." In this letter (of 29 December 1927) he points out that he had made no "Christmas communion," although he had attended the British Church [in Paris] on Sunday, but having "breakfasted ... did not communicate" (*L3* 872).

Like many Anglo-Catholics, in the matter of Eucharistic teaching and of other issues of doctrine and practice, Eliot was often critical of and exasperated by what he saw as the theological imprecision of mainstream Anglicanism and especially of what he regarded as the compromising of Catholic teaching that was characterising the growing ecumenical movement in its overtures to Protestant Churches. In both "Thoughts after Lambeth" and the later pamphlet, "Reunion by Destruction" (1943), in which he inveighed against the proposal for the Church of South India, whereby Anglicans would recognise non-episcopal bodies, he particularly focused on one of the cardinal points of Anglo-Catholic principle, the importance of episcopal ordination of priests and of the so-called Apostolic Succession of bishops that made those ordinations – and the subsequent sacramental ministrations of those so ordained – valid: "[W]hat is required is some theory of degrees of reception of the Blessed Sacrament, as well as the validity of the ministration of a celebrant not episcopally ordained ... if the Church of England cannot find these reasons, and make them intelligible to the more philosophically trained among the faithful, what can it do?" (*CP4* 233).

That Eliot took these matters as seriously as he did, and was prepared – unusually, with regard to his personal religion – to enter into public controversy about them, not only indicates how important they were to him but should make us realise how significant the precise matters of Anglo-Catholic teaching were to him. When he writes, in the last of the *Quartets*, that "You are here to kneel / Where prayer has been valid" (*CPP* 192), our interpretation of that adjective is impoverished if we are unaware of the deep resonance of the term within Anglo-Catholic discourse. The Laudian basis of sacramental worship at the Little Gidding church in the time of Nicholas Ferrar was for Eliot exemplary of such valid liturgy.

The High Mass was the glory of triumphant Anglo-Catholicism, following the order in *The English Missal*, the Anglo-Catholic conflation of The Book of Common Prayer and the *Missale Romanum*. In weekly attendance on Sundays, as well as on great holy days, Eliot, genuflecting to the Real Presence in the sanctuary on entering St Stephen's, would have found the high altar's six candles ablaze and the air redolent with the preparation of incense for the ensuing ceremony, most of which was sung by the three sacred ministers, vested in chasuble, dalmatic and tunicle, with Gregorian chant and polyphony from the choir (Palestrina, then, was a favourite[8]), much of it in Latin. During the "Canon" of the Mass, its central, most solemn section, wherein the consecration of the bread and wine took place, uttered by the celebrant *in secreto* – silently – Eliot and his fellow congregants would have peered through the incense-clouded sanctuary to the elevation of the Host and of the chalice of the Blood, accompanied by the ringing of the sanctuary bell, crossing themselves and bowing their heads in prayer as the Canon drew to its conclusion. They would lift their eyes again a few minutes later when the priest, turning to the people, after having made his communion, holding the paten aloft with the Host just above it, enunciated the words "Behold the Lamb of God." To this they would have responded three times, striking their breasts in rhythm with the words that made their way into *Ash-Wednesday*:

> Lord, I am not worthy that thou shouldest enter under my roof;
> But speak the word only, and my soul shall be healed.

Holy Week was the climax of the worshipping year. An altar server from the days of Eliot's attendance at St Stephen's, under its rector, Eric Cheetham, recalled for me the dramatic characteristics of the observance of the various ceremonies: "It was very liturgical and adhered strictly to the *then* Roman rite according to the English Missal and *Ritual Notes*. Everything was very dramatic and to an extent theatrical as was Fr Cheetham's wish with fading house lights, spotlights on the pulpit, tabernacle etc. I remember that only rattles *not* bells were used on Maundy Thursday."[9] On Good Friday, Christ's reproaches were sung during the third part of the liturgy on that day, "The Solemn Adoration of the Holy Cross": "O my people, what have I done unto thee? or wherein have I wearied thee? Answer me!" Eliot punctuates the fifth section of *Ash-Wednesday* with the first reproach, but concludes it with the warmth of "O my people" (*CPP* 96), the reproachful phrase having been removed, as the spirituality of the poem moves towards a vision of redemption, the six-section work at large proceeding through Lent, from Ash Wednesday to Good Friday.

"I like a full liturgy myself,"[10] Eliot wrote, and his Anglo-Catholic preference in this regard is given expression in his poetry. With regard to the Mass, for example, the doctrine of transubstantiation is strikingly enunciated in the last stanza of the theological lyric in *East Coker*. But Eliot also recognised that such ceremonial preferences had a temperamental, even sensual basis, in addition to their theological justification. In a letter to Geoffrey Faber, he noted that he found pleasure in a range of experiences: "Paul Whiteman [the popular bandleader known as the "King of Jazz"], in High Mass at the Madeleine [a neo-classical Catholic church in Paris] and in the Café des Ambassadeurs [a restaurant and nightclub, also in Paris]" (*L3* 712).

Yet it was the sacrament of penance, or confession, that was most characteristic of Eliot's Christianity – not in terms of his frequency of recourse to it (in the Anglican way, he used it occasionally, a few times each year; not weekly, in the once-usual manner of devout Roman Catholics), but with regard to its sacramental expression of his conviction that "penitence and humility are the foundation of the Christian life"[11] and the two are, of course, inextricably linked. Baudelaire, Eliot judged, possessed "the greatest, the most difficult, of the Christian virtues, the virtue of humility" (*CP3* 77) and "perceived that what really matters is Sin and Redemption" (*CP4* 161), while Simone Weil, a Jewish convert to Christianity, had "an almost superhuman humility."[12] Of Pascal, Eliot exclaimed: "how fast a hold he has of humility!" (*CP4* 347). In his poetry, Eliot declared that "humility is endless" (*CPP* 179) and in an unusually public expression (on BBC radio) of the private persuasion of his faith, its ascetic qualities emerge with a focus on this virtue: "[T]he Christian scheme seemed the only possible scheme which found a place for values which I must maintain or perish (and belief comes first and practice second), the belief, for instance, in holy living and holy dying, in sanctity, chastity, humility, austerity" (*CP4* 428).

This observation incorporates the titles of the two best-known devotional works of the seventeenth-century bishop, Jeremy Taylor: *The Rule and Exercise of Holy Living* (1650) and … *of Holy Dying* (1651). Taylor was a champion of sacramental confession, urging the clergy on in its practice. A fortnight later – also in the *Listener* – Eliot confesses to "low appetites" and "vulgar tastes" and how they have been assuaged in his life: "I have perceived their transience, their unsatisfactoriness, and the horror of satiety which is far beyond the famine of deprivation … Without the love of God there is no love at all" (*CP4* 449, 451). This restraint in not naming and specifying these appetites and tastes while admitting to them – a similar strategy to John Donne's non-specific catalogue of his sins in the lyric "Wilt thou forgive that sin" – makes them seem even more terrible for being unspeakable, or at least unspoken.

Eliot preferred to have as his confessor a priest distinct from his vicar at St Stephen's. His first was Francis Underhill (cousin of Evelyn Underhill, the famous author of *Mysticism* [1911]) who went on to become, as Bishop of Bath and Wells, one of the first definite Anglo-Catholic prelates in the Church of England. Next was the Reverend Sir Percy Maryon-Wilson, vicar of St Mary's, Somers Town, by Euston Station, and he was followed by the Reverends P. G. Bacon and F. L. Hillier (whom Eliot had met on retreat at St Silas's, Kentish Town).

Mary Trevelyan records Eliot's account, in 1953, of his settled custom in the matter of this sacrament:

> I write to my Confessor [by this stage, Father Bacon] for an appointment. He always says 12.30 and invites me to lunch afterwards and I always accept as part of my penance. Sometimes I wonder if he remembers what I said last time and the time before and every time – always the same. When it is over, I say my penance.[13]

The phrase, "Bless me father," which we find in the final section of Eliot's most confessional poem, *Ash-Wednesday*, is the penitent's opening phrase in the rite: "Bless me, Father, for I have sinned."

In the penitential season of Lent, Eliot observed its first day, Ash Wednesday, in traditional Anglo-Catholic style – as Trevelyan recalled in her diary for 1950: "On Ash Wednesday we attended Matins and Ante-Communion and the Imposition of the Ashes at 11 a.m., then drove through St. James's Park to our respective offices." "Ashed," to remind him of his humble status, Eliot would have spent the rest of the day at Faber & Faber with the remains of the black cross, inscribed by the priest, on his forehead.

It is in Eliot's plays that the value he placed on the confession of sin is most strongly reflected in his creative work. In *Murder in the Cathedral*

(1935), the references are most explicit with repeated references to the "divine appointment" of Christ to Peter and his successors to absolve the penitent. At his martyrdom, in Thomas's last words, as he commends his soul to God, Eliot uses phrases from the confessional formula, the *Confiteor*, from the priest's introductory prayers prior to Mass: "Now to Almighty God, to the Blessed Mary ever Virgin" (*CPP* 275).

At the very core of Eliot's next play, *The Family Reunion* (1939), where the setting is, contrastingly, in the modern world, the age-old discipline of concentration on the recollection of sin and the desire for repentance is seen to be a fundamental human process. Harry retreats to Wishwood for a contemplative experience of self-discovery (Anglo-Catholic retreats, frequently engaged in by Eliot, customarily feature sacramental confession). Harry is haunted by the faces and circumstances of a traumatic past and he needs, if he is ever to be freed from the despair they are daily imposing on his spirit, to encounter them courageously and (in humility) to be purged from their influence. Agatha (the name of the virgin martyr who is listed in the Canon of the Mass and who is invoked against fire) promises that, at this moment of grace, all time will be gathered together and stand still. Harry's situation is given dramatic force by his impatience for confession and, hence, liberation from his sinfulness. He bares his soul to Warburton, the family's doctor.

Aloneness as the necessary prelude to atonement for sin is stressed in Eliot's last plays, *The Confidential Clerk* (1954) and *The Elder Statesman* (1959). But it is in that final play where, repeatedly, the characters insist upon the need for confession ("confession" and "confess" are used several times), and the attainment of ultimate peace, arising out of the act of contrition, is celebrated in Claverton's assertion that he has been "brushed by the wing of happiness" (*CPP* 581), reflecting that familiar emotion of relief and release to which many penitents refer, especially after their first experience of confession and absolution in its sacramental form. The lovely phrase may also allude, in a play dedicated "To My Wife," to Eliot's own experience of absolving and solving human love in his 1957 marriage to Valerie Fletcher, when he appeared to all who knew him to have been born again, as it were.

Anglo-Catholicism would seem to have prepared Eliot, in a particular way, for the complete enjoyment of this unexpected happiness. Early in his experience of the practice of the faith, he wrote to Geoffrey Faber: "I have found my own love for a woman enhanced, intensified and purified by meditation on the Virgin" (*L3* 711). As surely as any other aspect of his Christianity, Eliot's devotion to Mary places him securely in the Anglo-Catholic tradition. It was one of the hallmarks of its advanced expression, the restoration in the 1930s of the medieval shrine of Our Lady of Walsingham in

Norfolk being its most obvious manifestation. Eliot had no reservations about the various Marian dogmas, and when Pope Pius XII defined her Assumption in 1950, to the dismay of many Anglican theologians – even of moderate Catholic persuasion, like Austin Farrer – Eliot, as Mary Trevelyan recalls, expressed no difficulty and was content to explain it as "Our Lady by-passing Purgatory,"[14] alluding, in the process, to another contentious and allegedly unscriptural Catholic teaching to which only Anglo-Catholics, in Anglicanism, subscribe.

It is in the context of Eliot's Marianism that we do find a sharp contrast between his earlier and later poetry. Prior to *Ash-Wednesday*, female figures are presented negatively, almost without exception. In *The Waste Land*, for example, we have a cavalcade of suicidal sybils, false prophetesses and neurotic and promiscuous denizens of the debauched metropolis. In "The Hollow Men" (1925), there is a brief glimpse of hopefulness in the midst of the abject despair of these wastelanders, consigned to Hell, as they cast desperate eyes on "the perpetual star / Multifoliate rose" (*CPP* 85) of the redemptive dispensation, recalling Dante's vision of the Virgin in his *Paradiso*. But the allusion is oblique, and a hopeless hope, in fact, in this context. Nonetheless, it is a significant moment in Eliot's poetry as the very first sign of the possibility of redeemed life, and, crucially, this is communicated through a vision of the Mediatrix. Christopher Ricks points out that, originally, "The Hollow Men" ended on this optimistic note – very different from its ultimately despairing close with "a whimper."[15] And although the "silken girls" (*CPP* 103) in "Journey of the Magi" are beautiful, they are distractions from the wise men's quest. It is not until *Ash-Wednesday*, the most important Marian poem, in English, of the twentieth century that we encounter the wholehearted appreciation of the ways in which meditation on the divine in female form can be so profoundly restorative.[16]

The importance of Mary to Eliot is also clearly demonstrated in *Four Quartets*, where the four theological lyrics, in each poem, are devoted, in turn, to the Persons of the Trinity and – in *The Dry Salvages* – to Mary, conferring high status on her by that inclusion with Father, Son and Spirit. The lyric for her is in the form of a prayer for protection for those at sea (in this watery third Quartet), based on the understanding that she is the one who, like so many fishermen's mothers and wives, saw her son setting forth on a dangerous journey, Jonah-like, to "the dark throat" of death. To begin the poem, Eliot notes a "shrine" of the "Lady" (*CPP* 189), having in mind the church of Notre Dame de la Garde, high up overlooking the Mediterranean at Marseilles, but he also insisted in a letter that it could be any shrine to the Virgin.[17] From his childhood, Eliot was familiar with the image of Mary atop the church of Our Lady of Good Voyage in Gloucester, Massachusetts, even if the Unitarian lad had never entered this Catholic building.[18]

As the essential philosophico-theological teaching of *Four Quartets* is the apprehension of the intersection of the timeless with time, the necessity to be alive to the intimations of spiritual insight which may be revealed in the midst of ordinary activity, the appropriateness of the Virgin, whose annunciation is the Christian archetype of such a "still point" (*CPP* 173), initiating the mystery of the Incarnation, is evident. But in addition to the Virgin of the Annunciation, Eliot embraces the idea of Mary as *Mater Dolorosa*, the mother of Sorrows; and she is also here, crowned, as the "Queen of Heaven," *Regina Coeli*.

These various "mysteries" of the Virgin are concentrated in the rosary devotion which was a daily element in Eliot's private prayer life, including the repeated "*Ave Maria*" petition ("Hail Mary ... Pray for us sinners now and at the hour of our death"). Phrases from this, and from the "*salve Regina*" ("Hail, holy Queen ... After this our exile, show unto us the blessed fruit of thy womb, Jesus") make their way, in various forms, into his poetry. Writing to Trevelyan on 11 January 1948, and noting the feast of St Honoré du Faubourg, Eliot offers her the choice of one of two rosaries blessed and given to him by Pius XII (with whom he had had an audience the previous week). In a subsequent letter (26 January), he repeats the offer of a good rosary (with the words in block letters this time), pointing out that he will not give it to anyone who would not keep it in constant use. In her diary for 1950, Trevelyan notes how Eliot's papal rosary lost a bead and "put him off his stride."

Eliot's praying the rosary points to the fact that prayer and meditation were, for him, the bedrock of faith, sustaining the Christian in daily life, especially in the modern secular world. There were "only four ways of thinking," Eliot asserted in 1931, "to talk to others, or to one other, or to talk to oneself, or to talk to God" (*CP4* 390), and the greatest of these was the last – that is, prayer. Eliot reflected that "the highest life is the life of contemplation" (*OPP* 126). But, typically, for him, even this activity, outside the structures of public worship, had to be ordered and part of a routine. So he was strongly drawn to the life of religious communities, where prayer could be pursued in a highly disciplined environment of individual as well as communal devotion. Again, this is a specifically Anglo-Catholic element in his Christianity, as such communities, flourishing for a century after the Oxford Movement, were concentrated centres of Anglo-Catholic faith and practice, uninhibited by Protestantising influences in diocesan and parochial Anglicanism. By the 1950s, Eliot had determined to retire permanently, as a lay member, to the Benedictine house at Nashdom in Buckinghamshire, remarking to a friend in 1952: "One day I will go there to stay permanently. It suits me. I would have no guests then, but you could come every year for a week or two, being a priest."[19] Had events in his personal life not turned out differently, culminating in his marriage five years later, this is how Eliot's life would have ended. He believed, moreover, that the modern world at large had much to learn from the monastic vocation: "It will become more and more a question whether something corresponding to the monastic seclusion, some form of complete or temporary withdrawal from the affairs of the world, will be one of the great remedies for the dehumanizing effect of a civilization of busybodies."[20]

Anglo-Catholicism was the central element, the still point in T. S. Eliot's world picture, from 1927 until his death in 1965, informing all that he did in his creative work and, of course, in his personal life. We cannot enter fully into the mind of this great poet or into his work (including that prior to his "conversion," for he was journeying towards this understanding of human life well before his Baptism and Confirmation in 1927), until we have learnt of his faith, the ground of his being.

NOTES

1 Quoted in Kenneth Asher, *T. S. Eliot and Ideology* (Cambridge: Cambridge University Press, 1995), p. 9.

2 Kenneth Graham, "Devotional Poetry," in Roland Greene *et al.* (eds.), *The Princeton Encyclopedia of Poetry and Poetics* (Princeton: Princeton University Press, 2012), p. 354.

3 Writing to his Unitarian mother, towards the end of her life, about his belief in their meeting in a "future life," Eliot reflects the gulf between Unitarianism's casting-off of orthodox Christianity's transcendental teachings, and his embrace of them, when, recording his hope that "I shall see you in another life," he gently notes that "I somehow have a much firmer conviction than you have, and I wish that you felt as I do ... I should like to feel that you felt sure as I do of our meeting again." 22 August 1927 (*L3* 647).

4 J. G. Lockhart, *Charles Lindley – Viscount Halifax*, Part II: 1885–1934 (London: Geoffrey Bles, 1936), p. 368.

5 Robert Sencourt, *T. S. Eliot: A Memoir* (London: Garnstone Press, 1971), p. 104.

6 Mary Trevelyan, unpublished diary, photocopy of typescript in my possession.

7 Herbert Read, "T. S. E. – A Memoir," *T. S. Eliot: The Man and His Work*, ed. Allen Tate (London: Chatto & Windus, 1967), p. 27.

8 Information from an altar server at St Stephen's in the 1950s.

9 Delian Bower, letter to me, 22 October 1975. The Roman rite for Holy Week was extensively revised in the 1950s by Pope Pius XII. Mr Bower was referring to the rite before the revisions, as observed by Roman and Anglo-Catholics.

10 T. S. Eliot, *The Value and Use of Cathedrals in England Today* (Chichester: Friends of Chichester Cathedral, 1952), p. 6.

11 *A Sermon preached in Magdalene College Chapel* (Cambridge: Cambridge University Press, 1948), p. 8.
12 Preface to *The Need for Roots* (London: Routledge and Kegan Paul, 1952), p. vi.
13 Trevelyan, unpublished diary, 1953.
14 Trevelyan, unpublished diary, 1956.
15 Christopher Ricks, *Decisions and Revisions in T. S. Eliot* (London: The British Library, 2003), p. 96.
16 For a full account of this poem, from this perspective, see Barry Spurr *See the Virgin Blest: Representations of the Virgin Mary in English Poetry* (New York: Palgrave Macmillan, 2007), pp. 177–82.
17 Quoted in Helen Gardner, *The Composition of* Four Quartets (London: Faber and Faber, 1978), p. 141.
18 See Nancy Hargrove, *Landscape as Symbol in the Poetry of T. S. Eliot* (Jackson: University Press of Mississippi, 1978), p. 165.
19 To Father William Levy, in William Turner Levy and Victor Scherle, *Affectionately, T. S. Eliot: The Story of a Friendship 1947–1965* (London: Dent, 1968), p. 43.
20 "Planning and Religion," *Theology* (May 1943), p. 104.

SELECT BIBLIOGRAPHY

Multi-volume authorised editions of Eliot's texts are in production at the time of writing: *T. S. Eliot: The Poems*, 2 vols., edited by Christopher Ricks and Jim McCue (London: Faber, 2015); *The Complete Prose of T. S. Eliot: The Critical Edition*, 8 vols., under the general editorship of Ronald Schuchard (Baltimore: John Hopkins & London: Faber, 2014-); *The Letters of T. S. Eliot*, under the general editorship of John Haffenden (London: Faber, 2009-), who will also complete a new edition of Eliot's plays.

Ackroyd, Peter, *T. S. Eliot: A Life*. London: Hamish Hamilton, 1984.

Albright, Daniel, *Quantum Poetics: Yeats, Pound, Eliot, and the Science of Modernism*. Cambridge: Cambridge University Press, 1997.

Altieri, Charles, *Painterly Abstraction in Modernist American Poetry: The Contemporaneity of Modernism*. Cambridge: Cambridge University Press, 1989.

Asher, Kenneth, *T. S. Eliot and Ideology*. Cambridge: Cambridge University Press, 1995.

Badenhausen, Richard, *T. S. Eliot and the Art of Collaboration*. Cambridge: Cambridge University Press, 2004.

Bergonzi, Bernard, *T. S. Eliot*. London: Macmillan, 1978.

Bornstein, George, *Transformations of Romanticism in Yeats, Eliot and Stevens*. Chicago: University of Chicago Press, 1976.

Brooker, Jewel Spears, *Mastery and Escape: T. S. Eliot and the Dialectic of Modernism*. Amherst: University of Massachusetts Press, 1994.

ed., *T. S. Eliot: The Contemporary Reviews*. Cambridge: Cambridge University Press, 2004.

Browne, E. Martin, *The Making of T. S. Eliot's Plays*. London: Cambridge University Press, 1969.

Bush, Ronald, *T. S. Eliot: A Study in Character and Style*. New York: Oxford University Press, 1983.

ed., *T. S. Eliot: The Modernist in History*. Cambridge: Cambridge University Press, 1991.

Chace, W. M., *The Political Identities of Ezra Pound and T. S. Eliot*. Stanford: Stanford University Press, 1973.

Chinitz, David, ed., *A Companion to T. S. Eliot*. Chichester: Wiley-Blackwell, 2009.

T. S. Eliot and the Cultural Divide. Chicago: University of Chicago Press, 2003.

Cianci, Giovanni, and Jason Harding, eds. *T. S. Eliot and the Concept of Tradition.* Cambridge: Cambridge University Press, 2007.
Collini, Stefan, *Absent Minds: Intellectuals in Britain*, Oxford: Oxford University Press, 2006.
Cooper, John Xiros, *T. S. Eliot and the Ideology of Four Quartets.* Cambridge: Cambridge University Press, 1995.
The Cambridge Introduction to T. S. Eliot, Cambridge: Cambridge University Press, 2006.
Corcoran, Neil, *Shakespeare and the Modern Poet*, Cambridge: Cambridge University Press, 2010.
Crawford, Robert, *The Savage and the City in the Work of T. S. Eliot*. Oxford: Clarendon Press, 1987.
Young Eliot: From St. Louis to "The Waste Land". London: Jonathan Cape, 2015.
Cuda, Anthony, *The Passions of Modernism: Eliot, Yeats, Woolf, Mann.* Columbia: University of South Carolina Press, 2010.
Däumer, Elisabeth, and Shyamal Bagchee, eds., *The International Reception of T. S. Eliot*. London: Continuum, 2007.
Davie, Donald, *Modernist Essays*, ed. Clive Wilmer. Manchester: Carcanet, 2004.
Donoghue, Denis, *Words Alone: The Poet, T. S. Eliot*. New Haven: Yale University Press, 2000.
Ellis, Steve, *The English Eliot: Dream, Language and Landscape in "Four Quartets"*. London: Routledge, 1991.
T. S. Eliot: A Guide for the Perplexed. London: Continuum, 2009.
Ellmann, Maud, *The Poetics of Impersonality: T. S. Eliot and Ezra Pound*. Brighton: Harvester, 1987.
Freed, Lewis, *T. S. Eliot: The Critic as Philosopher*, West Lafayette: Purdue University Press, 1979.
Gallop, Jane, *Around 1981: Academic Feminist Literary Theory*. New York: Routledge, 1991.
Gallup, Donald, *T. S. Eliot: A Bibliography*. London: Faber, 1969.
Gardner, Helen, *The Art of T. S. Eliot*. London: The Cresset Press, 1968.
Goldie, David, *A Critical Difference: T. S. Eliot and John Middleton Murry in English Literary Criticism, 1919–1928*. Oxford: Oxford University Press, 1998.
Gordon, Lyndall, *T. S. Eliot: An Imperfect Life*. London: Vintage, 1998.
Gray, Piers, *T. S. Eliot's Intellectual and Poetic Development*. Brighton: Harvester, 1982.
Habib, M. A. R., *The Early T. S. Eliot and Western Philosophy*. Cambridge: Cambridge University Press, 1999.
Harding, Jason, *"The Criterion": Cultural Politics and Periodical Networks in Interwar Britain*. Oxford: Oxford University Press, 2002.
ed., *T. S. Eliot in Context*. Cambridge: Cambridge University Press, 2011.
Hargrove, Nancy Duvall, *T. S. Eliot's Parisian Year*. Gainesville: University Press of Florida, 2009.
Howarth, Herbert, *Notes on Some Figures Behind T. S. Eliot*. London: Chatto & Windus, 1965.
Jain, Manju, *T. S. Eliot and American Philosophy: The Harvard Years*. Cambridge: Cambridge University Press, 1992.

Julius, Anthony, *T. S. Eliot, Anti-Semitism and Literary Form*. London: Thames & Hudson, 2003.

Kearns, Cleo McNelly, *T. S. Eliot and Indic Traditions: A Study in Poetry and Belief*. Cambridge: Cambridge University Press, 1987.

Kenner, Hugh, *The Invisible Poet: T. S. Eliot*. London: Methuen, 1960.

Kirk, Russell, *Eliot and His Age: T. S. Eliot's Moral Imagination in the Twentieth Century*. Wilmington: ISI Books, 2008.

Kojecký, Roger, *T. S. Eliot's Social Criticism*. London: Faber, 1971.

Laity, Cassandra, and Nancy K. Gish, eds., *Gender, Desire and Sexuality in T. S. Eliot*. Cambridge: Cambridge University Press, 2004.

Lamos, Colleen, *Deviant Modernism: Sexual and Textual Errancy in T. S. Eliot, James Joyce, and Marcel Proust*. Cambridge: Cambridge University Press, 2004.

Leavis, F. R., *New Bearings in English Poetry*. London: Chatto & Windus, 1950.

Lentricchia, Frank, *Modernist Quartet*. Cambridge: Cambridge University Press, 1994.

Levenson, Michael, *A Genealogy of Modernism: A Study of English Literary Doctrine, 1908–1922*. Cambridge: Cambridge University Press, 1984.

Litz, A. Walton, ed., *Eliot in His Time: Essays on the Occasion of the Fiftieth Anniversary of The Waste Land*. Princeton: Princeton University Press, 1973.

Lobb, Edward, *T. S. Eliot and the Romantic Critical Tradition*. London: Routledge, 1981.

Lockerd, Benjamin, *Aetherial Rumours: T. S. Eliot's Physics and Poetics*. Cranbury: Associated University Presses, 1998.

McDonald, Gail, *Learning to be Modern: Pound, Eliot, and the American University*. Oxford: Clarendon Press, 1993.

Malamud, Randy, *T. S. Eliot's Drama: A Research and Production Sourcebook*. New York: Greenwood Press, 1992.

Manganiello, Dominic. *T. S. Eliot and Dante*. Basingstoke: Macmillan, 1989.

Margolis, J. D., *T. S. Eliot's Intellectual Development 1922–1939*. Chicago: University of Chicago Press, 1972.

Materer, Timothy, *Vortex: Pound, Eliot, and Lewis*. Ithaca: Cornell University Press, 1979.

Matthews, Steven, *T. S. Eliot and Early Modern Literature*. Oxford: Oxford University Press, 2013.

Menand, Louis, *Discovering Modernism: T. S. Eliot and His Context*, New York: Oxford University Press, 1987.

Moody, A. D., ed., *The Cambridge Companion to T. S. Eliot*. Cambridge: Cambridge University Press, 1994.

Thomas Stearns Eliot: Poet. Cambridge: Cambridge University Press, 1994.

North, Michael, *The Political Aesthetics of Yeats, Eliot, and Pound*. Cambridge: Cambridge University Press, 1991.

Reading 1922: A Return to the Scene of the Modern. New York: 1999.

Olney, James, ed., *T. S. Eliot: Essays from the "Southern Review"*. Oxford: Clarendon Press, 1988.

O'Neill, Michael, *The All-Sustaining Air: Romantic Legacies and Renewals in British, American, and Irish Poetry since 1900*. Oxford: Oxford University Press, 2007.

Oser, Lee, *T. S. Eliot and American Poetry*. Columbia: University of Missouri Press, 1998.

The Ethics of Modernism: Moral Ideas in Yeats, Eliot, Joyce, Woolf and Beckett. Cambridge: Cambridge University Press, 2007.

Perl, Jeffrey M., *Skepticism and Modern Enmity: Before and After Eliot*. Baltimore: Johns Hopkins University Press, 1989.

Perloff, Marjorie, *21st Century Modernism: The "New Poetics"*. Oxford: Blackwell, 2002.

Perry, Seamus, *The Connell Guide to T. S. Eliot's "The Waste Land"*. London: Connell, 2014.

Pinkney, T., *Women in the Poetry of T. S. Eliot*. London: Macmillan, 1984.

Raine, Craig, *T. S. Eliot*. Oxford: Oxford University Press, 2006.

Rainey, Lawrence, *Revisiting "The Waste Land"*. New Haven: Yale University Press, 2005.

Reeves, Gareth, *T. S. Eliot: A Virgilian Poet*. London: Macmillan, 1989.

Ricks, Christopher, *T. S. Eliot and Prejudice*. London: Faber, 1988.

Decisions and Revisions in T. S. Eliot. London: British Library, 2003.

True Friendship: Geoffrey Hill, Anthony Hecht, and Robert Lowell Under the Sign of Eliot and Pound. New Haven: Yale University Press, 2010.

Riquelme, John Paul, *Harmony of Dissonances: T. S. Eliot, Romanticism, and Imagination*. Baltimore: Johns Hopkins University Press, 1991.

Schuchard, Ronald, *Eliot's Dark Angel: Intersections of Life and Art*. New York: Oxford University Press, 1999.

Schwartz, Sanford, *The Matrix of Modernism: Pound, Eliot, and Early Twentieth-Century Thought*. Princeton: Princeton University Press, 1985.

Sherry, Vincent, *The Great War and the Language of Modernism*. Oxford: Oxford University Press, 2003.

Sigg, Eric. *The American T. S. Eliot: A Study of the Early Writings*. Cambridge: Cambridge University Press, 1989.

Smith, Carol, *T. S. Eliot's Dramatic Theory and Practice: from "Sweeney Agonistes" to "The Elder Statesman"*. Cambridge: Cambridge University Press, 1963.

Smith, Grover, *T. S. Eliot's Poetry and Plays: A Study in Sources and Meaning*. Chicago: Chicago University Press, 1974.

Smith, Stan, *The Origins of Modernism: Eliot, Pound and the Rhetorics of Renewal*. 1994.

Southam, B. C., *A Student's Guide to the Selected Poems of T. S. Eliot*. London: Faber, 1994.

Spender, Stephen, *T. S. Eliot*. London: Fontana, 1975.

Spurr, Barry, *"Anglo-Catholic in Religion": T. S. Eliot and Christianity*. Cambridge: Lutterworth Press, 2010.

Sullivan, Hannah, *The Work of Revision*. Cambridge, MA: Harvard University Press, 2013.

Svarny, Erik, *"The Men of 1914": T. S. Eliot and Early Modernism*. Milton Keynes: Open University Press, 1988.

Tate, Allen, *T. S. Eliot: The Man and His Work*, London: Chatto & Windus, 1967.

Thaventhiran, Helen. *Radical Empiricists: Five Modernist Close Readers*. Oxford: Oxford University Press, 2015.

Thormählen, Marianne, *"The Waste Land": A Fragmentary Wholeness*. Lund: Gleerup, 1978.

INDEX

Cambridge Companions to...

AUTHORS

Edward Albee edited by Stephen J. Bottoms
Margaret Atwood edited by Coral Ann Howells
W. H. Auden edited by Stan Smith
Jane Austen edited by Edward Copeland and Juliet McMaster (second edition)
James Baldwin edited by Michele Elam
Beckett edited by John Pilling
Bede edited by Scott DeGregorio
Aphra Behn edited by Derek Hughes and Janet Todd
Walter Benjamin edited by David S. Ferris
William Blake edited by Morris Eaves
Boccaccio edited by Guyda Armstrong, Rhiannon Daniels, and Stephen J. Milner
Jorge Luis Borges edited by Edwin Williamson
Brecht edited by Peter Thomson and Glendyr Sacks (second edition)
The Brontës edited by Heather Glen
Bunyan edited by Anne Dunan-Page
Frances Burney edited by Peter Sabor
Byron edited by Drummond Bone
Albert Camus edited by Edward J. Hughes
Willa Cather edited by Marilee Lindemann
Cervantes edited by Anthony J. Cascardi
Chaucer edited by Piero Boitani and Jill Mann (second edition)
Chekhov edited by Vera Gottlieb and Paul Allain
Kate Chopin edited by Janet Beer
Caryl Churchill edited by Elaine Aston and Elin Diamond
Cicero edited by Catherine Steel
Coleridge edited by Lucy Newlyn
Wilkie Collins edited by Jenny Bourne Taylor
Joseph Conrad edited by J. H. Stape
H. D. edited by Nephie J. Christodoulides and Polina Mackay
Dante edited by Rachel Jacoff (second edition)
Daniel Defoe edited by John Richetti
Don DeLillo edited by John N. Duvall
Charles Dickens edited by John O. Jordan
Emily Dickinson edited by Wendy Martin
John Donne edited by Achsah Guibbory
Dostoevskii edited by W. J. Leatherbarrow
Theodore Dreiser edited by Leonard Cassuto and Claire Virginia Eby
John Dryden edited by Steven N. Zwicker
W. E. B. Du Bois edited by Shamoon Zamir
George Eliot edited by George Levine
T. S. Eliot edited by A. David Moody
Ralph Ellison edited by Ross Posnock
Ralph Waldo Emerson edited by Joel Porte and Saundra Morris
William Faulkner edited by Philip M. Weinstein
Henry Fielding edited by Claude Rawson
F. Scott Fitzgerald edited by Ruth Prigozy
Flaubert edited by Timothy Unwin
E. M. Forster edited by David Bradshaw
Benjamin Franklin edited by Carla Mulford
Brian Friel edited by Anthony Roche
Robert Frost edited by Robert Faggen
Gabriel García Márquez edited by Philip Swanson
Elizabeth Gaskell edited by Jill L. Matus
Goethe edited by Lesley Sharpe
Günter Grass edited by Stuart Taberner
Thomas Hardy edited by Dale Kramer
David Hare edited by Richard Boon
Nathaniel Hawthorne edited by Richard Millington
Seamus Heaney edited by Bernard O'Donoghue
Ernest Hemingway edited by Scott Donaldson
Homer edited by Robert Fowler
Horace edited by Stephen Harrison
Ted Hughes edited by Terry Gifford

Ibsen edited by James McFarlane
Henry James edited by Jonathan Freedman
Samuel Johnson edited by Greg Clingham
Ben Jonson edited by Richard Harp and Stanley Stewart
James Joyce edited by Derek Attridge (second edition)
Kafka edited by Julian Preece
Keats edited by Susan J. Wolfson
Rudyard Kipling edited by Howard J. Booth
Lacan edited by Jean-Michel Rabaté
D. H. Lawrence edited by Anne Fernihough
Primo Levi edited by Robert Gordon
Wyndham Lewis edited by Tyrus Miller
Lucretius edited by Stuart Gillespie and Philip Hardie
Machiavelli edited by John M. Najemy
David Mamet edited by Christopher Bigsby
Nelson Mandela edited by Rita Barnard
Thomas Mann edited by Ritchie Robertson
Christopher Marlowe edited by Patrick Cheney
Andrew Marvell edited by Derek Hirst and Steven N. Zwicker
Herman Melville edited by Robert S. Levine
Arthur Miller edited by Christopher Bigsby (second edition)
Milton edited by Dennis Danielson (second edition)
Molière edited by David Bradby and Andrew Calder
Toni Morrison edited by Justine Tally
Nabokov edited by Julian W. Connolly
Eugene O'Neill edited by Michael Manheim
George Orwell edited by John Rodden
Ovid edited by Philip Hardie
Petrarch edited by Albert Russell Ascoli
Harold Pinter edited by Peter Raby (second edition)
Sylvia Plath edited by Jo Gill
Edgar Allan Poe edited by Kevin J. Hayes
Alexander Pope edited by Pat Rogers
Ezra Pound edited by Ira B. Nadel
Proust edited by Richard Bales
Pushkin edited by Andrew Kahn
Rabelais edited by John O'Brien
Rilke edited by Karen Leeder and Robert Vilain
Philip Roth edited by Timothy Parrish
Salman Rushdie edited by Abdulrazak Gurnah
John Ruskin edited by Francis O'Gorman
Seneca edited by Shadi Bartsch and Alessandro Schiesaro
Shakespeare edited by Margareta de Grazia and Stanley Wells (second edition)
Shakespeare and Contemporary Dramatists edited by Ton Hoenselaars
Shakespeare and Popular Culture edited by Robert Shaughnessy
Shakespearean Comedy edited by Alexander Leggatt
Shakespearean Tragedy edited by Claire McEachern (second edition)
Shakespeare on Film edited by Russell Jackson (second edition)
Shakespeare on Stage edited by Stanley Wells and Sarah Stanton
Shakespeare's History Plays edited by Michael Hattaway
Shakespeare's Last Plays edited by Catherine M. S. Alexander
Shakespeare's Poetry edited by Patrick Cheney
George Bernard Shaw edited by Christopher Innes
Shelley edited by Timothy Morton
Mary Shelley edited by Esther Schor
Sam Shepard edited by Matthew C. Roudané
Spenser edited by Andrew Hadfield
Laurence Sterne edited by Thomas Keymer
Wallace Stevens edited by John N. Serio
Tom Stoppard edited by Katherine E. Kelly
Harriet Beecher Stowe edited by Cindy Weinstein

August Strindberg edited by Michael Robinson
Jonathan Swift edited by Christopher Fox
J. M. Synge edited by P. J. Mathews
Tacitus edited by A. J. Woodman
Henry David Thoreau edited by Joel Myerson
Tolstoy edited by Donna Tussing Orwin
Anthony Trollope edited by Carolyn Dever and Lisa Niles
Mark Twain edited by Forrest G. Robinson
John Updike edited by Stacey Olster
Mario Vargas Llosa edited by Efrain Kristal and John King
Virgil edited by Charles Martindale
Voltaire edited by Nicholas Cronk
Edith Wharton edited by Millicent Bell
Walt Whitman edited by Ezra Greenspan
Oscar Wilde edited by Peter Raby
Tennessee Williams edited by Matthew C. Roudané
August Wilson edited by Christopher Bigsby
Mary Wollstonecraft edited by Claudia L. Johnson
Virginia Woolf edited by Susan Sellers (second edition)
Wordsworth edited by Stephen Gill
W. B. Yeats edited by Marjorie Howes and John Kelly*Zola* edited by Brian Nelson

TOPICS

The Actress edited by Maggie B. Gale and John Stokes
The African American Novel edited by Maryemma Graham
The African American Slave Narrative edited by Audrey A. Fisch
African American Theatre by Harvey Young
Allegory edited by Rita Copeland and Peter Struck
American Crime Fiction edited by Catherine Ross Nickerson
American Gay and Lesbian Literature edited by Scott Herring
American Modernism edited by Walter Kalaidjian
The American Modernist Novel edited by Joshua Miller
American Poetry since 1945 edited by Jennifer Ashton
American Poets edited by Mark Richardson
American Realism and Naturalism edited by Donald Pizer
American Science Fiction edited by Gerry Canavan and Eric Carl Link
American Travel Writing edited by Alfred Bendixen and Judith Hamera
American Women Playwrights edited by Brenda Murphy
Ancient Rhetoric edited by Erik Gunderson
Arthurian Legend edited by Elizabeth Archibald and Ad Putter
Asian American Literature edited by Crystal Parikh and Daniel Y. Kim
Australian Literature edited by Elizabeth Webby
Autobiography edited by Maria DiBattista and Emily Wittman
The Body in Literature edited by David Hillman and Ulrika Maude
British Fiction since 1945 edited by David James
British Literature of the French Revolution edited by Pamela Clemit
British Poetry, 1945–2010 edited by Edward Larrissy
British Romanticism edited by Stuart Curran (second edition)
British Romantic Poetry edited by James Chandler and Maureen N. McLane
British Theatre, 1730–1830 edited by Jane Moody and Daniel O'Quinn
Canadian Literature edited by Eva-Marie Kröller

Children's Literature edited by M. O. Grenby and Andrea Immel
The Classic Russian Novel edited by Malcolm V. Jones and Robin Feuer Miller
Contemporary Irish Poetry edited by Matthew Campbell
Creative Writing edited by David Morley and Philip Neilsen
Crime Fiction edited by Martin Priestman
Early Modern Women's Writing edited by Laura Lunger Knoppers
The Eighteenth-Century Novel edited by John Richetti
Eighteenth-Century Poetry edited by John Sitter
English Literature, 1500–1600 edited by Arthur F. Kinney
English Literature, 1650–1740 edited by Steven N. Zwicker
English Literature, 1740–1830 edited by Thomas Keymer and Jon Mee
English Literature, 1830–1914 edited by Joanne Shattock
English Novelists edited by Adrian Poole
English Poetry, Donne to Marvell edited by Thomas N. Corns
English Poets edited by Claude Rawson
English Renaissance Drama edited by A. R. Braunmuller and Michael Hattaway (second edition)
English Renaissance Tragedy edited by Emma Smith and Garrett A. Sullivan, Jr.
English Restoration Theatre edited by Deborah C. Payne Fisk
The Epic edited by Catherine Bates
European Modernism edited by Pericles Lewis
European Novelists edited by Michael Bell
Fairy Tales edited by Maria Tatar
Fantasy Literature edited by Edward James and Farah Mendlesohn
Feminist Literary Theory edited by Ellen Rooney
Fiction in the Romantic Period edited by Richard Maxwell and Katie Trumpener
The Fin de Siècle edited by Gail Marshall
The French Enlightenment edited by Daniel Brewer
French Literature edited by John D. Lyons
The French Novel: from 1800 to the Present edited by Timothy Unwin
Gay and Lesbian Writing edited by Hugh Stevens
German Romanticism edited by Nicholas Saul
Gothic Fiction edited by Jerrold E. Hogle
The Greek and Roman Novel edited by Tim Whitmarsh
Greek and Roman Theatre edited by Marianne McDonald and J. Michael Walton
Greek Comedy edited by Martin Revermann
Greek Lyric edited by Felix Budelmann
Greek Mythology edited by Roger D. Woodard
Greek Tragedy edited by P. E. Easterling
The Harlem Renaissance edited by George Hutchinson
The History of the Book edited by Leslie Howsam
The Irish Novel edited by John Wilson Foster
The Italian Novel edited by Peter Bondanella and Andrea Ciccarelli
The Italian Renaissance edited by Michael Wyatt
Jewish American Literature edited by Hana Wirth-Nesher and Michael P. Kramer
The Latin American Novel edited by Efraín Kristal
The Literature of the First World War edited by Vincent Sherry
The Literature of London edited by Lawrence Manley
The Literature of Los Angeles edited by Kevin R. McNamara
The Literature of New York edited by Cyrus Patell and Bryan Waterman
The Literature of Paris edited by Anna-Louise Milne
The Literature of World War II edited by Marina MacKay

Literature on Screen edited by Deborah Cartmell and Imelda Whelehan
Medieval English Culture edited by Andrew Galloway
Medieval English Literature edited by Larry Scanlon
Medieval English Mysticism edited by Samuel Fanous and Vincent Gillespie
Medieval English Theatre edited by Richard Beadle and Alan J. Fletcher (second edition)
Medieval French Literature edited by Simon Gaunt and Sarah Kay
Medieval Romance edited by Roberta L. Krueger
Medieval Women's Writing edited by Carolyn Dinshaw and David Wallace
Modern American Culture edited by Christopher Bigsby
Modern American Poetry edited by Walter Kalaidjian
Modern British Women Playwrights edited by Elaine Aston and Janelle Reinelt
Modern French Culture edited by Nicholas Hewitt
Modern German Culture edited by Eva Kolinsky and Wilfried van der Will
The Modern German Novel edited by Graham Bartram
The Modern Gothic edited by Jerrold E. Hogle
Modern Irish Culture edited by Joe Cleary and Claire Connolly
Modern Italian Culture edited by Zygmunt G. Baranski and Rebecca J. West
Modern Latin American Culture edited by John King
Modern Russian Culture edited by Nicholas Rzhevsky
Modern Spanish Culture edited by David T. Gies
Modernism edited by Michael Levenson (second edition)
The Modernist Novel edited by Morag Shiach
Modernist Poetry edited by Alex Davis and Lee M. Jenkins
Modernist Women Writers edited by Maren Tova Linett
Narrative edited by David Herman
Native American Literature edited by Joy Porter and Kenneth M. Roemer
Nineteenth-Century American Women's Writing edited by Dale M. Bauer and Philip Gould
Old English Literature edited by Malcolm Godden and Michael Lapidge (second edition)
Performance Studies edited by Tracy C. Davis
The Poetry of the First World War edited by Santanu Das
Popular Fiction edited by David Glover and Scott McCracken
Postcolonial Literary Studies edited by Neil Lazarus
The Postcolonial Novel edited by Ato Quayson
Postmodernism edited by Steven Connor
The Pre-Raphaelites edited by Elizabeth Prettejohn
Renaissance Humanism edited by Jill Kraye
The Roman Historians edited by Andrew Feldherr
Roman Satire edited by Kirk Freudenburg
Science Fiction edited by Edward James and Farah Mendlesohn
Scottish Literature edited by Gerald Carruthers and Liam McIlvanney
Sensation Fiction edited by Andrew Mangham
Slavery in American Literature edited by Ezra Tawil
The Sonnet edited by A. D. Cousins and Peter Howarth
The Spanish Novel: from 1600 to the Present edited by Harriet Turner and Adelaida López de Martínez
Textual Scholarship edited by Neil Fraistat and Julia Flanders
Theatre History by David Wiles and Christine Dymkowski
Travel Writing edited by Peter Hulme and Tim Youngs

Twentieth-Century British and Irish Women's Poetry edited by Jane Dowson
The Twentieth-Century English Novel edited by Robert L. Caserio
Twentieth-Century English Poetry edited by Neil Corcoran
Twentieth-Century Irish Drama edited by Shaun Richards
Twentieth-Century Russian Literature edited by Marina Balina and Evgeny Dobrenko
Utopian Literature edited by Gregory Claeys
Victorian and Edwardian Theatre edited by Kerry Powell
The Victorian Novel edited by Deirdre David (second edition)
Victorian Poetry edited by Joseph Bristow
Victorian Women's Writing edited by Linda H. Peterson
War Writing edited by Kate McLoughlin
Women's Writing in Britain, 1660–1789 edited by Catherine Ingrassia
Women's Writing in the Romantic Period edited by Devoney Looser
Writing of the English Revolution edited by N. H. Keeble